TO

CARY GRANT

the suave sophisticate whose talent and irresistible appeal earned for him a place among the world's most popular and best loved film stars.

JANE FONDA and JON VOIGHT
in "Coming Home"
1978 Academy Award Winners for Best Actress and Best Actor

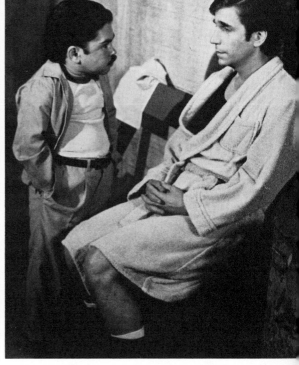

**Henry Winkler Top: Kim Darby,
Charles Victor, Henry Winkler**

Herve Villechaize, Henry Winkler

Richard Widmark, Genevieve Bujold

COMA

(UNITED ARTISTS) Producer, Martin Erlichman; Direction and Screenplay, Michael Crichton; Based on novel by Robin Cook; Photography, Victor J. Kemper, Gerald Hirschfeld; Editor, David Bretherton; Music, Jerry Goldsmith; Design, Albert Brenner; Costumes, Eddie Marks, Yvonne Kubis; Assistant Directors, William McGarry, Ron Grow; In Metrocolor; 113 minutes; Rated PG; January release.

CAST

Dr. Susan Wheeler	Genevieve Bujold
Dr. Mark Bellows	Michael Douglas
Mrs. Emerson	Elizabeth Ashley
Dr. George	Rip Torn
Dr. Harris	Richard Widmark
Nancy Greenly	Lois Chiles
Dr. Morelind	Harry Rhodes
Computer Technician	Gary Barton
Kelly	Frank Downing
Jim	Richard Doyle
Dr. Marcus	Alan Haufrect
Vince	Lance LeGault
Chief Resident	Michael MacRae
Nurse	Betty McGuire
Murphy	Tom Selleck
Dr. Goodman	Charles Siebert
Lab Technician	William Wintersole

Top: (L) Michael Douglas, Genevieve
Bujold (R) Elizabeth Ashley

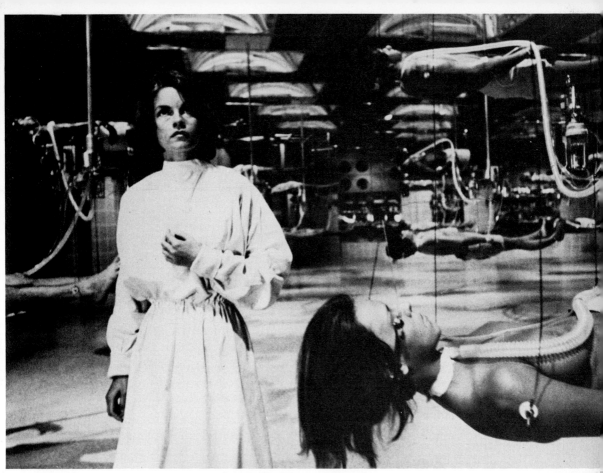

Genevieve Bujold, Michael Douglas
Top: Genevieve Bujold

Rip Torn, Genevieve Bujold

BLUE COLLAR

(UNIVERSAL) Executive Producer, Robin French; Producer, Don Guest; Director, Paul Schrader; Screenplay, Paul Schrader, Leonard Schrader; Source material, Sydney A. Glass; Photography, Bobby Byrne; Associate Producer, David Nichols; Music, Jack Nitzsche; Editor, Tom Rolf; Designer, Lawrence G. Paull; Assistant Directors, G. C. Rusty Meek, Dan Franklin, George Marshall; Costumes, Ron Dawson, Alice Rush; In Technicolor; 110 minutes; Rated R; February release.

CAST

Zeke	Richard Pryor
Jerry	Harvey Keitel
Smokey	Yaphet Kotto
Bobby Joe	Ed Begley, Jr.
Eddie Johnson	Harry Bellaver
Jenkins	George Memmoli
Arlene Bartowski	Lucy Saroyan
Clarence Hill	Lane Smith
John Burrows	Cliff DeYoung
Dogshit Miller	Borah Silver
Caroline Brown	Chip Fields
Hank	Harry Northup
IRS Man	Leonard Gaines
Sumabitch	Milton Selzer
Barney	Sammy Warren
Charlie T. Hernandez	Jimmy Martinez
Superintendent	Jerry Dahlmann
Unshaven Thug	Denny Arnold
Blonde Thug	Rock Riddle
Debby Bartowski	Stacey Baldwin
Bob Bartowski	Steve Butts
Flannigan	Stephen P. Dunn
Slim	Speedy Brown
Frazier Brown	Davone Florence
Ali Brown	Eddie Singleton
Aretha Brown	Rya Singleton
Neighbor	Vermetta Royster
Little Joe	Jaime Carreire
Doris	Victoria McFarland

and Gloria Delaney, Rosa Flores, Crystal McCarey, Debra Fay Walker, Gino Ardito, Sean Fallon Walsh, Vincent Lucchesi, Jerry Snider, Colby Chester, Donl Morse, William Pert, Tracey Walter, Almeria Quinn, Lee McDonald, Rodney Lee Walker, Glenn Wilder, Frank Orsatti, Matt (Jim) Connors

Top Right: Davone Florence, Richard Pryor
Below: Richard Pryor, Harvey Keitel

Chip Fields, Richard Pryor

Yaphet Kotto, Harvey Keitel
Richard Pryor

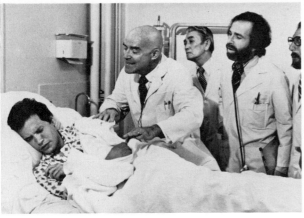

RABBIT TEST

(AVCO EMBASSY) Producer, Edgar Rosenberg; Director, Joan Rivers; Screenplay, Joan Rivers, Jay Redack; Photography, Lucien Ballard; Editor, Stanford C. Allen; Music; Mike Post, Peter Carpenter; Art Director, Robert Kinoshita; Associate Producer, Melissa Rosenberg; Assistant Directors, Joseph M. Ellis, Billy Ray Smith; In color; 84 minutes; Rated PG; February release.

CAST

Lionel	Billy Crystal
Segoynia	Joan Prather
Danny	Alex Rocco
Mrs. Carpenter	Doris Roberts
Newscaster	Edward Ansara
Madam Marie	Imogene Coca
Anthropologist	Jane Connell
Dr. Lasse-Braun	Keene Curtis
Segoynia's father	Norman Fell
President's wife	Fannie Flagg
The Pope	Jack Fletcher
Nurse Tunn	Alice Ghostley
President of U.S.	George Gobel
Taxi Driver	Roosevelt Grier
Dr. Vidal	Paul Lynde
Dr. Lowell	Murray Matheson
Gypsy Grandmother/Dr. Fishbind	Roddy McDowall
Mystery Lady	Sheree North
Minister	Tom Poston
Cousin Clare	Charlotte Rae
Second Nurse	Joan Rivers
Chinese Leader	Sab Shimono
Melody Carpenter	Mary Steelsmith
Umbuto	Jimmie Walker

Top: Norman Fell, Joan Prather, Billy Crystal, Imogene Coca, Roddy McDowall Below: Crystal, Keene Curtis

Billy Crystal, George Gobel Top: Paul Lynde

13

COMING HOME

(UNITED ARTISTS) Producer, Jerome Hellman; Director, Hal Ashby; Screenplay, Waldo Salt, Robert C. Jones; Based on story by Nancy Dowd; Photography, Haskell Wexler; Editor, Don Zimmerman; Design, Mike Haller; Costumes, Ann Roth, Mike Hoffman, Silvio Scarano, Jennifer Parson; Assistant Director, Chuck Myers; In DeLuxe Color; 126 minutes; Rated R; February release.

CAST

Sally Hyde	Jane Fonda
Luke Martin	Jon Voight
Capt. Bob Hyde	Bruce Dern
Sgt. Dink Mobley	Robert Ginty
Viola Munson	Penelope Milford
Bill Munson	Robert Carradine

Left: Jane Fonda, Bruce Dern
*1978 Academy Awards for Best Actor (Jon Voight),
Best Actress (Jane Fonda), and Best Original
Screenplay*

Jon Voight, Jane Fonda

Jon Voight, Jane Fonda Top: Penelope
Milford, Robert Carradine Right: Voight
and Carradine

Bruce Dern, Jane Fonda
Above: Penelope Milford, Jane Fonda

15

THE BETSY

(ALLIED ARTISTS) Producer, Robert R. Weston; Director, Daniel Petrie; Screenplay, Walter Bernstein, William Bast; Based on novel by Harold Robbins; Photography, Mario Tosi; Editor, Rita Roland; Designer, Herman A. Blumenthal; Music, John Barry; Associate Producer, Jack Grossberg; Costumes, Dorothy Jeakins; Assistant Directors, Wolfgang Glattes, Jack Sanders; Presented by Emanuel L. Wolf; In Technicolor; 120 minutes; Rated R; February release.

CAST

Loren Hardeman, Sr.	Laurence Olivier
Loren Hardeman III	Robert Duvall
Sally Hardeman	Katharine Ross
Angelo Perino	Tommy Lee Jones
Alicia Hardeman	Jane Alexander
Lady Bobby Ayres	Lesley-Anne Down
Jake Weinstein	Joseph Wiseman
Betsy Hardeman	Kathleen Beller
Dan Weyman	Edward Herrmann
Loren Hardeman, Jr.	Paul Rudd
Duncan	Roy Poole
Mark Sampson	Richard Venture
Angelo Luigi Perino	Titos Vandis
Joe Warren	Clifford David
Mrs. Craddock	Inga Swenson
Elizabeth Hardeman	Whitney Blake
Roxanne	Carol Williard
Donald	Read Morgan
Loren III (as a boy)	Charlie Fields

and Robert Phalen (Man), Nick Czmyr (Bellhop), Norman Palmer, Fred Carney, Maury Cooper, Russell Porter (Boardmembers), Teri Ralston (Hotel Clerk), Warney H. Ruhl (Security Guard), Patrick J. Monks (Helicopter Pilot), William Roerick (Secretary of Commerce), William B. Cain (Butler), Mary Petrie (Nurse), H. August Kuehl (Guest), Robert Hawkins (Retired Man), Sadie Hawkins (Retired Lady), Anthony Steere (Car Driver)

Left: Robert Duvall, Jane Alexander
Top: Laurence Olivier, Tommy Lee Jones

Standing: Robert Duvall, Edward Herrmann, Lesley-Anne Down, Paul Rudd, Kathleen Beller, Joseph Wiseman, Inga Swenson, Titos Vandis, Tommy Lee Jones, Seated: Jane Alexander, Laurence Olivier, Katharine Ross

Leo McKern, Jodie Foster,
David Niven, Helen Hayes

CANDLESHOE

(BUENA VISTA) Producer, Ron Miller; Director, Norman Tokar; Screenplay, David Swift, Rosemary Anne Sisson; Based on "Christmas at Candleshoe" by Michael Innes; Associate Producer, Hugh Attwooll; Photography, Paul Beeson; Music, Ron Goodwin; Art Director, Albert Witherick; Editor, Peter Boita; Costumes, Julie Harris; Assistant Director, Jack Causey; In Technicolor; 101 minutes; Rated G; February release.

CAST

Priory	David Niven
Lady St. Edmund	Helen Hayes
Casey	Jodie Foster
Bundage	Leo McKern
Grimsworthy	Vivian Pickles
Cluny	Veronica Quilligan
Peter	Ian Sharrock
Anna	Sarah Tamakuni
Bobby	David Samuels
Jenkins	John Alderson
Mrs. McCress	Mildred Shay
Mr. McCress	Michael Balfour
Mr. Thresher	Sydney Bromley
Train Guard	Michael Segal

Jodie Foster, David Niven,
Helen Hayes

THE BOYS IN COMPANY C

(COLUMBIA) Executive Producer, Raymond Chow; Producer, Andrew Morgan; Director, Sidney J. Furie; Screenplay, Rich Natkin, Sidney J. Furie; Photography, Godfrey A. Godar; Music, Jaime Mendoza-Nava; Song "Here I Am" by Craig Wasson; Designer, Robert Lang; Editors, Michael Berman, Frank J. Urioste, Allan Pattillo, James Benson; Associate Producer, Dennis Juban; Art Director, Laida Perez; Assistant Directors, Fred Slark, Hernan Robles, Ulysses Formanez, Madalena Chan; A Golden Harvest Production in Panavision and Technicolor; 125 minutes; Rated R; February release.

CAST

Tyrone Washington	Stan Shaw
Billy Ray Pike	Andrew Stevens
Alvin Foster	James Canning
Vinnie Fazio	Michael Lembeck
Dave Bisbee	Craig Wasson
Captain Collins	Scott Hylands
Lt. Archer	James Whitmore, Jr.
Sgt. Curry	Noble Willingham
Sgt. Loyce	Lee Ermey
Sgt. Aquilla	Santos Morales
Col. Metcalfe	Drew Michaels
Betsy	Karen Hilger
Nancy Bisbee	Peggy O'Neal
Roy Foster	Claude Wilson
George Pike	Chuck Doherty
Spoon	Cisco Oliver
Receiving Sergeant	Stan Johns
Junior D. I	Don Bell
Hank	Bob Mallett
Oates	Parris Hicks

and Frederick Matthews, Logan Clarke, Ray Wagner, Duane Mercier, Noel Kramer, Fred Smithson, Eazy Black, Rick Natkin, Helen McNeely, Charles Waters, Ken Metcalfe, Vic Diaz, Jose Mari Avellana, Victor Pinzon, Michael Cohen

STRAIGHT TIME

(WARNER BROS.) Producers, Stanley Beck, Tim Zinneman; Director, Ulu Grosbard; Screenplay, Alvin Sargent, Edward Bunker, Jeffrey Boam; Based on novel "No Beast So Fierce" by Edward Bunker; Photography, Owen Roizman; Designer, Stephen Grimes; Editors, Sam O'Steen, Randy Roberts; Music, David Shire; Executive Producer, Howard B. Pine; Associate Producer, Gail Mutrux; Assistant Director, Jack Roe; Art Director, Dick Lawrence; In Technicolor; 114 minutes; Rated R; A SeetWall Production; March release.

CAST

Max Dembo	Dustin Hoffman
Jenny Mercer	Theresa Russell
Jerry Schue	Harry Dean Stanton
Willy Darin	Gary Busey
Earl Frank	M. Emmet Walsh
Manny	Sandy Barron
Selma Darin	Kathy Bates
Mickey	Edward Bunker
Salesman #1	Stuart I. Berton
Salesman #2	Barry Cahill
Carlos	Corey Rand
Manager	James Ray
Cafe Owner	Fran Ryan
Carol Schue	Rita Taggart

Top Right: Dustin Hoffman

Dustin Hoffman
(also above)

Theresa Russell, Dustin Hoffman

AN UNMARRIED WOMAN

(20th CENTURY-FOX) Producers, Paul Mazursky, Tony Ray; Direction and Screenplay, Paul Mazursky; Music, Bill Conti; Photography, Arthur Ornitz; Designer, Pato Guzman; Editor, Stuart H. Pappe; Costumes, Albert Wolsky; Assistant Directors, Terry Donnelly, Tom Kane; In Movielab Color; 124 minutes; Rated R; March release.

CAST

Erica	Jill Clayburgh
Saul	Alan Bates
Martin	Michael Murphy
Charlie	Cliff Gorman
Sue	Pat Quinn
Elaine	Kelly Bishop
Patti	Lisa Lucas
Jeannette	Linda Miller
Bob	Andrew Duncan
Dr. Jacobs	Daniel Seltzer
Phil	Matthew Arkin
Tanya	Penelope Russianoff
Jean	Novella Nelson
Edward	Raymond J. Barry
Herb Rowan	Ivan Karp
Claire	Jill Eikenberry
Fred	Michael Tucker
Cabbie	Chico Martinez
Chinese Waiter	Clint Chin
Man at bar	Ken Chapin
Ice Vendor	Tom Elios
Executive Secretary	Karen Ford
Waitress	Alice J. Kane
Hal	Paul Mazursky
Hatcheck Girl	Pamela Meunier
Sophie	Donna Perich
Man at party	Vincent Schiavelli
Bartender	John Stravinsky
Lady MacBeth	Ultra Violet

Lisa Lucas, Alan Bates, Jill Clayburgh
Top Left: Jill Clayburgh

Jill Clayburgh, Lisa Lucas
Top: Cliff Gorman, Jill Clayburgh

Alan Bates, Jill Clayburgh

25

A LITTLE NIGHT MUSIC

(NEW WORLD) Executive Producer, Heinz Lazek; Producer, Elliott Kastner; Director, Harold Prince; Screenplay, Hugh Wheeler; Based on New York stage musical of same title; Music and Lyrics, Stephen Sondheim; Suggested by film "Smiles of a Summer Night" by Ingmar Bergman; Choreography, Patricia Birch; Editor, John Jympson; Photography, Arthur Ibbetson; Costumes, Florence Klotz; Production Supervisor, Laci von Ronay; Musical Director, Paul Gemignani; Assistant Director, Kip Gowans; Art Director, Herta Pischinger; An S&T Production; A Roger Corman Presentation; In color; 124 minutes; Rated PG; March release.

CAST

Desiree Armfeldt	Elizabeth Taylor
Charlotte Mittelheim	Diana Rigg
Frederick Egerman	Len Cariou
Anne Egerman	Lesley-Anne Down
Mme. Armfeldt	Hermione Gingold
Carl-Magnus Mittelheim	Laurence Guittard
Erich Egerman	Christopher Guard
Fredericka Armfeldt	Chloe Franks
Kurt	Heimz Maracek
Petra	Lesley Dunlop
Conductor	Jonathan Tunick
Franz	Hubert Tscheppe
Band Conductor	Rudolf Schrympf
Mayor	Franz Schussler
Mayoress	Johanna Schussler
BoxOffice Lady	Jean Sincere
First Lady	Dagmar Koller
Second Lady	Ruth Brinkman
Concierge	Anna Veigl
Uniformed Sergeant	Stefan Paryla
First Whore	Eva Dvorska
Second Whore	Lisa De Cohen
Major Domo	Kurt Martynow
Cook	Gerty Barek
Footman	James De Graot

Top: Diana Rigg, Lesley-Anne Down,
Christopher Guard Left: Len Cariou,
Elizabeth Taylor

Len Cariou, Elizabeth Taylor, Laurence
Guittard, Diana Rigg Above: Hermione
Gingold, Chloe Franks

AMERICAN HOT WAX

(PARAMOUNT) Producer, Art Linson; Director, Floyd Mutrux; Screenplay, John Kaye; Photography, William A. Fraker; Editors, Melvin Shapiro, Ronald J. Fagan; Art Director, Elayne Barbara Ceder; Assistant Director, Joe Wallenstein; In Metrocolor; 91 minutes; Rated PG; March release.

CAST

Alan Freed	Tim McIntire
Sheryl	Fran Drescher
Mookie	Jay Leno
Teenage Louise	Laraine Newman
The Chesterfields	Carl Earl Weaver, Al Chalk, Sam Harkness, Arnold McCuller
Lennie Richfield	Jeff Altman
Artie Moress	Moosie Drier
District Attorney	John Lehne
Prof. La Plano	Kenny Vane
Themselves	Chuck Berry, Jerry Lee Lewis, Screamin' Jay Hawkins

Right: Tim McIntire

The Chesterfields

THE FURY

(20th CENTURY-FOX) Executive Producer, Ron Preissman; Producer, Frank Yablans; Director, Brian De Palma; Screenplay, John Farris from his novel; Photography, Richard H. Kline; Music, John Williams; Editor, Paul Hirsch; In DeLuxe Color; 117 minutes; Rated R; March release.

CAST

Peter	Kirk Douglas
Childress	John Cassavetes
Hester	Carrie Snodgress
Gillian	Amy Irving
Susan Charles	Fiona Lewis
Robin	Andrew Stevens
Dr. Ellen Lindstrom	Carol Rossen
Dr. Jim McKeever	Charles Durning
Katherine Bellaver	Joyce Easton
Raymond	William Finley
Robertson	J. Patrick McNamara
Vivian Nuckles	Jane Lambert
Nuckles	Bernie Kuby
Kristen	Rutanya Alda
Larue	Melody Thomas
Cheryl	Hilary Thomas
Mrs. Callahan	Alice Nunn
Blackfish	Sam Laws

Left: Amy Irving

Kirk Douglas, Carrie Snodgress

Fiona Lewis, Andrew Stevens
Top: Amy Irving

CROSSED SWORDS

(WARNER BROS.) Executive Producer, Ilya Salkind; Producer, Pierre Spengler; Director, Richard Fleischer; Screenplay, George MacDonald Fraser, Berta Dominguez, Pierre Spengler; Based on novel by Mark Twain; Photography, Jack Cardiff; Music, Maurice Jarre; Editor, Ernest Walter; Designer, Tony Pratt; Costumes, Judy Moorcroft; Assistant Directors, Vilmos Kolba, Michael Green, Zsuzsanna Szemes; Choreographer, Sally Gilpin; In Panavision and Technicolor; 113 minutes; Rated PG; March release.

CAST

Miles Hendon	Oliver Reed
Lady Edith	Raquel Welch
Edward/Tom	Mark Lester
John Canty	Ernest Borgnine
Ruffler	George C. Scott
Duke of Norfolk	Rex Harrison
Hugh Hendon	David Hemmings
Hertford	Harry Andrews
St. John	Julian Orchard
Prince's Dresser	Murray Melvin
Jester	Graham Stark
Mother Canty	Sybil Danning
Princess Elizabeth	Lalla Ward
Lady Jane	Felicity Dean
Henry VIII	Charlton Heston

Top: George C. Scott
Below: Rex Harrison

Mark Lester, Felicity Dean Above:
Oliver Reed, Mark Lester, Top:
Charlton Heston

CASEY'S SHADOW

(COLUMBIA) Producer, Ray Stark; Director, Martin Ritt; Screenplay, Carol Sobieski; Based on short story "Ruidoso" by John McPhee; Photography, John A. Alonzo; Executive Producer, Michael Levee; Music, Patrick Williams; Songs, Patrick Williams and Will Jennings, Dr. John, Richard Betts; Performed by Dobie Gray, Dr. John, Allman Brothers Band; Designer, Robert Luthardt; Editor, Sidney Levinn; Costumes, Moss Mabry; Assistant Directors, Ronald L. Schwary, Steve H. Perry, William P. Scott; In Panavision and color; 116 minutes; Rated PG; March release.

CAST

Lloyd Bourdell	Walter Matthau
Sarah Blue	Alexis Smith
Mike Marsh	Robert Webber
Tom Patterson	Murray Hamilton
Buddy Bourdelle	Andrew A. Rubin
Randy Bourdelle	Stephen Burns
Kelly Marsh	Susan Myers
Casey Bourdelle	Michael Hershewe
Calvin Lebec	Harry Caesar
Jimmy Judson	Joel Fluellen
Dr. Williamson	Whit Bissell
Donovan	Jimmy Halty
Dr. Pitt	William Pitt
Dean	Dean Turpitt
Old Cajun	Sanders Delhomme
Lenny	Richard Thompson
Indian	Galbert Wanoskia
Old Man	William Karn
All American Network Announcer	Ed Hyman
Auctioneers	Thomas Caldwell, Bill Tackett
Starting Gate Announcer	Tom Dawson
Weight Scales Jockey Room	William Thomas
Race Announcer	Robert Dudich
Guard	Warren Richardson

and Ronald L. Schwary (Ticketseller), Leonard Blach (Veterinarian), Justin Buford (Kid), Dean Cormier (Barmaid), Thelma Cormier, Ronald Benoit (Dealers), Norman Faulk (Track Timer), Gene Norman (Head Wrangler), Paul Uccello (Track Timer), W. Patrick Scott (Veterinarian), James Hutchinson, Jr. (Bar Man)

Right: Walter Matthau, Andrew Rubin
Top: Alexis Smith

Walter Matthau

Michael Hershewe

THE OTHER SIDE OF THE MOUNTAIN PART 2

(UNIVERSAL) Producer, Edward S. Feldman; Director, Larry Peerce; Screenplay, Douglas Day Stewart; Photography, Ric Waite; Associate Producer, Donna R. Dubrow; Art Director, William Campbell; Music, Lee Holdridge; Lyrics, Molly-Ann Leikin; Vocalist, Merrily Webber; Editors, Eve Newman, Walter Hannemann; Assistant Directors, Cliff Coleman, Robert Latham Brown; In Panavision and Technicolor; 105 minutes, Rated PG; March release.

CAST

Jill Kinmont	Marilyn Hassett
John Boothe	Timothy Bottoms
June Kinmont	Nan Martin
Audra-Jo	Belinda J. Montgomery
Linda	Gretchen Corbett
Bill Kinmont	William Bryant
Mr. Boothe	James A. Bottoms
Mrs. Boothe	June Dayton
Roy Boothe	Curtis Credel
Beverly Boothe	Carole Tru Foster
Mel	Charles Frank
Doctor in Los Angeles	George Petrie
Presenter at luncheon	Ross Durfee
Woman at bar	Jackie Russell
Waitress	Gerri Nelson
Bob Kinmont	Tom Jordan
Jerry Kinmont	Harry Moses
Doctor in Bishop	Myron Healey
Minister	Rev. Bee Landis
Wrangler	Steve Conte
Gary	Craig Chudy
Indian Boy	David Yanez
Indian Girl	Marlina Vega

Left: Timothy Bottoms, Marilyn Hassett are married Top: Nan Martin, Marilyn Hassett

Marilyn Hassett, Timothy Bottoms

June Dayton, James Bottoms

FM

(UNIVERSAL) Producer, Rand Holston; Co-Producer, Robert Larson; Director, John A. Alonzo; Screenplay, Ezra Sacks; Photography, David Myers; Editor, Jeff Gourson; Designer, Lawrence G. Paull; Title song composed and performed by Steely Dan; Assistant Directors, Bert Gold, Peter Burrell, Candace C. Suerstedt; Costumes, Kent Warner; In Dolby Sound, Panavision and Technicolor; 110 minutes; Rated PG; April release

CAST

Jeff Dugan	Michael Brandon
Mother	Eileen Brennan
Doc Holiday	Alex Karras
Prince	Cleavon Little
Eric Swan	Martin Mull
Laura Coe	Cassie Yates
Carl Billings	Norman Lloyd
Bobby Douglas	Jay Fenichel
Lt. Reach	James Keach
Albert Driscoll	Joe Smith
Regis Lamar	Tom Tarpey
Alice	Janet Brandt
Cathy	Mary Torrey
Shari Smith	Roberta Wallach
Michael J. Carlyle	Terry Jastrow
Maggie	Cissy Wellman
Jack Rapp	Robert Patten
Buxom Blonde	Karen Ciral
Delores Deluxe	Brenda Venus
Alice's Assistant	Tina Ritt
Police Captain	Don Dolan

and David Matthau, John Larson, Phillip Epstein, Peter Fox, Bo Kaprall, Keith Jensen, Patricia Marlowe, Tammy Masters, Paul Menzel, Louis Messina, Andrea Claudio, Linda Ronstadt, Jimmy Buffett, Tom Petty, Reo Speedwagon, Kevin Cronin, Gary Richrath, Alan Gratzer, Bruce Hall, Neal Doughty

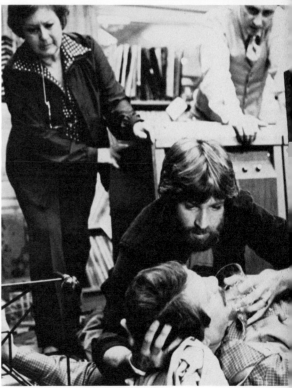

Top: Michael Brandon, Alex Karras
Below: Eileen Brennan, Cleavon Little,
Karras, Martin Mull

Janet Brandt, Michael Brandon,
Alex Karras

THE SEA GYPSIES

(WARNER BROS.) Executive Producer, Peter R. Simpson; Producer, Joseph C. Raffill; Direction and Screenplay, Stewart Raffill; Editors, Dan Greer, R. Hansel Brown, Art Stafford; Photography, Thomas McHugh; Music, Fred Steiner; Associate Producer, Gerald Alcan; Assistant Director, Hal Schwartz; In CFI Color; 101 minutes; Rated G; April release.

CAST

Travis	Robert Logan
Kelly	Mikki Jamison-Olsen
Courtney	Heather Rattray
Jesse	Cjon Damitri Patterson
Samantha	Shannon Saylor

© Warner Bros. 1978
Top: Mikki Jamison-Olsen, Shannon
Saylor, Robert Logan, Heather Rattray, Cjon
Damitri Patterson

Robert Logan

I WANNA HOLD YOUR HAND

(UNIVERSAL) Executive Producer, Steven Spielberg; Producers, Tamara Asseyev, Alex Rose; Director, Robert Zemeckis; Screenplay, Robert Zemeckis, Bob Gale; Associate Producer, Bob Gale; Photography, Donald M. Morgan; Art Director, Peter Jamison; Editor, Frank Morriss; Assistant Directors, Newton Arnold, Dan Kolsrud, Robert Villar; Music, The Beatles; Costumes, Roseanna Norton; In Panavision and Technicolor; 104 minutes; Rated PG; April release.

CAST

Pam Mitchell	Nancy Allen
Tony Smerko	Bobby DiCicco
Larry Dubois	Marc McClure
Janis Goldman	Susan Kendall Newman
Grace Corrigan	Theresa Saldana
Rosie Petrofsky	Wendie Jo Sperber
Richard "Ringo" Klaus	Eddie Deezen
Peter Plimpton	Christian Juttner
Ed Sullivan	Will Jordan
Peter's father	Read Morgan
Al	Claude Earl Jones
Eddie	James Houghton
Neil	Michael Hewitson
Sgt. Bresner	Dick Miller
CBS Security Guard	Vito Carenzo
Police Officer in alley	Luke Andreas
Cafeteria girls	Roberta Lee Carroll, Sherry Lynn
Sheet Girl	Irene Arranga
Club Leader	Carole H. Field
Amazon	Nancy Osborne

and Newton Arnold (Barber), Murray the K, Wil Albert (Goldman), Troy Melton (Guard), Nick Pellegrino (Lou), Martin Fiscoe (Elevator Operator), Marilyn Moe (On elevator), Michael Ross Verona (Reporter), Marilyn Fox (Interviewee), Kristine DeBell (Cindy), Gene LeBell (Reese), Victor Brandt (Foley), Roger Pancake (Sgt.), Kimberly Spengel (Sheet Girl), Bob Maroff (Bartender), Ivy Bethune (Foreigner), Craig Spengel, Frank Verroca (Protestors), Derek Barton (Driver), Edward Call, John Malloy, Larry Pines, Dave Adams, Poppy Lagos, Robyn Petti, Paula Watson, Leslie Hoffman, Chuck Waters, Rick Sawaya, Jim Nickerson, George Sawaya, The Romanos.

Right: Theresa Saldana, Marc McClure, Nancy Osborne Top: Nancy Allen (Center)

Susan Kendall Newman

Will Jordan as Ed Sullivan

SILVER BEARS

(COLUMBIA) Producers, Alex Winitsky, Arlene Sellers; Director, Ivan Passer; Screenplay, Peter Stone; Based on novel by Paul E. Erdman; Music, Claude Bolling; Photography, Anthony Richmond; Editor, Bernard Gribble; Art Director, Edward Marshall; Costumes, Ruth Myers; Assistant Directors, Mike Gowans, Bob Howard; In Technicolor; 113 minutes; Rated PG; April release.

CAST

Doc Fletcher	Michael Caine
Debbie Luckman	Cybill Shepherd
Prince di Siracusa	Louis Jourdan
Shireen Firdausi	Stephane Audran
Agha Firdausi	David Warner
Donald Luckman	Tom Smothers
Joe Fiore	Martin Balsam
Albert Fiore	Jay Leno
Marvin Skinner	Tony Mascia
Charles Cook	Charles Gray
Henry Foreman	Joss Ackland
Nick Topping	Jeremy Clyde
Signore Bendetti	Moustache
Boston	Mike Falco
St. Louis	Philip Mascellino
New York	Leni Del-Genio
Chicago	Gus Giuffre
Miami	Tommy Rundell
Los Angeles	Max Starky
Clerk	Steve Plytas

and Victor Baring (Accountant), Joe Treggonino (Chef), Patricia Lecchi (Maid), Tom Andrew (Dorso), Phil Brown, Bruce Boa, Shane Rimmer, Robert Robinson (Bankers), Anthony Broad, David English, Phil Caton, Edward Duke, Mark Penfold, Nigel Nevinson (Stockbrokers)

Right: Louis Jourdan

Jay Leno, Cybill Shepherd, Michael Caine, Louis Jourdan, Stephane Audran, Tony Mascia

PRETTY BABY

(PARAMOUNT) Producer-Director, Louis Malle; Screenplay, Polly Platt; Based on story by Polly Platt, Louis Malle from material in "Storyville" by Al Rose; Photography, Maureen Lambray; Editors, Suzanne Baron, Suzanne Fenn; Music, Jerry Wexler; Piano solos, Bob Greene; Design, Trevor Williams; Costumes, Mina Mittelman; Assistant Directors, John M. Poer, Don Heitzer; In MetroColor; 109 minutes; Rated R; April release.

CAST

Bellocq	Keith Carradine
Hattie	Susan Sarandon
Violet	Brooke Shields
Nell	Frances Faye
Piano Player	Antonio Fargas
Highpockets	Gerrit Graham
Mama Mosebery	Mae Mercer
Frieda	Diana Scarwid
Josephine	Barbara Steele
Red Top	Matthew Anton
Flora	Secret Scott
Gussie	Cheryl Markowitz
Fanny	Susan Manskey
Agnes	Laura Zimmerman
Odette	Miz Mary
Alfred Fuller	Don Hood
Ola Mae	Pat Perkins
Nonny	Von Eric Perkins
Justine	Sasha Holliday
Antonia	Lisa Shames
Harry	Harry Braden
Senator	Philip H. Sizeler
Violet's First Customer	Don K. Lutenbacher

Right: Brooke Shields, Susan Sarandon
Center: Susan Manskey, Diana Scarwid, Cheryl Markowitz, Susan Sarandon, Seret Scott, Keith Carradine, Brooke Shields, Miz Mary, Barbara Steele

Miz Mary, Brooke Shields, Susan Manskey, Keith Carradine

Brooke Shields, Keith Carradine

THE LAST WALTZ

(UNITED ARTISTS) Producer, Robbie Robertson; Executive Producer, Jonathan Taplin; Director, Martin Scorsese; Photography, Michael Chapman, Laszlo Kovacs, Vilmos Zsigmond, David Myers, Bobby Byrne, Michale Watkins, Hiro Narita; Editors, Yeu-Bun Yee, Jan Roblee; Design, Boris Leven; Associate Producer, Steven Prince; Assistant Directors, Jerry Grandey, James Quinn; In Dolby Stereo and DeLuxe Color; 115 minutes; Rated PG; April release.

A rock documentary of the last concert by the Band on Thanksgiving 1976 at Winterland in San Francisco, with Bob Dylan, Joni Mitchell, Neil Diamond, Emmylou Harris, Neil Young, Van Morrison, Ron Wood, Muddy Waters, Eric Clapton, the Staples, Ringo Starr, Dr. John, Ronnie Hawkins, Paul Betterfield, The Band

Left: Richard Manuel, Rick Danko, Robbie Robertson, Garth Hudson, Levon Helm

Rick Danko, Robbie Robertson Above: Van Morrison, Bob Dylan, Robertson

Neil Young, Joni Mitchell Above: The Staple Singers

F. I. S. T.

(UNITED ARTISTS) Producer-Director, Norman Jewison; Executive Producer, Gene Corman; Screenplay, Joe Eszterhas, Sylvester Stallone; From a story by Joe Eszterhas; Photography, Laszlo Kovacs; Editors, Tony Gibbs, Graeme Clifford; Music, Bill Conti; Design, Richard MacDonald; Art Director, Angelo Graham; Costumes, Anthea Sylbert, Tony Scarano, Thalia Phillips; Assistant Director, Andrew Stone; In Technicolor; 145 minutes; Rated PG; April release.

CAST

Johnny Kovak	Syvester Stallone
Senator Madison	Rod Steiger
Max Graham	Peter Boyle
Anna Zerinkas	Melinda Dillon
Abe Belkin	David Huffman
Babe Milano	Tony Lo Bianco
Vince Doyle	Kevin Conway
Molly	Cassie Yates
Arthur St. Clarie	Peter Donat
Win Talbot	Henry Wilcoxon
Gant	John Lehne
Mike Monahan	Richard Herd
Mrs. Zerinkas	Elena Karam
Bernie Marr	Ken Kercheval
Tom Higgins	Tony Mockus
Frank Vasko	Brian Dennehy
Andrews	James Karen

Top: Sylvester Stallone, David Huffman
Below: Melinda Dillon, Stallone Top
Right: Stallone, Peter Boyle, Rod
Steiger

Sylvester Stallone, also above
with David Huffman

39

THE END

(UNITED ARTISTS) Producer, Lawrence Gordon; Executive Producer, Hank Moonjean; Director, Burt Reynolds; Screenplay, Jerry Belson; Photography, Bobby Byrne; Editor, Donn Cambern; Music, Paul Williams; Design, Jan Scott; Costumes, Norman Salling; Assistant Director, Kurt Baker; In DeLuxe Color; 100 minutes; Rated R; May release.

CAST

Sonny Lawson	Burt Reynolds
Marlon Boruiki	Dom DeLuise
Mary Ellen	Sally Field
Dr. Kling	Strother Martin
Marty Lieberman	David Steinberg
Jessica	Joanne Woodward
Dr. Krugman	Norman Fell
Maureen Lawson	Myrna Loy
Julie Lawson	Kristy McNichol
Ben Lawson	Pat O'Brien
Priest	Robby Benson
Dr. Maneet	Carl Reiner
Pacemaker Patient	James Best
Old Man	Jock Mahoney

**Left: Burt Reynolds, Joanne Woodward
Below: Myrna Loy, Reynolds, Pat O'Brien**

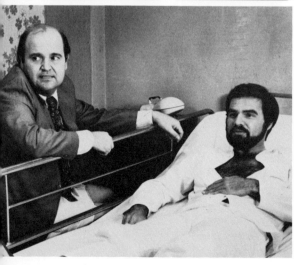

Dom DeLuise, Burt Reynolds

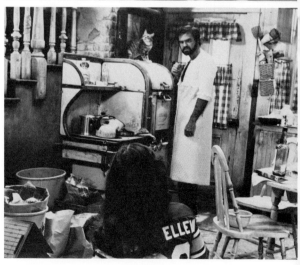

**Sally Field, Burt Reynolds
Above: Kristy McNichol, Burt Reynolds**

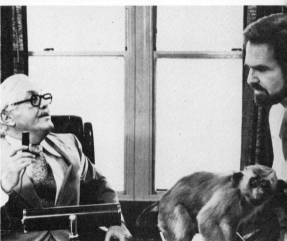

Burt Reynolds, David Steinberg Above: Carl
Reiner, Reynolds, Top: Robby Benson,
Burt Reynolds

Burt Reynolds, Dom DeLuise Above: Strother
Martin, Reynolds Top: Sally Field

THE GREEK TYCOON

(UNIVERSAL) Producers, Allen Klein, Ely Landau; Director, J. Lee Thompson; Screenplay, Mort Fine; Story, Nico Mastorakis, Win Wells, Mort Fine; Co-Producers, Nico Mastorakis, Lawrence Myers; Photography, Tony Richmond; Designer, Michael Stringer; Editor, Alan Strachan; Executive Producers, Mort Abrahams, Peter Howard, Les Landau; Associate Producer, Eric Rattray; Music, Stanley Myers; Assistant Directors, Ariel Levy, Michael Stevenson, Bob Wright, Anthony Mixaleas, Steve Barnett; An ABKCO Films Production in Technovision and Technicolor; 105 minutes; Rated R; May release.

CAST

Theo Tomasis	Anthony Quinn
Liz Cassidy	Jacqueline Bisset
Spyros Tomasis	Raf Vallone
Nico Tomasis	Edward Albert
James Cassidy	James Franciscus
Simi Tomasis	Camilla Sparv
Sophia Matalas	Marilu Tolo
Michael Russell	Charles Durning
Paola Scotti	Luciana Paluzzi
John Cassidy	Robin Clarke
Nancy Cassidy	Kathryn Leigh Scott
Robert Keith	Roland Culver
Doctor	Tony Jay
Servant	John Bennett
Helena	Katharine Schofield
Lady Allison	Joan Benham
Angela	Linda Thorson
Tahlib	Guy Deghy
Magda	Jill Melford
Mia	Lucy Gutteridge

and Nasis Kedrakas, John Denison, Carolle Rousseau, Danos Lygizos, Cassandra Harris, Patricia Kendall-John, Sandor Eles, Beulah Hughes, Vicki Michelle, Carol Royle, Mimi Denissi, Athene Fielding, Bonnie George, Charles Maggiore, Jeff Pomerantz, Richard Fasciano, John Bolt, Henderson Forsythe, Michael Prince, Gordon Oas-Heim, William Stelling, John Hoffmeister, Carinthia West, Dimitri Nikolaidis, Dimos Starenios, John Ioannou, David Masterman

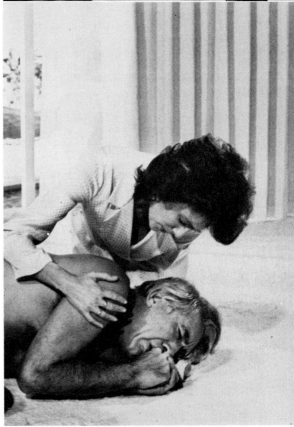

Top: Jacqueline Bisset, Anthony Quinn
Below: Edward Albert, Quinn, Charles Durning

Jacqueline Bisset, Anthony Quinn
Above: Anthony Quinn

NUNZIO

(UNIVERSAL) Producer, Jennings Lang; Director, Paul Williams; Screenplay, James Andronica; Photography, Edward R. Brown; Music, Lalo Schifrin; Designer, Mel Bourne; Editor, Johanna Demetrakes; Costumes, Ann Roth; Art Director, Richard Fuhrman; Assistant Directors, J. Allan Hopkins, Joseph Ray; In Panavision and Technicolor; 85 minutes; Rated PG; May release.

CAST

Nunzio	David Proval
Jamesie	James Adronica
Mrs. Sabatino	Morgana King
Angelo	Joe Spinell
Michelle	Tovah Feldshuh
Carol Sabatino	Maria Smith-Caffey
JoJo	Vincent Russo
Bobby	Jamie Alba
MaryAnn	Theresa Saldana
Georgia	Glenn Scarpelli
Georgie's friend	Tony Panetta
Carmine	Steve Gucciardo
Customer	Charlet Oberley
JoJo's friends	Sal Maneri, Anthony Esemplare, Robert Hayden
Mrs. Shuman	Sonia Zomina
Crystal Sabatino	Crystal Hayden
Vincent Sabatino	Vincent Igneri
Pete	Tom Quinn

and Joseph Tripi, Anthony Gilberti, Jennifer Gilberti, Guy Spennato, Nicole DeMaio, Jerry Tambasco, John Di Giso, Jr., Brian Brennan, Bill Hickey, Walter Gorney, Monica Lewis, Dorene Belleus, Lenore Volpe, Angela Pietropinto, Amanda Hope Lipnick, P. W. Williams, Zoe Clarke-Williams, Joseph Sullivan, Filomena Spagnuolo, Joe Adamo, Tony DiBenedetto, Leo Ciani, Jack Meeks, Bob Scarantino, Larry Silvestri, James Anthony, Jenny Shawn, Pasquale Igneri, Randall Andronica, Sal LaPera

Top: David Proval Below: James Andronica, Proval

David Proval, Glenn Scarpelli

Tovah Feldshuh, David Proval

JAWS 2

(UNIVERSAL) Producers, Richard D. Zanuck, David Brown; Director, Jeannot Szwarc; Screenplay, Carl Gottlieb, Howard Sackler; Based on characters created by Peter Benchley; Photography, Michael Butler; Editor, Neil Travis; Music, John Williams; Designer-Associate Producer, Joe Alves; Art Directors, Gene Johnson, Stu Campbell; Special Effects, Robert A. Mattey, Roy Arbogast; Assistant Directors, Scott Maitland, Don Zepfel, Kathy Marie Emde, Beau Marks; Editors, Steve Potter, Arthur Schmidt; Costumes, Bill Jobe; In Panavision and Technicolor; 123 minutes; Rated PG; June release.

CAST

Brody	Roy Scheider
Ellen Brody	Lorraine Gary
Mayor Vaughan	Murray Hamilton
Peterson	Joseph Mascolo
Hendricks	Jeffrey Kramer
Dr. Elkins	Collin Wilcox
Tina	Ann Dusenberry
Mike	Mark Gruner
Andrews	Barry Coe
Old Lady	Susan French
Andy	Gary Springer
Jackie	Donna Wilkes
Ed	Gary Dubin
Polo	John Dukakis
Timmy	G. Thomas Dunlop
Larry	David Elliott
Sean	Marc Gilpin
Doug	Keith Gordon
Lucy	Cynthia Grover
Patrick	Ben Marley

and Martha Swatek (Marge), Billy Van Zandt (Bob), Gigi Vorgan (Brook), Jerry M. Baxter (Pilot), Jean Coulter (Boat Driver), Daphne Dibble, David Tintle (Swimmers), Christine Freeman (Skier), April Gilpin (Renee), William Griffith (Lifeguard), Frank Sparks, Greg Harris (Divers), Coll Red McLean (Red), Susan O. McMillan, David Owsley (Sailors), Allan L. Paddack (Crosby), Oneida Rollins (Ambulance Driver), Kathy Wilson (Mrs. Bryant)

Marc Gilpin, Roy Scheider, Lorraine Gary
Top Left: Roy Scheider, and below with
Collin Wilcox

A DIFFERENT STORY

(AVCO EMBASSY) Executive Producer, Michael F. Leone; Producer, Alan Belkin; Director, Paul Aaron; Screenplay, Henry Olek; Photography, Philip Lathrop; Songs, Bob Wahler; Associate Producers, James Freiburger, Joy Shelton Davis; Costumes, Robert Demora; Music, David Frank; Editor, Lynn McCallon; Assistant Director, Donald Gold; In color; A Petersen Company Presentation; 107 minutes; Rated PG; June release.

CAST

Albert	Perry King
Stella	Meg Foster
Phyllis	Valerie Curtin
Sills	Peter Donat
Mr. Cooke	Richard Bull
Mrs. Cooke	Barbara Collentine
Ned	Guerin Barry
Roger	Doug Higgins
Chris	Lisa James
Sam	Eugene Butler
Chastity	Linda Carpenter
Richard I	Allan Hunt
Richard II	Burke Byrnes
Bernie	Eddy C. Dyer
Phyllis' Neighbor	Richard Altman
Justice of the Peace	Richard Seff
Mr. Hashmoni	George Skaff
Salesman	Sid Conrad

and Trent Dolan, Dan Mahar (Deputies), Ted Richards III (Justin), Clarke Gordon (Taylor), Gypsi DeYoung (Mrs. Taylor), Marion Perkins (Receptionist), Florence Di Re (Fitter), Gay Kleimenhapen (Pattern Maker), Marie Denn (Coordiniator), Kathryn Jackson (Nurse), Hatsuo Uda, Peter Furuta (Businessmen), Jennifer Dumas (Model), Eric Helland (Doorman), Philip Levien (Chicken Man), Stephen Nichols (Man at bath), Derek Flint (Little Albert 1), Joshua Hansen (Little Albert 2)

Top: Meg Foster, Perry King, also
below with Joshua Hansen

Meg Foster, Perry King
Top: Guerin Barry, Perry King

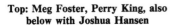

HEAVEN CAN WAIT

(PARAMOUNT) Producer, Warren Beatty; Directors, Warren Beatty, Buck Henry; Screenplay, Warren Beatty, Elaine May; Based on play of same title by Harry Segall; Executive Producers, Howard W. Koch, Jr., Charles H. Maguire; Photography, William A. Fraker; Designer, Paul Sylbert; Editors, Robert C. Jones, Don Zimmerman; Music, Dave Grusin; Costumes, Theodora Van Runkle, Richard Bruno; Assistant Directors, Howard W. Koch, Jr., Craig Huston; Art Director, Edwin O'Donovan; Special Effects, Robert MacDonald; In Panavision and Movielab Color; 101 minutes; Rated PG; June release.

CAST

Joe Pendleton	Warren Beatty
Betty Logan	Julie Christie
Mr. Jordan	James Mason
Max Corkle	Jack Warden
Tony Abbott	Charles Grodin
Julia Farnsworth	Dyan Cannon
The Escort	Buck Henry
Krim	Vincent Gardenia
Sisk	Joseph Maher
Bentley	Hamilton Camp
Everett	Arthur Malet
Corinne	Stephanie Faracy
Lavinia	Jeannie Linero
Gardener	Harry D. K. Wong
Security Guard	George J. Manos
Peters	Larry Block
Conway	Frank Campanella
Tomarken	Bill Sorrells
TV Interviewer	Dick Enberg
Head Coach	Dolph Sweet
General Manager	R. G. Armstrong
Trainer	Ed V. Peck
Former Owner	John Randolph
Oppenheim	Keene Curtis
Renfield	William Larsen
Nuclear Reporter	William Sylvester

and Morgan Farley (Middleton), William Bogert (Lawson), Robert E. Leonard, Joel Marston, Earl Montgomery, Robert C. Stevens (Board Members), Bernie Massa (Guard), Peter Tomarken (Reporter), Richard O'Brien (Adviser), Joseph F. Makel (Ambassador), Will Hare (Doctor), Lee Weaver (Attendant), Roger Bowen (Newspaperman), Lisa Blake Richards (Reporter), Charlie Charles (Highwire Artist), Nick Outin (Chauffeur), Jerry Scanlan (Hodges), Jim Boeke (Kowalsky), Marvin Fleming (Gudnitz), Deacon Jones (Gorman), Les Josephson (Owens), Jack T. Snow (Cassidy), Curt Gowdy (TV Commentator), Al DeRogatis (TV Analyst)

Top: Jack Warden

1978 Academy Award for Best Art Direction

Julie Christie, Warren Beatty
Above: James Mason, Beatty (also at top)

46

Frankie Avalon Top: Annette Charles
John Travolta, Eve Arden

Olivia Newton-John, John Travolta

49

CAPRICORN ONE

(WARNER BROS.)Producer, Paul N. Lazarus III; Direction and Screenplay, Peter Hyams; Photography, Bill Butler; Music, Jerry Goldsmith; Editor, James Mitchell; Designer, Albert Brenner; Associate Producer, Michael Rachmil; Art Director, David M. Haber; Costumes, Patricia Norris; Assistant Directors, Irby Smith, Jack Sanders; In Panavision and color; 127 minutes; Rated PG; June release.

CAST

Robert Caulfield ....Elliott Gould
Charles Brubaker ....James Brolin
Kay Brubaker ....Brenda Vaccaro
Peter Willis .... Sam Waterston
John Walker .... O. J. Simpson
Dr. James Kelloway ....Hal Holbrook
Hollis Peaker...David Huddleston
Walter Loughlin ....David Doyle
Betty Walker .... Denise Nicholas
Elliot Whittier..Robert Walden
Sharon Willis... Lee Bryant
Capsule Communicator ....Alan Fudge
Judy Drinkwater .... Karen Black
Albain .... Telly Savalas

**Top: Sam Waterston, James Brolin,
O. J. Simpson**

James Brolin, Brenda Vaccaro

O. J. Simpson, James Brolin, Sam
Waterston Top: Elliott Gould, Telly
Savalas

Hal Holbrook

THE CAT FROM OUTER SPACE

(BUENA VISTA) Producer, Ron Miller; Co-Producer, Norman Tokar; Director, Norman Tokar: Screenplay, Ted Key; Photography, Charles F. Wheeler; Music, Lalo Schifrin; Art Directors, John B. Mansbridge, Preston Ames; Editor, Cotton Warburton; Associate Producer, Jan Williams; Assistant Directors, Gene Sultan, William Carroll; In Technicolor; 103 minutes; Rated G; June release.

CAST

Frank	Ken Berry
Liz	Sandy Duncan
General Stilton	Harry Morgan
Mr. Stallwood	Roddy McDowall
Link	McLean Stevenson
Earnest Ernie	Jesse White
Dr. Wenger	Alan Young
Dr. Heffel	Hans Conried
Sgt. Duffy	Ronnie Schell
Capt. Anderson	James Hampton
Col. Woodruff	Howard T. Platt
Mr. Olympus	William Prince
Weasel	Ralph Manza
Honest Harry	Tom Pedi
Officer	Hank Jones
Dydee Guard	Rick Hurst
Mr. Smith	John Alderson
Omar	Tiger Joe Marsh
NASA Executive	Arnold Soboloff

and Mel Carter, Dallas McKennon, Alice Backes, Henry Slate, Roger Pancake, Roger Price, Jerry Fujikawa, Jim Begg, Pete Renaday, Rick Sorensen, Tom Jackman, Fred L. Whalen, Joe Medalis, Gil Stratton, Jana Milo, Richard Warlock

Left: McLean Stevenson, Sandy Duncan, Ken Berry, Jake

Ronnie Schell, Harry Morgan, James Hampton, Howard Platt

Annie Potts, Mark Hamill (also Top Right)
Right Center: Eugene Roche, Mark Hamill

CORVETTE SUMMER

(UNITED ARTISTS) Producer, Hal Barwood; Director, Matthew Robbins; Screenplay, Hal Barwood, Matthew Robbins; Photography, Frank Stanley; Editor, Amy Jones; Music, Craig Safan; Art Director, James Schoppe; Costumes, Aggie Guerard Rodgers; Assistant Director, Jim Bloom; In Panavision and Metrocolor; 105 minutes; Rated PG; June release.

CAST
Ken Dantley	Mark Hamill
Vanessa	Annie Potts
Ed McGrath	Eugene Roche
Wayne Lowry	Kim Milford
Principal	Richard McKenzie
Police P. R	William Bryant
Gil	Philip Bruns
Kootz	Danny Bonaduce
Mrs. Dantley	Jane A. Johnston
Ricci	Albert Insinnia
Tico	Isaac Ruiz, Jr.
Con Man	Stanley Kamel
Tony	Jason Ronard
Jeff	Brion James

Annie Potts, Mark Hamill

53

Jonathan Scott-Taylor

DAMIEN - OMEN II

(20th CENTURY-FOX) Producer, Harvey Bernhard; Director, Don Taylor; Screenplay, Stanley Mann, Michael Hodges; Story, Harvey Bernhard; Based on characters created by David Seltzer; Co-Producer, Charles Orme; Photography, Bill Butler; Music, Jerry Goldsmith; Editor, Robert Brown, Jr.; Associate Producer, Joseph "Pepi" Lenzi; Designers, Philip M. Jefferies, Fred Harpman; Assistant Directors, Al Nicholson, Jerry Balle, Richard Luke Rothschild; In Panavision and DeLuxe Color; 110 minutes; Rated R; June release.

CAST

Richard Thorn	William Holden
Ann Thorn	Lee Grant
Damien Thorn	Jonathan Scott-Taylor
Paul Buher	Robert Foxworth
Charles Warren	Nicholas Pryor
Bill Atherton	Lew Ayres
Aunt Marion	Sylvia Sidney
Sgt. Neff	Lance Henriksen
Joan Hart	Elizabeth Shepherd
Mark Thorn	Lucas Donat
Pasarian	Alan Arbus
Murray	Fritz Ford
Dr. Kane	Meshach Taylor
Teddy	John J. Newcombe
Butler	John Charles Burns
Colonel	Paul Cook
Jane	Diane Daniels
Teacher	Robert E. Ingham
Minister	William B. Fosser
Greenhouse Technician	Corney Morgan
Truck Driver	Russell P. Delia
Maid	Judith Dowd

and Thomas O. Erhart, Jr. (Sgt.), Anthony Hawkins (Pasarian's Assistant), Robert J. Jones, Jr. (Guide), Rusdi Lane (Jim), Charles Mountain (Priest), Cornelia Sanders (Girl), Felix Shuman (Dr. Fiedler), James Spinks (Technician), Owen Sullivan (Byron), William J. Whelehan (Guard)

Top: William Holden, Lee Grant

THE DRIVER

(20th CENTURY-FOX) Producer, Lawrence Gordon; Associate Producer, Frank Marshall; Direction and Screenplay, Walter Hill; Photography, Philip Lathrop; Designer, Harry Horner; Music, Michael Small; Editors, Tina Hirsch, Robert K. Lambert; Assistant Directors, Pat Kehoe, Lisa Hallas; Art Director, David Haber; In Panavision and DeLuxe Color; 91 minutes; Rated R; July release.

CAST

The Driver	Ryan O'Neal
The Detective	Bruce Dern
The Player	Isabelle Adjani
The Connection	Ronee Blakley
Red Plainclothesman	Matt Clark
Gold Plainclothesman	Felice Orlandi
Glasses	Joseph Walsh
Teeth	Rudy Ramos
Exchange Man	Denny Macko
The Kid	Frank Bruno
Fingers	Will Walker
Split	Sandy Brown Wyeth
Frizzy	Tara King
Floorman	Richard Carey
Card Player	Fidel Corona
Boardman	Victor Gilmour
Blue Mask	Nick Dimitri
Green Mask	Bob Minor
Patrons	Angelo Lamonea, Patrick Burns, Karen Kleiman
Passengers	Thomas Myers, Bill McConnell
Commuters	Peter Jason, William Hasley
Uniformed Cop	Allan Graf

Right: Joseph Walsh, Bruce Dern
Top: Ronee Blakley, Ryan O'Neal

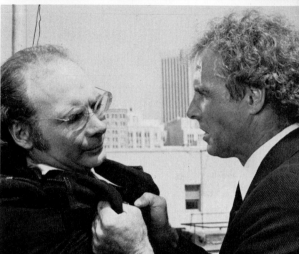

Ryan O'Neal, Bruce Dern

Isabelle Adjani

REVENGE OF THE PINK PANTHER

(UNITED ARTISTS) Producer-Director, Blake Edwards; Executive Producer, Tony Adams; Screenplay, Frank Waldman, Ron Clark, Blake Edwards; Based on story by Mr. Edwards; Photography, Ernie Day; Editor, Alan Jones; Music, Henry Mancini; Design, Peter Mullins; Art Director, John Siddall; Costumes, Tiny Nichols; Assistant Director, Terry Marcel; In Panavision and Technicolor; 98 minutes; Rated PG; July release.

CAST

Clouseau	Peter Sellers
Dreyfus	Herbert Lom
Simone Legree	Dyan Cannon
Douvier	Robert Webber
Cato	Burk Kwouk
Scallini	Paul Stewart
Marchione	Robert Loggia
Auguste Balls	Graham Stark
Claude Russo	Sue Lloyd
Guy Algo	Tony Beckley
Tanya	Valerie Leon

Left: Peter Sellers

Peter Sellers, Burt Kwouk

Dyan Cannon, Peter Sellers

**Peter Sellers, and above with Burt Kwouk,
Dyan Cannon Top with Valerie Leon**

**Dyan Cannon, Peter Sellers
Top: Herbert Lom, Valerie Leon**

SERGEANT PEPPER'S LONELY HEARTS CLUB BAND

(UNIVERSAL) Producer, Robert Stigwood; Director, Michael Schultz; Screenplay, Henry Edwards; Executive Producer, Dee Anthony; Photography, Owen Roizman; Associate Producer, Bill Oakes; Music, John Lennon, Paul McCartney; Arranged by George Martin; Choreography, Patricia Birch; Designer, Brian Eatwell; Editor, Christopher Holmes; Costumes, May Routh; Assistant Directors, L. Andrew Stone, Jerram Swartz, Chris Soldo; A Geria Production: In Dolby Stereo, Panavision and color; 111 minutes; Rated PG; July release.

CAST

Billy Shears	Peter Frampton
Mark Henderson	Barry Gibb
Dave Henderson	Robin Gibb
Bob Henderson	Maurice Gibb
Mean Mr. Mustard	Frankie Howerd
Dougie Shears	Paul Nicholas
B. D. Brockhurst	Donald Pleasence
Strawberry Fields	Sandy Farina
Lucy	Dianne Steinberg
Dr. Maxwell Edison	Steve Martin
Future Villain	Aerosmith
Father Sun	Alice Cooper
Benefit Performers	Earth, Wind & Fire
Sgt. Pepper	Billy Preston
The Diamonds	Stargard
Mr. Kite	George Burns
The Brute	Carel Struycken
Saralinda Shears	Patti Jerome
Ernest Shears	Max Showalter
Mr. Fields	John Wheeler

and Jay W. MacIntosh, Eleanor Zee, Scott Manners, Stanley Coles, Stanley Sheldon, Bob Mayo, Woodrow Chambliss, Hank Worden, Morgan Farley, Delos V. Smith, Pat Cranshaw, Teri Lynn Wood, Tracy Justrich, Anna Rodzianko, Rose Aragon.

Top: Robin, Barry and Maurice Gibb
(The Bee Gees)

George Burns

Sandy Farina with the Bee Gees and Peter Frampton Above: Billy Preston Top: Steve Martin

George Burns Above: Donald Pleasence, Paul Nicholas, Dianne Steinberg Top: Frankie Howerd

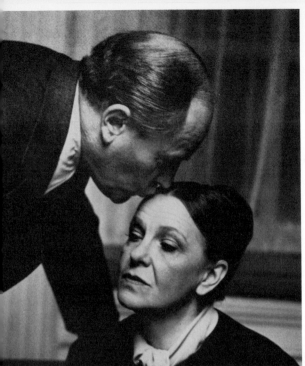

INTERIORS

(UNITED ARTISTS) Producers, Charles H. Joffe; Executive Producer, Robert Greenhut; Direction and Screenplay, Woody Allen; Photography, Gordon Willis; Editor, Ralph Rosenblum; Design, Mel Bourn; Costumes, Joel Schumacher; Assistant Director, Martin Berman; In Technicolor; 93 minutes; Rated PG; July release.

CAST

Flyn	Kristin Griffith
Joey	Marybeth Hurt
Frederick	Richard Jordan
Renata	Diane Keaton
Arthur	E. G. Marshall
Eve	Geraldine Page
Pearl	Maureeen Stapleton
Mike	Sam Waterston

Left: E. G. Marshall, Geraldine Page

Kristin Griffith, Sam Waterston, Marybeth Hurt, Diane Keaton, Geraldine Page

**Diane Keaton, Richard Jordan Above: Sam
Waterston, Marybeth Hurt Top: Keaton,
Kristin Griffith, Hurt**

**Richard Jordan, Marybeth Hurt
Above: Kristin Griffith**

NATIONAL LAMPOON'S ANIMAL HOUSE

(UNIVERSAL) Producers, Matty Simmons, Ivan Reitman; Director, John Landis; Screenplay, Harold Ramis, Douglas Kenney, Chris Miller; Photography, Charles Correll; Editor, George Folsey, Jr.; Music, Elmer Bernstein; Art Director, John J. Lloyd; Costumes, Deborah Nadoolman; Assistant Directors, Cliff Coleman, Ed Milkovich; Songs performed by Stephen Bishop, John Belushi, The Kingsmen, Bobby Lewis, Sam Cooke, Chris Montez, Connie Francis, Paul and Paula; In Panavision and Technicolor; 109 minutes; Rated R; July release.

CAST

Larry Kroger	Thomas Hulce
Kent Dorfman	Stephen Furst
Doug Neidermeyer	Mark Metcalf
Mandy Pepperidge	Mary Louise Weller
Babs Jansen	Martha Smith
Greg Marmalard	James Daughton
Chip Diller	Kevin Bacon
John Blutarsky	John Belushi
Stork	Douglas Kenney
Hardbar	Christian Miller
B.B.	Bruce Bonnheim
Katy	Karen Allen
Robert Hoover	James Widdoes
Eric Stratton	Tim Matheson
Donald Schoenstein	Peter Riegert
Daniel Simpson Day	Bruce McGill
Mothball	Joshua Daniel
Dave Jennings	Donald Sutherland
Dean Vernon Wormer	John Vernon
Trooper	Junior
Mayor Carmine DePasto	Cesare Danova
Otter's Co-Ed	Sunny Johnson
Marion Wormer	Verna Bloom
Clorette DePasto	Sarah Holcomb
Sissy	Stacy Grooman

and Stephen Bishop, DeWayne Jessie, Eliza Garrett, Lisa Baur, Aseneth Jurgenson, Katherine Denning, Raymone Robinson, Robert Elliott, Reginald H. Farmer, Jebidiah R. Dumas, Priscilla Lauris, Rick Eby, John Freeman, Sean McCartin, Helen Vick, Rich Greenough, Gary McLarty, Albert M. Mauro, Karen Werner, Fred Hice, Bill Hooker, Clifford Happy, Pam Bebermeyer, Bud Ekins, Jim Halty, R. A. Rondell, Walter Wyatt, Gilbert Combs

Left: James Daughton, John Vernon
Top: John Belushi

Mark Metcalf

James Widdoes, Tim Matheson

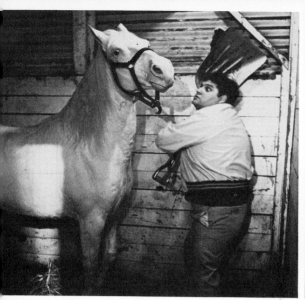

Verna Bloom, Tim Matheson Above: Mary
Louise Weller, Martha Smith Top: Stephen
Furst

John Vernon, Cesare Danova Above: Stephen
Furst, John Belushi, Bruce McGill
Top: Martha Smith

FOUL PLAY

(PARAMOUNT) Producers, Thomas L. Miller, Edward K. Milkis; Direction and Screenplay, Colin Higgins; Photography, David M. Walsh; Designer, Alfred Sweeney; Editor, Pembroke Herring; Associate Producer, Peter V. Herald; Assistant Directors, Gary D. Daigler, Larry J. Franco; Songs sung by Barry Manilow, The Bee Gees; Music, Charles Fox; Lyrics, Norman Gimbel; In Panavision and Movielab Color; 116 minutes; Rated PG; July release.

CAST

Gloria	Goldie Hawn
Tony	Chevy Chase
Hennessey	Burgess Meredith
Gerda	Rachel Roberts
Archbishop Thorncrest	Eugene Roche
Stanley Tibbets	Dudley Moore
Stella	Marilyn Sokol
Fergie	Brian Dennehey
Stiltskin	Marc Lawrence
Theatre Manager	Chuck McCann
MacKuen	Billy Barty
Scarface	Don Calfa
Scott	Bruce Solomon
Sandy	Cooper Huckabee
Mrs. Venus	Pat Ast
Mrs. Russel	Frances Bay
House Manager	Lou Cutell
Albino	William Frankfather
Capt. Coleman	John Hancock
Sally	Barbara Sammeth
Elsie	Queenie Smith
Ethel	Hope Summers
Mrs. Monk	Irene Tedrow
Turk	Ion Teodorescu
Sylvia	Janet Wood

and David Cole, Bill Gamble, Cyril Magnin, Michael David Lee, Neno Russo, Rollin Moriyama, Mitsu Yashima, M. James Arnett, Jophery Brown, John Hatfield, Joe Bellan, Chuck Walsh, Connie Sawyer, F. Jo Mohrbach, Garry Goodrow, Enrico DiGiuseppe, Glenys Fowles, Kathleen Hegierski, Sandra Walker, Thomas Jamerson, Richard McKee, Jane Shaulis, Craig Baxley, Hal Needham, Glynn Rubin, Shirley Python

Top: Chevy Chase

Goldie Hawn

68

Goldie Hawn Above: Dudley Moore
Top: Goldie Hawn

Chevy Chase, Goldie Hawn Above: Goldie
Hawn, Marilyn Sokol Top: Rachel Roberts

THE BUDDY HOLLY STORY

(COLUMBIA) Executive Producer, Edward H. Cohen; Co-Executive Producer, Fred T. Kuehnert; Associate Producer, Frances Avrut-Bauer; Producer, Fred Bauer; Director, Steve Rash; Screenplay, Robert Gittler; Story, Steve Rash, Fred Bauer; Photography, Stevan Larner; Editor, David Blewitt; Designer, Joel Schiller; Assistant Directors, Carol Himes, Bob Smally; In color; 113 minutes; July release.

CAST

Buddy Holly	Gary Busey
Jesse	Don Stroud
Ray Bob	Charles Martin Smith
Riley Randolph	Bill Jordan
Maria Elena Holly	Maria Richwine
Ross Turner	Conrad Janis
Eddie Foster	Albert Popwell
Jenny Lou	Amy Johnston
Mr. Wilson	Jim Beach
T. J.	John F. Goff
Madman Mancuso	Fred Travalena
Sol Zuckerman	Dick O'Neil
Luther	Stymie Beard
M.C. (Buffalo)	M. G. Kelly
Sam Cooke	Paul Mooney
Desk Clerk	Bill Phillips Murry
Tyrone	Freeman King
Cook	Steve Camp
Engineer Sam	Jody Berry
Cadillac Salesman	Bob Christopher
Mr. Holly	Arch Johnson
Mrs. Holly	Neva Patterson

and Gloria Irricari (Mrs. Santiago), Rajah Bergman, Joe Renzetti (Violinists), Gilbert Melgar (Richie), Gailaird Sartain (Big Bopper), George Simonelli (Dion), Steve Doubet (Roger), Jack Dembo (Cabbie), Richard Kennedy (Rev. Hargiss), Anthony Johnson (Singer on bus), Rod Grier (Singer on show), Peter Griffin (Director), Maxine Green, Mary Hyland, Susan Morse (Group Singers), Buster Jones (Soloist), Jerry Zaremba (Eddie), Paul Carmello (Parker), Bill Lytle (Delbert), Raymond Schockey (Sheriff), Loutz Gage (Producer), John Waldron, Alan Peterson (Little Boys), Jack Jozefson (Stage Manager), Craig White (King Curtis)

Left: Gary Busey, Don Stroud, Charlie Martin Smith, Conrad Janis Top: Gary Busey
1978 Academy Award for Best Scoring

Gary Busey, Amy Johnston

Gary Busey, Maria Richwine

Kevin McKenzie, Dennis Dimster,
Katharine Hepburn

Katharine Hepburn

OLLY OLLY OXEN FREE

(SANRIO) Producer-Director, Richard A. Colla; Screenplay, Eugene Poinc; Story, Maria L. de Ossio, Richard A. Colla, Eugene Poinc, Photography, Gayne Rescher; Designer, Peter Wooley; Music, Bob Alcivar; Editor, Lee Burch; Miss Hepburn's wardrobe, Edith Head; Associate Producers, Mark Lisson, Bill Froehlich; Executive Producer, Don Henderson; A Rico-Lion Film in color; 93 minutes; Rated G; August release

CAST

Miss Pudd .... Katharine Hepburn
Alby ....Kevin McKenzie
Chris ....Dennis Dimster
Mailman .... Peter Kilman
Joshua .... Obie

HOOPER

(WARNER BROS.) Producer, Hank Moonjean; Director, Hal Needham; Screenplay, Thomas Rickman, Bill Kerby; Story, Walt Green, Walter S. Herndon; Photography, Bobby Byrne; Art Director, Hilyard Brown; Editor, Donn Cambern; Music, Bill Justis; Assistant Directors, David Hamburger, Bill Scott; Title song written and sung by Bent Myggen; In color; 99 minutes; Rated PG; August release.

CAST

Sonny Hooper	Burt Reynolds
Ski	Jan-Michael Vincent
Gwen	Sally Field
Jocko	Brian Keith
Max Berns	John Marley
Cully	James Best
Adam	Adam West
Tony	Alfie Wise
Roger Deal	Robert Klein

© Warner Bros. 1978
Left: Jan-Michael Vincent, Burt Reynolds

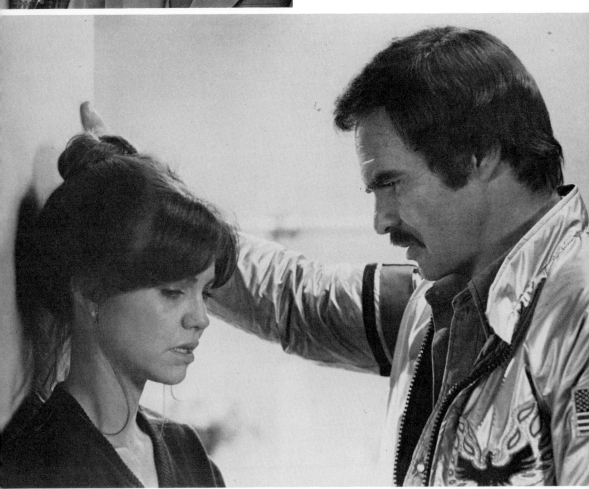

Sally Field, Burt Reynolds

Sally Field, Burt Reynolds, Jan-Michael Vincent, Robert Klein
Top: Burt Reynolds

WHO'LL STOP THE RAIN?

(UNITED ARTISTS) Producers, Herb Jaffe, Gabriel Katzka; Director, Karel Reisz; Screenplay, Judith Roscoe, Robert Stone; From novel "Dog Soldiers" by Robert Stone; Photography, Richard H. Kline; Editor, John Bloom; Music, Laurence Rosenthal; In color; 125 minutes; August release.

CAST

Ray	Nick Nolte
Marge	Tuesday Weld
John	Michael Moriarty
Antheil	Anthony Zerbe
Danskin	Richard Masur
Smitty	Ray Sharkey
Chairman	Gail Strickland
Eddy	Charles Haid
Bender	David O. Opatoshu

Top: Nick Nolte, Tuesday Weld
Below: Michael Moriarty, Richard Masur

Michael Moriarty, Nick Nolte Above: Nolte,
Jose Carlos Ruiz Top: Moriarty, Tuesday Weld

THE MANITOU

(AVCO EMBASSY) Producer-Director, William Girdler; Executive Producer, Melvin G. Gordy; Screenplay, William Girdler, Jon Cedar, Tom Pope; Based on novel of same title by Graham Masterson; Music, Lalo Schifrin; Associate Producers, Gilles A. DeTurenne, Jon Cedar; Editor, Bub Asman; Photography, Michel Hugo; Designer, Walter Scott Herndon; Assistant Directors, Bob Bender, Alain Silver; In Panavision, Dolby Stereo and color by CFI; 104 minutes; Rated PG; August release

CAST

Harry Erskine	Tony Curtis
Singing Rock	Michael Ansara
Karen Tandy	Susan Strasberg
Amelia Crusoe	Stella Stevens
Dr. Jack Hughes	Jon Cedar
Mrs. Karmann	Ann Sothern
Dr. Ernest Snow	Burgess Meredith
Dr. Robert McEvoy	Paul Mantee
Mrs. Winconis	Jeanette Nolan
Mrs. Hertz	Lurene Tuttle
Floor Nurse	Ann Mantee
MacArthur	Hugh Corcoran
Singing Rock's Wife	Tenaya
Prostitute	Carole Hemingway
Second Floor Nurse	Beverly Kushida
Wolf	Jan Heininger
Michael	Michael Laren

Right: Susan Strasberg Below: Tony Curtis, Burgess Meredith

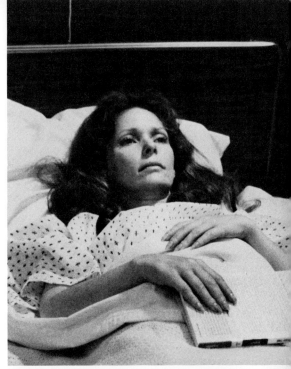

Susan Strasberg, Tony Curtis Above: Hugh Corcoran, Stella Stevens, Curtis, Ann Sothern

Ann Sothern, Stella Stevens

HOT LEAD AND COLD FEET

(BUENA VISTA) Producer, Ron Miller; Director, Robert Butler; Co-Producer, Christopher Hibler; Screenplay, Joe McEveety, Arthur Alsberg, Don Nelson; Based on story by Rod Piffath; Photography, Frank Phillips; Music, Buddy Baker; Associated Producer, Kevin Corcoran; Art Directors, John Mansbridge, Frank T. Smith; Costumes, Ron Talsky; Editor, Ray de Leuw; Assistant Directors, Paul "Tiny" Nichols, Jerram Swartz; In Technicolor; 90 minutes; Rated G; August release.

CAST

Eli/Wild Billy/Jasper Bloodshy	Jim Dale
Jenny	Karen Valentine
Denver Kid	Don Knotts
Rattlesnake	Jack Elam
Mayor Ragsdale	Darren McGavin
Mansfield	John Williams
Boss Snead	Warren Vanders
Roxanne	Debbie Lytton
Marcus	Michael Sharrett
Jack	Dave Cass
Pete	Richard Wright
Bartender	Don "Red" Barry
Jake	Jimmy Van Patten
Jeff	Gregg Palmer
Joshua	Ed Bakey
Old Codger	John Steadman

and Eric Server, Paul Lukather, Hap Lawrence, Robert Rothwell, Terry Nichols, Dallas McKennon, Stanley Clements, Don Brodie, Warde Donovan, Ron Honthaner, Norland Benson, Jim Whitecloud, Brad Weston, Russ Fast, Mike Howden, Art Burke, James Michaelford

Left: Jim Dale (R)

Jim Dale, Debbie Lytton, Karen Valentine, Michael Sharrett

GIRLFRIENDS

(WARNER BROS.) Producer-Director, Claudia Weill; Co-Producer, Jan Saunders; Screenplay, Vicki Polon; Story, Claudia Weill, Vicki Polon; Photography, Fred Murphy; Editor, Suzanna Pettit; Music, Michael Small; Art Director, Patrizia von Brandenstein; Associate Producers, Pat Churchill, Lilly Kilvert; Assistant Director, David Streit; A Cyclops Films Presentation in DuArt Color; 86 minutes; Rated PG; August release.

CAST

Susan Weinblatt	Melanie Mayron
Anne Munroe	Anita Skinner
Rabbi Gold	Eli Wallach
Eric	Christopher Guest
Martin	Bob Balaban
Julie	Gina Rogak
Ceil	Amy Wright
Beatrice	Viveca Lindfors
Abe	Mike Kellin
Terry	Jean de Baer
Cabbie	Ken McMillan
Photo Editor	Russell Horton
Rabbi's Wife	Tania Berezin
Carpel's Receptionist	Kathryn Walker
Carpel	Roderick Cook
Charlie	Kristoffer Tabori

© Warner Bros. 1978
Top: Christopher Guest, Melanie Mayron

Anita Skinner, Melanie Mayron

Raul Julia, Faye Dunaway

EYES OF LAURA MARS

(COLUMBIA) Producer, Jon Peters; Director, Irvin Kershner; Executive Producer, Jack H. Harris; Screenplay, John Carpenter, David Zelag Goodman; Story, John Carpenter; Photography, Victor J. Kemper; Music, Artie Kane; Love theme song "Prisoner" by Karen Lawrence and John DeSautels, sung by Barbara Streisand; Associate Producer, Laura Ziskin; Designer, Gene Callahan; Costumes, Theoni V. Aldredge; Editor, Michael Kahn; Art Director, Robert Gundlach; Assistant Directors, Louis A. Stroller, Mel Howard, Joseph Maimone, Jr.; In Panavision and color; 104 minutes; Rated R; August release.

CAST

Laura Mars	Faye Dunaway
John Neville	Tommy Lee Jones
Tommy Ludlow	Brad Dourif
Donald Phelps	Rene Auberjonois
Michael Reisler	Raul Julia
Sal Volpe	Frank Adonis
Michele	Lisa Taylor
Lulu	Darlanne Fluegel
Elaine Cassell	Rose Gregorio
Bill Boggs	Himself
Robert	Steve Marachuk
Doris Spenser	Meg Mundy
Sheila Weissman	Marilyn Meyers
Reporters	Gary Bayer, Mitchell Edmonds
Bert	Michael Tucker
Photo Assistants	Jeff Niki, Toshi Matsuo
Billy T	John E. Allen
Douglas	Dallas Edward Hayes
Aunt Caroline	Paula Lawrence
Make-up Person	Joey R. Mills
Hairdresser	John Sahag
Cab Driver	Hector Troy
Models	Anna Anderson, Deborah Beck, Jim Devine, Hanny Friedman, Winnie Hollman, Patty Oja, Donna Palmer, Sterling St. Jacques, Rita Tellone, Kari Page
Policemen	John Randolph Jones, Al Joseph, Gerald Kline, Sal Richards, Tom Degidon

Top: Tommy Lee Jones, Faye Dunaway

Rene Auberjonois, Faye Dunaway, Tommy Lee Jones
Top: (L) Brad Dourif (R) Faye Dunaway, Rene Auberjonois

UP IN SMOKE

(PARAMOUNT) Producers, Lou Adler, Lou Lombardo; Director, Lou Adler; Screenplay, Tommy Chong, Cheech Martin; Photography, Gene Polito; Associate Producer, John Beug; Editors, Lou Lombardo, Scott Conrad; Art Director, Leon Ericksen; Assistant Directors, Mike Moder, Bill Beasley; In Panavision and Metrocolor; 86 minutes; Rated R; September release.

CAST

Pedro	Cheech Marin
Man	Tommy Chong
Mr. Stoner	Strother Martin
Tempest Stoner	Edie Adams
Chauffeur	Harold Fong
Richard	Richard Novo
Jail Baits	Jane Moder, Pam Bille
Arresting Officer	Arthur Roberts
Judge Gladys Dykes	Marian Beeler
Bailiff	Donald Hotton
Prosecuting Attorney	Jon Ian Jacobs
Freak with basketball	Gary Mule Deer
Strawberry	Tom Skerritt
Ajax Lady	June Fairchild
Laughing Lady	Rainbeaux Smith
Aunt Bolita	Angelina Estrada
Upholstery Shop Foreman	Ernie Fuentes
Factory Boss	Val Avery
Bennie	Ben Marino
Toyota Kawasaki	Akemi Kikumura
Border Guards	Joe Creaghe, Roy Stocking
Jade East	Zane Buzby
Debbie	Anne Wharton
Gloria	Louisa Moritz
Motorcycle Cop	Otto Felix
Rodney Bingenheimer	Rodney Bingenheimer
Roxy Doormen	Kurt Kaufman, David Nelson
Punk on stairs	Hal Goplerud
Tow Truck Driver	Wayne Hazelhurst
Sgt. Stedenko	Stacy Keach
Harry	Mills Watson
Clyde	Karl Johnson
Murphy	Rick Beckner

Nuns .... Marcia Wolf, Andi Nachman, Betty McGuire, Cheryl Jeffrey, Gayna Shernen, June Creaghe, Patty Proudfoot

Cheech Marin, Tommy Chong

Tommy Chong, Cheech Marin, Jon Ian Jacobs, Marian Beeler
Top: (L) Edie Adams (R) Cheech Marin, Tommy Chong

SOMEBODY KILLED HER HUSBAND

(COLUMBIA) Producer, Martin Poll; Director, Lamont Johnson; Screenplay, Reginald Rose; Music, Alex North; Song "Love Keeps Getting Stronger Every Day" by Neil Sedaka, Howard Greenfield, Sung by Neil Sedaka; Photography, Andrew Laszlo, Ralf D. Bode; Editor, Barry Malkin; Designer, Ted Haworth; Costumes, Joseph G. Aulisi; Art Director, David Chapman; Assistant Directors, Alex Hapsas, Thomas John Kane; Associate Producer, William Craver; In Movielab Color; A Melvin Simon Presentation; 97 minutes; Rated PG; September release.

CAST

Jenny Moore	Farrah Fawcett-Majors
Jerry Green	Jeff Bridges
Ernest Van Santen	John Wood
Audrey Van Santen	Tammy Grimes
Hubert Little	John Glover
Helene	Patricia Elliott
Flora	Mary McCarty
Preston Moore	Laurence Guittard
Benjamin	Vincent Robert Santa Lucia
Frank Danziger	Beeson Carroll
Other Neighbor	Eddie Lawrence
Customer	Arthur Rhytis
Man in beret	Jean-Pierre Stewart
Lulu's Mother	Terri DuHaime
Girl Typist	Sands Hall
Night Doorman	Joseph Culliton
Day Doorman	Dave Johnson
Employee	Melissa Ferris
Odd Couple Husband	Jeremiah Sullivan
Odd Couple Wife	Sloan Shelton
Indignant Woman	Mary Alan Hokanson
Macy's Night Watchman	John Corcoran
Elf	Mark Haber

and Tony Farentino, Jim Lovelett, Liz Kallimeyer, Bill Anagnos, John Gibson

Jeff Bridges, Farrah Fawcett-Majors
(also Top)

PARADISE ALLEY

(UNIVERSAL) Producers, John F. Roach, Ronald A. Suppa; Executive Producer, Edward Pressman; Direction and Screenplay, Sylvester Stallone; Associate Producer, Arthur Chobanian; Photography, Laszlo Kovacs; Designer, John W. Corso; Editor, Eve Newman; Music, Bill Conti; Art Director, Deborah Beaudet; Assistant Directors, Cliff Coleman, Mark R. Schilz; In Panavision and Technicolor; A Force Ten Production; A Moonblood Film; Song "Too Close to Paradise" by Bill Conti, sung by Sylvester Stallone; 108 minutes; Rated PG; September release.

CAST

Cosmo Carboni	Sylvester Stallone
Victor	Lee Canalito
Lenny	Armand Assante
Big Glory	Frank McRae
Annie	Anne Archer
Stitch	Kevin Conway
Franky the Thumper	Terry Funk
Bunchie	Joyce Ingalls
Burp	Joe Spinell
Susan Chow	Aimee Eccles
Mumbles	Tom Waits
Doorman	Chick Casey
Paradise Bartender	James J. Casino
Paradise Alley Hooker	Fredi O. Gordon
Bar Room Hookers	Lydia Goya, Patricia Spann
Paradise Alley Bum	Michael Jeffers
Mr. Giambelli	Max Leavitt
Rat	Paul Mace
Fat Lady	Polli Magaro
Vonny	Pamela Miller
Mickey the bartender	John Monks, Jr.
Store Owner	Leo Nanas
Singer	Frank Stallone, Jr.
Skinny the Hand	Frank Pesce
Towel Boy	Stuart K. Robinson
Legs	Ray Sharkey
Sticky	Jeff Waid

**Right: Paul Mace, Kevin Conway, Terry Funk, Frank Pesce, Sylvester Stallone, Lee Canalito
Top: Armand Assante, Lee Canalito, Sylvester Stallone**

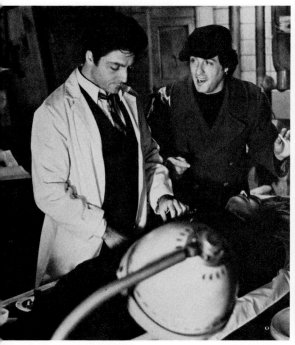

Armand Assante, Sylvester Stallone

Anne Archer, Sylvester Stallone

DEATH ON THE NILE

(PARAMOUNT) Producers, John Brabourne, Richard Goodwin; Director, John Guillermin; Screenplay, Anthony Shaffer; Editor, Malcolm Cooke; Designer, Peter Murton; Costumes, Anthony Powell; Photography, Jack Cardiff; Music, Nino Rota; Assistant Director, Chris Carreras; Associate Producer, Norton Knatchbull; Art Directors, Brian and Terry Ackland; An EMI Film in Panavision and Technicolor; 140 minutes; Rated PG; September release.

CAST

Hercule Poirot	Peter Ustinov
Louise Bourget	Jane Birkin
Linnet Ridgeway	Lois Chiles
Mrs. Van Schuyler	Bette Davis
Jacqueline de Bellefort	Mia Farrow
Mr. Ferguson	Jon Finch
Rosalie Otterbourne	Olivia Hussey
Manager of the Karnak	I. S. Johar
Andrew Pennington	George Kennedy
Mrs. Salome Otterbourne	Angela Lansbury
Simon Doyle	Simon MacCorkindale
Colonel Rice	David Niven
Miss Bowers	Maggie Smith
Dr. Bessner	Jack Warden
Barnstaple	Harry Andrews
Rockford	Sam Wanamaker

Left: Mia Farrow, Simon MacCorkindale
Top: David Niven, Peter Ustinov, Bette Davis
1978 Academy Award for Best Costume Design

David Niven, George Kennedy, Peter Ustinov, Lois Chiles, Simon MacCorkindale, Jack Warden, Maggie Smith, Angela Lansbury, I. S. Johar

Simon MacCorkindale, Mia Farrow, Jack Warden, Maggie Smith, Bette Davis, Jon Finch, Olivia Hussey, George Kennedy,
I. S. Johar Top Left: Bette Davis, Angela Lansbury, Maggie Smith Below: Simon MacCorkindale, Jack Warden,
Peter Ustinov Top Right: Lois Chiles, Angela Lansbury Below: Mia Farrow, Olivia Hussey

GO TELL THE SPARTANS

(AVCO EMBASSY) Producers, Allan F. Bodoh, Mitchell Cannold; Director, Ted Post; Executive Producer, Michael Leone; Screenplay, Wendell Mayes; Based on novel "Incident at Muc Wa" by Daniel Ford; Associate Producer, Jesse Corallo; Photography, Harry Stradling, Jr.; Art Director, Jack Senter; Editor, Millie Moore; Music, Dick Halligan; Assistant Directors, Jesse Corallo, Michael Kane; A Mar Vista Productions Presentation; A Spartan Company Production; IN CFI Color; 114 minutes; Rated R; September release

CAST

Major Asa Barker	Burt Lancaster
Cpl. Stephen Courcey	Craig Wasson
Sgt. Oleonowski	Jonathan Goldsmith
Capt. Al Olivetti	Marc Singer
Lt. Raymond Hamilton	Joe Unger
Cpl. Abraham Lincoln	Dennis Howard
Lt. Finley Wattsberg	David Clennon
Cowboy	Evan Kim
Cpl. Ackley	John Megna
Signalman Toffer	Hilly Hicks
Gen. Harnitz	Dolph Sweet
Colonel Minh	Clyde Kasatsu
Corporal Oldman	James Hong
Butterfly	Denice Kumagai
One-Eyed Charlie	Tad Horino
Minh's Interpreter	Phong Diep
Minh's Aid-de-Camp	Ralph Brannen
Captain Schlitz	Mark Carlton

Top: Burt Lancaster, Dennis Howard, John Megna, Craig Wasson, Evan Kim, Jonathan Goldsmith

Burt Lancaster

AVALANCHE

(NEW WORLD) Producer, Roger Corman; Executive Producer, Paul Rapp; Director, Corey Allen; Screenplay, Claude Pola, Corey Allen; Story, Frances Doel; Photography, Pierre-William Glenn; Editors, Stuart Schoolnik, Larry Bock; Music, William Kraft; Assistant Directors, Russell Vreeland, Roger Carlton; Designer, Sharon Compton: Art Director, Phillip Thomas; In MetroColor; 91 minutes; Rated PG; September release.

CAST

David Shelby	Rock Hudson
Caroline Brace	Mia Farrow
Nick Throne	Robert Forster
Florence Shelby	Jeanette Nolan
Bruce Scott	Rick Moses
Henry McDade	Steve Franken
Mark Elliott	Barry Primus
Tina Elliott	Cathey Paine
Phil Prentiss	Jerry Douglas
Leo the Coach	Tony Carbone
Annette Rivers	Peggy Browne
Cathy Jordan	Pat Egan
TV Director	Joby Baker
Marty Brenner	X Brands
Susan Maxwell	Cindy Luedke
Ed the Pilot	John Cathey
Bruce's Coach	Angelo Lamonea

and Buzz Bundy, Bill Catching, Dottie Catching, Sandy Gimpel, Fred Hice, Leslie Hoffman, Keith Lane Jensen, Dennis Madalone, Cindy Perpiche, Sandy Robertson, Jerry Summers, Chuck Tamburro, Allen Wyatt, Jr.

Right: Rock Hudson

Rock Hudson, Mia Farrow, Robert Forster

DAYS OF HEAVEN

(PARAMOUNT) Executive Producer, Jacob Brackman; Producers, Bert and Harold Schneider; Direction and Screenplay, Terrence Malick; Photography, Nestor Almendros; Art Director, Jack Fisk; Editor, Billy Weber; Music, Ennio Morricone; Costumes, Patricia Norris; In Dolby Stereo and color; 95 minutes; Rated PG; September release.

CAST

Bill	Richard Gere
Abby	Brooke Adams
The Farmer	Sam Shepard
Linda	Linda Manz
Farm Foreman	Robert Wilke
Linda's Friend	Jackie Shultis
Mill Foreman	Stuart Margolin
Harvest Hand	Tim Scott
Dancer	Gene Bell
Fiddler	Doug Kershaw
Vaudeville Leader	Richard Libertini
Vaudeville Wrestler	Frenchie Lemond
Vaudeville Dancer	Sahbra Markus
Accountant	Bob Wilson
Headmistress	Muriel Jolliffe
Preacher	John Wilkinson
Farm Worker	King Cole

Left: Linda Manz
1978 Academy Award for Best Cinematography

Brooke Adams, Richard Gere

Linda Manz
Top: Richard Gere

Brooke Adams, Sam Shepard
Top: Brooke Adams

COMES A HORSEMAN

(UNITED ARTISTS) Producers, Gene Kirkwood, Dan Paulson; Executive Producers, Robert Chartoff, Irwin Winkler; Director, Alan J. Pakula; Screenplay, Dennis Lynton Clark; Photography, Gordon Willis; Designer, George Jenkins; Editor, Marion Rothman; Music, Michael Small; Costumes, Luster Bayless; Associate Producer, Ronald Caan; Assistant Director, Paul Helmick; In Panavision and color; 118 minutes; Rated PG; October release.

CAST

Frank	James Caan
Ella	Jane Fonda
Ewing	Jason Robards
Neil Atkinson	George Grizzard
Dodger	Richard Farnsworth
Julie Blocker	Jim Davis
Billy Joe Meynert	Mark Harmon
Hoverton	Macon McCalman
George Bascomb	Basil Hoffman
Ralph Cole	James Kline
Kroegh	James Keach
Cattle Buyer	Clifford A. Pellow

Jane Fonda, James Caan (also Top)
Above: Richard Farnsworth

Top: Jim Davis, Jason Robards, James
Kline Below: Jason Robards, George
Grizzard

90

WHO IS KILLING THE GREAT CHEFS OF EUROPE?

(WARNER BROS.) Producer, William Aldrich; Director, Ted Kotcheff; Screenplay, Peter Stone; Based on "Someone Is Killing the Great Chefs of Europe" by Nan and Ivan Lyons; Executive Producers, Merv Adelson, Lee Rich; Music, Henry Mancini; Assistant Director, Wolfgang Glattes; Art Director, Werner Achman; Costumes, Judy Moorcroft; In color; 112 minutes; Rated PG; October release.

CAST

Robby	George Segal
Natasha	Jacqueline Bisset
Max	Robert Morley
Kohner	Jean-Pierre Cassel
Moulineau	Philippe Noiret
Grandvilliers	Jean Rochefort
Ravello	Luigi Proietti
Fausto Zoppi	Stefano Satta Flores
Beecham	Madge Ryan
Blodgett	Frank Windsor
St. Claire	Peter Sallis
Doyle	Tim Barlow
Dr. Deere	John Lemesurier
Cantrell	Joss Ackland
Salpetre	Jean Gaven
Saint-Juste	Daniel Emilfork
Massenet	Jacques Marin
Chappemain	Jacques Balutin
Brissac	Jean Paredes
Soong	Michael Chow
Blonde	Anita Graham
Skeffington	Nicholas Ball
Bussingbill	David Cook

and Nigel Havers (Counterman), John Carlisle (Actor), Sheila Ruskin (Actress), Kenneth Fortescue (Director), Strewan Rodger (Asst. Director), Derek Smith (In Corridor), Marjorie Smith (Receptionist), Sylvia Kay (Reporter), Aimee Delamain (Old Woman), Lyall Jones (Driver), Eddie Tagoe (Mumbala), Caroline Langrishe (Loretta)

Right: Robert Morley © 1978 Warner Bros.

George Segal, Robert Morley, Jacqueline Bisset

Jacqueline Bisset, George Segal

THE WIZ

(UNIVERSAL) Executive Producer, Ken Harper; Producer, Rob Cohen; Director, Sidney Lumet; Screenplay, Joel Schumacher; From the book "The Wonderful Wizard of Oz" by L. Frank Baum, and the musical "The Wiz" with book by William F. Brown, and music and lyrics by Charlie Smalls; Photography, Oswald Morris; Editor, Dede Allen; Design and Costumes, Tony Walton; Visual effects, Albert Whitlock; Choreography, Louis Johnson; Associate Producer, Burtt Harris; Art Director, Philip Rosenberg; Assistant Directors, Burtt Harris, Alan Hopkins; Assistant Choreographers, Carlton Johnson, Mabel Robinson; A Motown Production in Dolby Stereo and Technicolor; 133 minutes; Rated G; October release.

CAST

Dorothy	Diana Ross
Scarecrow	Michael Jackson
Tinman	Nipsey Russell
Lion	Ted Ross
Evillene	Mabel King
Aunt Em	Theresa Merritt
Miss One	Thelma Carpenter
Glinda the Good	Lena Horne
The Wiz	Richard Pryor
Uncle Henry	Stanley Greene
Subway Peddler	Clyde J. Barrett
Head Winkie	Carlton Johnson
Cheetah	Harry Madsen
Rolls Royce Lady	Glory Van Scott
Green Lady	Vicki Baltimore
Crows	Derrick Bell, Roderick Spencer Sibert, Kashka Banjoko, Ronald Smokey Stevens
Gold Footmen	Tony Brealond, Joe Lynn
Green Footmen	Clinton Jackson, Charles Rodriguez
Munchkins	Ted Williams, Mabel Robinson, Damon Pearce, Donna Patrice Ingram

and Carlos Cleveland, Mariann Aalda, Aaron Boddie, Gay Faulkner, Ted Butler, T. B. Skinner, Jamie Perry, Daphne McWilliams, Douglas Berring, James Shaw, Johnny Brown, Gyle Waddy, Dorothy Fox, Frances Salisbury, Beatrice Dunmore, Traci Core, Donald King, Claude Brooks, Billie Allen, Willie Carpenter, Denise DeJon, Kevin Stockton, Alvin Alexis

Left: Diana Ross

Michael Jackson

Richard Pryor

**Mabel King Top: Ted Ross, Michael
Jackson, Diana Ross, Nipsey Russell**

GOIN' SOUTH

(PARAMOUNT) Producers, Harry Gittes, Harold Schneider; Director, Jack Nicholson; Screenplay, John Herman Shaner, Al Ramrus, Charles Shyer, Alan Mandel; Photography, Nestor Almendros; Story, John Herman Shanner, Al Ramrus; Designer, Roby Carr Rafelson; Editors, Richard Chew, John Fitzgerald Beck; Music, Van Dyke Parks, Perry Botkin, Jr.; Costumes, William Ware Theiss; Assistant Director, Michael Daves; In Panavision and Metrocolor; 105 minutes; Rated PG; October release.

CAST

Henry Moon	Jack Nicholson
Julia Tate	Mary Steenburgen
Towfield	Christopher Lloyd
Hector	John Belushi
Hermine	Veronica Cartwright
Sheriff Kyle	Richard Bradford
Big Abe	Jeff Morris
Hog	Danny DeVito
Coogan	Tracey Walter
Polty	Gerald H. Reynolds
Mrs. Anderson	Luana Anders
Mr. Anderson	George W. Smith
Mrs. Haber	Lucy Lee Flippin
Mr. Haber	Ed Begley, Jr.
Mrs. Warren	Maureen Byrnes
Mr. Warren	B. J. Merholz
Parson Weems	Britt Leach
Florence	Georgia Schmidt
Mrs. Standard	Nancy Coan Kaclik
Farmer Standard	R. L. Armstrong

and Barbara Ann Walters, Anne Ramsey, Marsha Ferri, Lin Shaye, Don McGovern, Dennis Fimple, Anne T. Marshall, Anita Terrian, Rogert L. Wilson, Carlton Risdon, May R. Boss, Loren Janes

Top: Christopher Lloyd, Richard Bradford, Jack Nicholson, John Belushi

Mary Steenburgen, Jack Nicholson

A WEDDING

(20th CENTURY-FOX) Producer-Director, Robert Altman; Executive Producer, Tommy Thompson; Screenplay, John Considine, Patricia Resnick, Allan Nicholls, Robert Altman; Story Robert Altman, John Considine; Associate Producers, Robert Eggenweiler, Scott Bushnell; Photography, Charles Rosher; Editor, Tony Lombardo; Assistant Directors, Tommy Thompson, Peter Berquist, Bob Dahlin; In Panavision, Dolby Stereo and DeLuxe Color; A Lion's Gate Films Production; 125 minutes; Rated PG; October release.

CAST

The Groom's Family: (Corelli): Lillian Gish (Grandmother), Ruth Nelson (Her Sister Beatrice) Ann Ryerson (Victoria, Beatrice's granddaughter), Desi Arnaz, Jr. (Dino the groom), Belita Moreno (Daphne, his twin), Vittorio Gassman (Luigi the groom's father), Nina Van Pallandt (Regina, groom's mother), Virginia Vestoff (Clarice, groom's aunt), Dina Merrill (Antoinette, groom's aunt), Pat McCormick (Mackenzie, groom's uncle), Luigi Proietti (Little Dino, groom's uncle)
The Bride's Family: (Brenner); Carol Burnett (Tulip, bride's mother), Paul Dooley (Snooks, bride's father), Amy Stryker (Muffin, the bride), Mia Farrow (Buffy, her sister), Dennis Christopher (Hughie, her brother), Mary Seibel (Aunt Marge, Snook's sister), Margaret Ladd (Ruby, Marge's daughter), Gerald Busby (David, Tulip's brother), Peggy Ann Garner (David's wife), Mark R. Deming (Matthew, David's son), David Brand, Chris Brand, Amy Brand, Jenny Brand, Jeffrey Jones, Jay D. Jones, Courtney MacArthur, Paul D. Keller III (David's children)

Corelli House Staff: Cedric Scott (Randolph, houseman), Robert Fortier (Jim, gardener), Maureen Steindler (Libby, cook)
The Wedding Staff: Geraldine Chaplin (Coordinator), Mona Abboud (Her Assistant), Viveca Lindfors (Ingrid, cateress), Lauren Hutton (Flo, film producer), Allan Nicholls (Jake, cameraman), Maysie Hoy (Casey, sound person), John Considine (Jeff, chief of security), Patricia Resnick (Redford, guard), Margery Bond (Lombardo, guard), Dennis Franz (Koons, Guard), Harold C. Johnson (Oscar, chef), Alexander Sopenar (Victor, photographer)
The Friends and Guests: Howard Duff (Dr. Meecham), John Cromwell (Bishop Martin), Bert Remsen (Only guest), Pamela Dawber (groom's ex-girlfriend), Gavan O'Herlihy (groom's ex-roommate), Craig Richard Nelson (teacher from groom's school), Jeffrey S. Perry (Bunky, groom's friend), Marta Heflin (Shelby, bridesmaid), Lesley Rogers (Rosie, bridesmaid), Timothy Thomerson (Russell, Rosie's husband), Beverly Ross (Nurse), David Fitzgerald (Kevin, cook's son), Susan Kendall Newman (Chris, Kevin's bride), Ellie Albers (Gypsy violinist), Tony Llorens (pianist), and Chuck Banks' Big Band with Chris La Kome

Right: Mia Farrow, Howard Duff Above: John Cromwell, Lillian Gish Top: Beverly Ross, Dina Merrill

Desi Arnaz, Jr., Nina Van Pallandt, Vittorio Gassman

Carol Burnett, Amy Stryker, Paul Dooley

BLOODBROTHERS

(WARNER BROS.) Producer, Stephen Friedman; Director, Robert Mulligan; Screenplay, Walter Newman; Based on novel by Richard Price; Music, Elmer Bernstein; Photography, Robert Surtees; Editor, Shelly Kahn; Designer, Gene Callahan; Assistant Directors, Howard Roessel, Robert Hargrove; In color; 116 minutes; Rated R; October release.

CAST

Chubby DeCoco	Paul Sorvino
Tommy DeCoco	Tony Lo Bianco
Stony DeCoco	Richard Gere
Marie	Lelia Goldoni
Phyllis	Yvonne Wilder
Banion	Kenneth McMillan
Dr. Harris	Floyd Levine
Annette	Marilu Henner
Albert	Michael Hershewe
Cheri	Christine DeBell
Mrs. Pitts	Pamela Myers
Sylvia	Gloria LeRoy
Paulie	Bruce French
Malfie	Peter Iacangelo
Butler	Kim Milford
Mott	Robert Englund
Jackie	Raymond Singer
Jackie's mother	Lila Teigh
Blackie	Eddie Jones
Artie	Danny Aiello

© Warner Bros. 1978
Left: Paul Sorvino, Richard Gere,
Tony Lo Bianco

Michael Hershewe, Richard Gere

Kristine DeBell, Richard Gere
Above: Richard Gere, Paul Sorvino

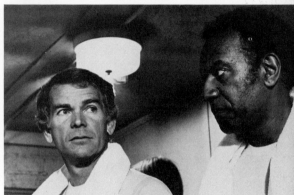

BORN AGAIN

(AVCO EMBASSY) Executive Producer, Robert L. Munger; Producer, Frank Capra, Jr.; Director, Irving Rapper; Screenplay, Walter Bloch; Music, Les Baxter; Associate Producer, Paul Temple; Photography, Harry Stradling, Jr.; Title Song sung by Larnell Harris; Lyrics, Craig Johnson; Designer, William J. Kenney; Editor, Axel Hubert; Assistant Directors, Bob Bender, Ed Milkovich; In color; 110 minutes; Rated PG; October release.

CAST

Chales Colson	Dean Jones
Patty Colson	Anne Francis
David Shapiro	Jay Robinson
Tom Phillips	Dana Andrews
Jimmy Newsom	Raymond St. Jacques
Judge Gerhard Gesell	George Brent
Senator Harold Hughes	Himself
President Richard M. Nixon	Harry Spillman
Scanlon	Scott Walker
Kramer	Robert Gray
Al Quie	Arthur Roberts
Douglas Coe	Ned Wilson
Dick Howard	Dean Brooks
Henry Kissinger	Peter Jurasik
Chris Colson	Christopher Conrad
Wendell Colson	Stuart Lee
Emily Colson	Alicia Fleer
H. R. Haldeman	Richard Caine
Holly Holm	Brigid O'Brien
John Erlichman	Robert Broyles
Archibald Cox	Byron Morrow
E. Howard Hunt	William Zukert
Leon Saworski	William Benedict

Anne Francis, Dean Jones

Top: Dana Andrews, Dean Jones
Below: Dean Jones, Harry Spillman
Top Right: Dean Jones, Jay Robinson
Below: Dean Jones, Raymond St. Jacques

MIDNIGHT EXPRESS

(COLUMBIA) Executive Producer, Peter Guber; Producers, Alan Marshall, David Puttnam; Director, Alan Parker; Screenplay, Oliver Stone; Based on book by Billy Hayes and William Hoffer; Designer, Geoffrey Kirkland; Art Director, Evan Hercules; Costumes, Milena Canonero; Assistant Director, Ray Corbett; Editor, Gerry Hambling; Music, Giorgio Moroder; In color; 120 minutes; Rated R; October release.

CAST

Billy Hayes	Brad Davis
Jimmy	Randy Quaid
Tex	Bo Hopkins
Max	John Hurt
Hamidou	Paul Smith
Mr. Hayes	Mike Kellin
Erich	Norbert Weisser
Susan	Irene Miracle
Rifki	Paolo Bonacelli
Stanley Daniels	Michael Ensign
Yesil	Franco Diogene
Prosecutor	Kevork Malikyan
Translator	Mihalis Yannatos
Chief Judge	Gigi Ballista
Aslan	Tony Boyd
Ahmet	Peter Jeffrey
Negdir	Ahmed El Shenawi
Turkish Detective	Zanninos Zanninou
Ticket Seller	Dimos Starenios

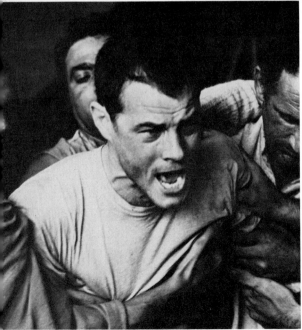

Brad Davis

Top: Mike Kellin, Brad Davis
*1978 Academy Award for Best Screenplay from
Another Medium*

Irene Miracle, Brad Davis Top Left: John Hurt, Brad Davis Below: Randy Quaid,
Brad Davis Top Right: Brad Davis, Norbert Weisser

THE BIG FIX

(UNIVERSAL) Producers, Carl Borack, Richard Dreyfuss; Director, Jeremy Paul Kagan; Screenplay, Roger L. Simon from his novel; Photography, Frank Stanley; Designer, Robert F. Boyle; Editor, Patrick Kennedy; Costumes, Edith Head; Music, Bill Conti; Art Director, Raymond Brandt; Assistant Directors, Jon C. Andersen, Robert Latham Brown, Candace Allen; In Panavision and Technicolor; 108 minutes; Rated PG; October release.

CAST

Moses Wine	Richard Dreyfuss
Lila	Susan Anspach
Suzanne	Bonnie Bedelia
Sam Sebastian	John Lithgow
Alora	Ofelia Medina
Spitzler	Nicolas Coster
Eppis	F. Murray Abraham
Oscar Procari, Sr.	Fritz Weaver
Jorge	Jorge Cervera, Jr.
Jacob	Michael Hershewe
Aunt Sonya	Rita Karin
Randy	Ron Rifkin
Wilson	Larry Bishop
Michael Linker	Andrew Bloch
Mr. Johnson	Sidney Clute
Hawthorne	John Cunningham
Jonah's Partner	Frank Doubleday
Woman in Mercedes	Joyce Easton
Bittleman	Martin Garner
Simon	Danny Gellis
Commentator	William Glover
Wendy Linker	Kathryn Grody
Perry	Murray MacLeod
Policemen	Ray Martucci, Bob O'Connell
Maid	Lupe Ontiveros

and Dick Whittington, Steven Benedict, Rene Botana, Harry Caesar, Billy Cardenas, Jane Chastain, Willie Covan, Fred Franklyn, Joel Fredrick, Margie Gordon, Chester Grimes, Pat Hustis, David Matthau, John Mayo, Mandy Patinkin, Raphael Simon, Gregory Prentiss, David Rowlands, Al Ruban, Running Deer, June Sanders, Caskey Swaim, Miiko Taka, Joe Warfield, James Wing Woo

Left: Nicolas Coster, Richard Dreyfuss, Susan Anspacher Top: Richard Dreyfuss, Bonnie Bedelia

Richard Dreyfuss, Fritz Weaver

Bonnie Bedelia, Ron Rifkin

SLOW DANCING IN THE BIG CITY

(UNITED ARTISTS) Producers, Michael Levee, John G. Avildsen; Directed and Edited by John G. Avildsen; Screenplay, Barra Grant; Photography, Ralf Bode; Music, Bill Conti; Art Director, Henry Shrady; Costumes, Ruth Morley; Choreographers, Robert North, Anne Ditchburn; Associate Producer, George Manasse; Assistant Director, Dwight Williams; In Dolby Stereo and color; 101 minutes; Rated PG; November release.

CAST

Lou Friedlander	Paul Sorvino
Sarah Gantz	Anne Ditchburn
David	Nicolas Coster
Franny	Anita Dangler
Roger	Hector Jaime Mercado
Christopher	Thaao Penghlis
Barbara	Linda Selman
Marty	G. Adam Gifford
Diana	Tara Mitton
George	Dick Carballo
Dr. Foster	Jack Ramage
T. C.	Daniel Faraldo

Top: Anita Dangler, Paul Sorvino
Below: G. Adam Gifford, Paul Sorvino
Top Right: Anne Ditchburn, Hector Jaime Mercado

Paul Sorvino, Anne Ditchburn

MOVIE MOVIE

(WARNER BROS.) Producer-Director, Stanley Donen; Screenplay, Larry Gelbart, Sheldon Keller; Executive Producer, Martin Starger; Photography, Charles Rosher, Jr. (Dynamite Hands), Bruce Surtees (Baxter's Beauties); Art Director, Jack Fisk; Editor, George Hively; Music, Ralph Burns; Musical Numbers Staged by Michael Kidd; Costumes, Patty Norris; Assistant Directors, Jonathan Sanger, Mark Johnson, Lorraine Senna; Designer, Chris Horner; In black and white and color; 105 minutes; Rated PG; November release.

CAST

"Dynamite Hands"

Gloves Malloy	George C. Scott
Betsy McGuire	Trish Van Devere
Peanuts	Red Buttons
Vince Marlowe	Eli Wallach
Joey Popchik	Harry Hamlin
Troubles Moran	Ann Reinking
Mama Popchik	Jocelyn Brando
Pop Popchik	Michael Kidd
Angie Popchik	Kathleen Beller
Johnny Danko	Barry Bostwick
Dr. Blaine	Art Carney
Sailor Lawson	Clay Hodges
Tony Norton	George P. Wilbur
Barney Keegle	Peter T. Stader

and James Lennon, John Hudkins, Robert Herron, Denver R. Mattson, James Nickerson, Harvey G. Parry, Wally Rose, Fred Scheiwiller, James J. Casino, John R. McKee, Gary Stokes, Garth Thompson, Clifford Happy, Terry L. Nichols, Larry Hayden, Patrick Omeirs, Michael Rodgers, Thomas Morga, Clarence Beatty, Charlie Murray, Evelyn Moriarty, June McCall, Jack Slate, Michael Lansing, Chuck Hicks, George Fisher, James Winburn, Bud Ekins

"Baxter's Beauties of 1933"

Spats Baxter	George C. Scott
Trixie Lane	Barbara Harris
Dick Cummings	Barry Bostwick
Isobel Stuart	Trish Van Devere
Jinks Murphy	Red Buttons
Pop	Eli Wallach
Kitty	Rebecca York
Dr. Bowers	Art Carney
Gussie	Maidie Norman
Mrs. Updike	Jocelyn Brando
Pennington	Charles Lane
Motorcycle Cop	Barney Martin
Tinkle Johnson	Dick Winslow
Fritz	Sebastian Brook
Theatre Workman	Jerry Von Hoeltke
Chorus Girl	Paula Jones
Chorus Boy	John Henry
Movers	John Hudkins, Robert Herron

© Warner Bros. 1978

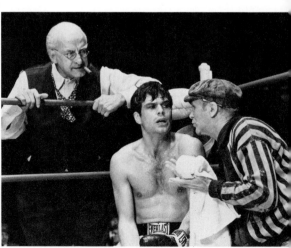

Ann Reinking
Above: Eli Wallach, George C. Scott

George C. Scott, Harry Hamlin, Red Buttons
Top Left: George C. Scott

Barry Bostwick, George C. Scott, Red Buttons
Top: George C. Scott, Trish Van Devere

THE LORD OF THE RINGS

(UNITED ARTISTS) Producer, Saul Zaentz; Director, Ralph Bakshi; Screenplay, Chris Conkling, Peter S. Beagle; Based on stories by J. R. R. Tolkien; Music, Leonard Rosenman; In Dolby Stereo and color; 131 minutes; Rated PG; A Fantasy Films Production; November release. An animated fantasy feature based on Tolkien's trilogy.

Top: Lady Galadriel
Below: Merry, Pippin, Boromir

Gollum and the Nine Companions
Top: Frodo, Gandalf, Sam

ONCE IN PARIS

(LEIGH-McLAUGHLIN) Produced, Directed and Written by Frank D. Gilroy; Co-Producers, Manny Fuchs, Gerard Croce; Photography, Claude Saunier; Editor, Robert Q. Lovett; Music, Mitch Leigh; Assistant Director, Francois X. Moullin; In TVC Labs Color; 100 minutes; Not rated; November release.

CAST

Michael Moore	Wayne Rogers
Susan Townsend	Gayle Hunnicutt
Jean-Paul Barbet	Jack Lenoir
Marcel Thery	Philippe March
Abe	Clement Harari
Eve Cartling	Tanya Lopert
Mme. Barbet	Marthe Mercadier
First man at party	Yves Massard
Second man at party	Sady Rebbot
Lars Brady	Matt Carney
His ex-wife	Doris Roberts
Monsieur Farny	Gerard Croce
Mme. Farny	Victoria Ville
First Waiter	Max Fournel
Young man at party	Frank Peyrinaud
His friend	Jean Jacques Charriere
Freddie	Andre Fetet
Woman in restaurant	Sylviane Charlet
Her friend	Pierre Dupray
Desk Clerk	Patrick Aubree
Bell Boy	Stephane Delcher

Gayle Hunnicutt, Wayne Rogers (also top right)

SAME TIME, NEXT YEAR

(UNIVERSAL) Producers, Walter Mirisch, Morton Gottlieb; Director, Robert Mulligan; Screenplay, Bernard Slade from his play of the same title; Music, Marvin Hamlisch; "The Last Time I Felt Like This" sung by Johnny Mathis and Jane Olivor; Photography, Robert Surtees; Designer, Henry Bumstead; Editor, Sheldon Kahn; Assistant Directors, Donald Roberts, Dan Kolsrud; In Panavision and Technicolor; 119 minutes; Rated PG; November release.

CAST

Doris	Ellen Burstyn
George	Alan Alda
Chalmers	Ivan Bonar
Waiter	Bernie Kuby
Second Waiter	Cosmo Sardo
Pilot #1	David Northcutt
Pilot #2	William Cantrell

Right: Alan Alda, Ellen Burstyn

Ellen Burstyn, Alan Alda

THE GREAT GEORGIA BANK HOAX

(WARNER BROS.) Formerly "Shenanigans"; Producers, Ralph Rosenblum, Joseph Jacoby; Executive Producers, Richard F. Bridges, T. Carlyle Scales, Lawrence Klausner; Direction and Screenplay, Joseph Jacoby; Photography, Walter Lassally; Designer, Gary Weist; Editor, Ralph Rosenblum; Associate Producer, Lester Berman; Costumes, Dianne Finn Chapman; Music, Arthur B. Rubinstein; Assistant Directors, Jeff Bricmont, Aralee Strange-Mason, Allan Coulter; In Movielab Color; 85 minutes; November release.

CAST

Manny Benchly	Richard Basehart
Julius Taggart	Ned Beatty
Cathy Bonano	Charlene Dallas
Jack Stutz	Burgess Meredith
Rev. Manigma	Michael Murphy
Richard Smedly	Paul Sand
Patricia Potter	Constance Forslund
Major Bryer	Arthur Godfrey

© Warner Bros. 1978
Right: Richard Basehart, Ned Beatty

Paul Sand

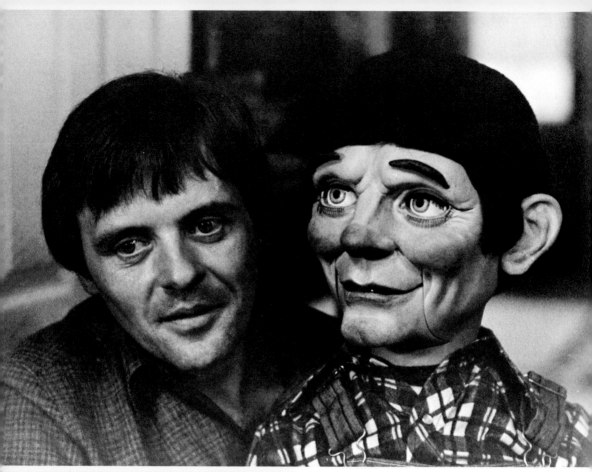

MAGIC

(20th CENTURY-FOX) Producers, Joseph E. Levine, Richard P. Levine; Director, Richard Attenborough; Screenplay, William Goldman from his novel; Executive Producer, C. O. Erickson; Photography, Victor J. Kemper; Designer, Terence Marsh; Music, Jerry Goldsmith; Editor, John Bloom; Assistant Directors, Arne Schmidt, Jerald Sobul; Art Director, Richard Lawrence; Costumes, Ruth Myers; In Technicolor; 106 minutes; Rated R; November release.

CAST

Corky	Anthony Hopkins
Peggy Ann Snow	Ann-Margret
Ben Greene	Burgess Meredith
Duke	Ed Lauter
Fats	Anthony Hopkins
Merlin	E. J. Andre
Cab Driver	Jerry Houser
Todson	David Ogden Stiers
Sadie	Lillian Randolph
Club M. C.	Joe Lowry
Laughing Lady	Beverly Sanders
Maitre d'	I. W. Klein
Captain	Stephen Hart
Doorman	Patrick McCullough
Father	Bob Hackman
Mother	Mary Munday
Corky's Brother	Scott Garrett
Young Corky	Brad Beesley
Minister	Michael Harte

Top: Anthony Hopkins and Fats

Ed Lauter, Anthony Hopkins

Ed Lauter, Ann-Margret Top: (L) Anthony Hopkins (R) Ann-Margret, Anthony Hopkins

CARAVANS

(UNIVERSAL) Producer, Elmo Williams; Director, James Fargo; Screenplay, Nancy Voyles Crawford, Thomas A. McMahon, Lorraine Williams; Based on book by James Michener; Photography, Douglas Slocombe; Music, Mike Batt; Editor, Richard Marden; Costumes, Renie Conley; Assistant Directors, Anthony Waye, Bozorgmehr Rafia, Gerry Gavigan; Song sung by Barbara Dickson; Art Directors, Ted Tester, Peter Williams, Peter James; Presented by Ibex Films and F.I.D.C.I.; In Panavision and Technicolor; 127 minutes; Rated PG; November release.

CAST

Zulfigar	Anthony Quinn
Mark Miller	Michael Sarrazin
Ellen Jasper	Jennifer O'Neill
Sardar Khan	Christopher Lee
Crandall	Joseph Cotten
Nazrullah	Behrooz Vosoughi
Richardson	Barry Sullivan
Dr. Smythe	Jeremy Kemp
Moheb	Duncan Quinn
Peasant Boy	Behrooz Gueramian
Shakkur	Mohammad Ali Keshavarz
Nur Mohammad	Parviz Gharib-Afshar
Mira	Fahimeh Amouzandeh
Dancing Boy	Khosrow Tabatabai
Maftoon	Mohammad Kahnemoui
Racha	Susan Vaziri
Capt. Majid	Mohammad Poursattar
Karima	Shahnaz Pakravan

Left: Barry Sullivan, Michael Sarrazin, Joseph Cotten Top: Michael Sarrazin, Anthony Quinn (C)

Anthony Quinn

Jennifer O'Neill, Michael Sarrazin

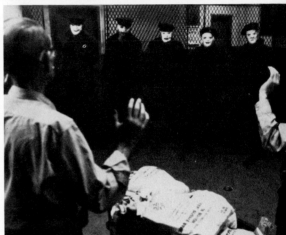

THE BRINK'S JOB

(UNIVERSAL) Producer, Ralph Serpe; Director, William Friedkin; Screenplay, Walon Green; Based on book "Big Stick Up at Brink's" by Noel Behn; Photography, Norman Leigh; Designer, Dean Tavoularis; Editors, Bud Smith, Robert K. Lambert; Music, Richard Rodney Bennett; Assistant Directors, Terence A. Donnelly, Mark Johnson; Art Director, Angelo Graham; Costumes, Ruth Morley; In Technicolor; 118 minutes; Rated PG; December release.

CAST

Tony Pino	Peter Falk
Joe McGinnis	Peter Boyle
Vinnie Costa	Allen Goorwitz
"Specs" O'Keefe	Warren Oates
Mary Pino	Gena Rowlands
Jazz Maffie	Paul Servino
J. Edgar Hoover	Sheldon Leonard
Sandy Richardson	Gerard Murphy
Stanley "Guss" Gusciora	Kevin O'Connor
Gladys	Claudia Peluso
H. H. Rightmire	Patrick Hines
Mutt Murphy	Malachy McCourt
Daniels	Walter Klavun
F.B.I. Agents	Randy Jurgensen, John Brandon, Earl Hindman, John Farrel

Top: Gena Rowlands, Peter Falk
Below: Allen Goorwitz, Gerard Murphy, Peter Falk,
Paul Sorvino, Warren Oates, Kevin O'Connor
Top Right: Peter Falk, Allen Goorwitz

Peter Falk

111

CALIFORNIA SUITE

(COLUMBIA) Producer, Ray Stark; Director, Herbert Ross; Screenplay, Neil Simon from his play of same title; Editor, Michael A. Stevenson; Designer, Albert Brenner; Music, Claude Bolling; Photography, David M. Walsh; Associate Producer, Ronald L. Schwary; Costumes, Ann Roth, Patricia Norris; Assistant Directors, Jack Roe, Carla Reinke; In Panavision and color; 103 minutes, Rated PG; December release.

CAST

Bill Warren	Alan Alda
Sidney Cochran	Michael Caine
Dr. Willis Panama	Bill Cosby
Hannah Warren	Jane Fonda
Marvin Michaels	Walter Matthau
Millie Michaels	Elaine May
Dr. Chauncy Gump	Richard Pryor
Diana Barrie	Maggie Smith
Lola Gump	Gloria Gifford
Bettina Panama	Sheila Frazier
Harry Michaels	Herbert Edelman

At the hotel: Denise Galik (Bunny), David Sheehan (Himself), Michael Boyle (Desk Clerk), Len Lawson (Frank), Gino Ardito (Plumber), Jerry Ziman (Man on phone), Clint Young (Doorman), David Matthau (Bellboy), James Espinoza (Busboy), Buddy Douglas (Page), Armand Cerami (Charley), Joseph Morena (Herb), Brian Cummings, William Kux, Zora Margolis (Autograph Seekers), Rita Gomez, Tina Menard (Maids), Lupe Ontiveros, Bert May, Eddie Villery (Waiters)
At the Academy Awards: Army Archerd (Army Archerd), Judith Hannah Brown (Oscar Winner), Gary Hendrix (Her date), Jack Scanlan, Bill Steinmetz (P.R. Men), Paolo Frediani (Young Man)
At the airport: Dana Plato (Jenny), Nora Boland (Passenger), David Rini (Airline Rep), John Hawker (Sky Cab), Frank Conn (Bobby), Colleen Drape, Kelly Harmon, Tawny Moyer, Leslie Pagett, Vicki Stephens, Nan Wylder, Linda Ewen (Stewardesses)
In Beverly Hills: David Sato (Salesman), Christopher Pennock (Cop)

Top: Michael Caine

Jane Fonda
Top: Alan Arkin

112

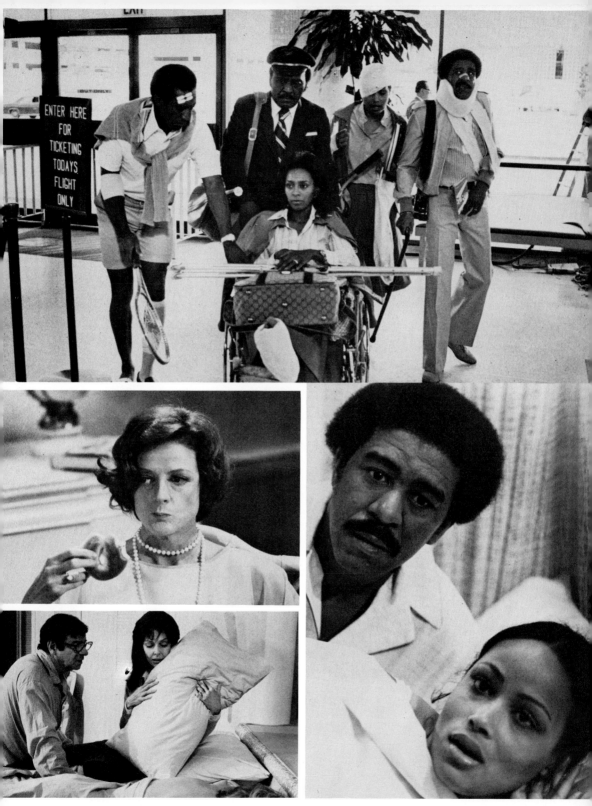

Walter Matthau, Elaine May, Denise Galik
Above: Maggie Smith Top: Bill Cosby, Sheila
Frazier, Gloria Gifford, Richard Pryor

Richard Pryor, Gloria Gifford

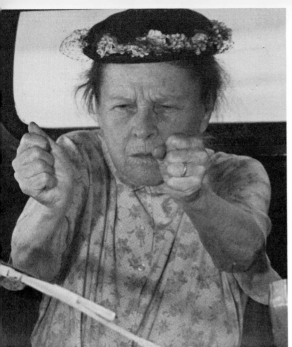

EVERY WHICH WAY BUT LOOSE

(WARNER BROS.) Producer, Robert Daley; Director, James Fargo; Screenplay, Jeremy Joe Kronsberg; Photography, Rexford Metz; Art Director, Elayne Ceder; Editors, Ferris Webster, Joel Cox; Associate Producers, Fritz Manes, Jeremy Joe Kronsberg; Assistant Directors, Larry Powell, Wendy Shear, Al Silvani, Alain J. Silver; A Malpaso Company Film in color; 119 minutes; Rated PG; December release.

CAST

Philo Beddoe	Clint Eastwood
Lynn Halsey-Taylor	Sondra Locke
Orville	Geoffrey Lewis
Echo	Beverly D'Angelo
Ma	Ruth Gordon

© Warner Bros. 1978
Left: Ruth Gordon

Clint Eastwood, Sondra Locke

KING OF THE GYPSIES

(PARAMOUNT) Producer, Federico De Laurentiis; Direction and Screenplay, Frank Pierson; Based on book by Peter Maas; Photography, Sven Nykvist; Design, Gene Callahan; Costumes, Anna Hill Johnstone; Editor, Paul Hirsch; Choreography, Julie Arenal; Music, David Grisman; Assistant Director, Allan Hopkins; Art Director, Jay Moore; A Dino De Laurentiis Presentation; In color; 112 minutes; Rated R; December release.

CAST

King Zharko Stepanovicz	Sterling Hayden
Queen Rachel	Shelley Winters
Rose	Susan Sarandon
Tita Stepanowicz	Brooke Shields
Sharon	Annette O'Toole
Dave Stepanowicz	Eric Roberts
Groffo	Judd Hirsch
Persa	Annie Potts
Spiro Georgio	Michael V. Gazzo
Danitza Georgio	Antonia Rey
Zio Miller	Daniel Spira
Adolf/Mikel	Stephen Mendillo
Rui Ilanovitch	Joe Zaloom
Pete Stepanowicz	Lou Cevetillo
Phuro	Zvee Scooler
Mr. Kessler	David Rounds
Judge	Michael Higgins
Willie	Mary Louise Wilson

and Robert Gerringer, Tom Quinn, Fred Coffin, Paul Sparer, William Duell, Harris Laskaway, Sam Coppola, Cory Einbinder, Matthew Laborteaux, Bliss Verdon, Danielle Brisebois, Tiffany Bogart, Marc Vahanian, Stephane Grappelli, Roy Brocksmith, Rebecca Darke, Glen Gianfrancisco, Patti LuPone, David Little, Joe Maruzzo, Robert Garcia, Linda Manz, C. A. R. Smith, James Shannon, MacIntyre Dixon, Mark Victor, Kathi Moss, Mary Wynn, Julie Garfield, Chris Manor, Jon Oppenheim, Bernie McInerney, Tom Mason, Jamil Zakkai, Ed Wagner, Leonard Jackson, William Thomas, Jr., Franklyn Scott, Jay Norman, Black-Eyed Susan, Kate Manheim, Sands Hall, Cecile Santos, Randy Danson, Richard Valladeres, John Del Ragno, Joe Ramezani

Top: Brooke Shields, Eric Roberts, Judd Hirsch, Susan Sarandon, Shelley Winters
Right Center: Shelley Winters, Sterling Hayden

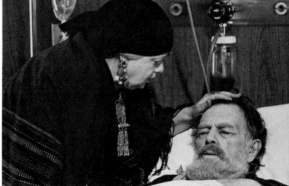

Susan Sarandon, Shelly Winters

OLIVER'S STORY

(PARAMOUNT) Producer, David V. Picker; Director, John Korty; Screenplay, Erich Segal, John Korty; Based on novel by Erich Segal; Photography, Arthur Ornitz; "Oliver's Theme" composed by Francis Lai; Music, Lee Holdridge; Art Director, Robert Gundlach; Editor, Stuart H. Pappe; Assistant Directors, Mel Howard, Candy Suerstedt; Costumes, Peggy Farrell; In Panavision and Movielab Color; 92 minutes; Rated PG; December release.

CAST

Oliver Barrett	Ryan O'Neal
Marcie Bonwit	Candice Bergen
Joanna Stone	Nicola Pagett
Phil Cavilleri	Edward Binns
John Hsiang	Benson Fong
Stephen Simpson	Charles Haid
James Francis	Kenneth McMillan
Mr. Barrett	Ray Milland
Dr. Dienhart	Josef Sommer
Mr. Gentilano	Sully Boyar
Gwen Simpson	Swoosie Kurtz
Mrs. Barrett	Meg Mundy
Waltereen	Beatrice Winde
Arlie	Sol Schwade
Father Giamatti	Father Frank Toste
Anita	Cynthia McPherson
Cleaning Woman	Gloria Irizarry
Waiter	Louis Turenne
Newscaster	Victor Gil de la Madrid

and Deborah Rush, Ann Risley, Jose L. Torres, Miguel Loperena, Sarah Beach, Wilfredo Hernandez, Dora Collazo-Levy, Herb Braha, Peter Looney

Top: Candice Bergen, Ryan O'Neal

Ryan O'Neal, Candice Bergen

Candice Bergen, Ryan O'Neal Top Left: Ryan O'Neal, Ray Milland Below: Nicola
Pagett, Ryan O'Neal Top Right: Ryan O'Neal

MOMENT BY MOMENT

(UNIVERSAL) Producer, Robert Stigwood; Executive Producer, Kevin McCormick; Direction and Screenplay, Jane Wagner; Photography, Phillip Lathrop; Editor, John F. Burnett; Design, Harry Horner; Music, Lee Holdridge; Costumes, Albert Wolsky; Assistant Director, Michael Grillo; In Dolby Stereo, Panavision and color; 105 minutes; Rated R; December release.

CAST

Trisha	Lily Tomlin
Strip	John Travolta
Naomi	Andra Akers
Stu	Bert Kramer
Peg	Shelley R. Bonus
Stacie	Debra Feuer
Dan Santini	James Luisi
Pharmacist	John O'Leary
Storekeeper	Neil Flanagan
Gas Station Attendant	Jarvais Hudson
Band Leader	Tom Slocum
Hotel Desk Clerk	Michael Consoldane
Bookstore Lady	Jo Jordan
Druggist	Joseph Schwab

Left: Lily Tomlin, John Travolta

Lily Tomlin, John Travolta, Andra Akers

BRASS TARGET

(UNITED ARTISTS) Executive Producer, Berle Adams; Producer, Arthur Lewis; Director, John Hough; Screenplay, Alvin Boretz; Based on novel "The Algonquin Project" by Frederick Nolan; Photography, Tony Imi; Editor, David Lane; Design, Rolf Zehetbauer; Music, Laurence Rosenthal; Costumes, Monika Bauert; Assistant Director, Bert Batt; In Panavision and color; 111 minutes; Rated PG; December release.

CAST

Mara	Sophia Loren
Maj. Joe DeLucca	John Cassavetes
Gen. George S. Patton, Jr.	George Kennedy
Col. Donald Rogers	Robert Vaughn
Col. Mike McCauley	Patrick McGoohan
Col. Robert Dawson	Bruce Davison
Col. Walter Gilchrist	Edward Herrmann
Shelley/Webber	Max von Sydow
Col. Elton F. Stewart	Ed Bishop
Lucky Luciano	Lee Montague

Top: John Cassavetes, Sophia Loren Below:
(L) Patrick McGoohan, Max von Sydow (R): George
Kennedy, Ed Bishop

Sophia Loren, Max von Sydow

Brooke Adams, Donald Sutherland

INVASION OF THE BODY SNATCHERS

(UNITED ARTISTS) Producer, Robert H. Solo; Director, Philip Kaufman; Screenplay, W. D. Richter; Based on novel by Jack Finney; Photography, Michael Chapman; Editor, Douglas Stewart; Design, Charles Rosen; Music, Denny Zeitlin; Assistant Director, Jim Bloom; Sepcial Effects, Dell Rheaume, Russ Hessey; In Dolby Stereo and Technicolor; 115 minutes; Rated PG; December release.

CAST

Matthew Bennell	Donald Sutherland
Elizabeth Driscoll	Brooke Adams
Dr. David Kibner	Leonard Nimoy
Nancy Bellicec	Veronica Cartwright
Jack Bellicec	Jeff Goldblum
Geoffrey	Art Hindle
Katherine	Lelia Goldoni
Running Man	Kevin McCarthy

Top: Jeff Goldblum, Donald Sutherland, Veronica Cartwright, Leonard Nimoy, Brooke Adams

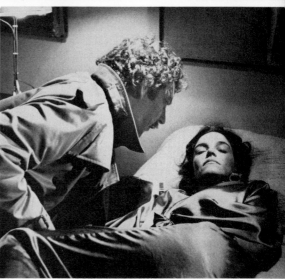

Leonard Nimoy, Donald Sutherland, Jeff Goldblum
Top: Leonard Nimoy, Lelia Goldon
Right: Donald Sutherland

Donald Sutherland, and above
with Brooke Adams

SUPERMAN

(WARNER BROS.) Producer, Pierre Spengler; Executive Producer, Ilya Salkind; Associate Producer, Charles F. Greenlaw; Director, Richard Donner; Screenplay, Mario Puzo, David Newman, Leslie Newman, Robert Benton; Based on characters created by Jerry Siegel and Joe Shuster; Story, Mario Puzo; Music, John Williams; Editor, Stuart Baird; Photography, Geoffrey Unsworth; Designer, John Barry; Special Effects, Colin Chivers; Assistant Directors, Vincent Winter, Michael Dryhurst, Allan James, Gareth Tandy; Costumes, Yvonne Blake; In Dolby Stereo, Panavision and Technicolor; Presented by Alexander Salkind; 143 minutes; Rated PG; December release.

CAST

Jor-El	Marlon Brando
Lex Luthor	Gene Hackman
Superman/Clark Kent	Christopher Reeve
Otis	Ned Beatty
Perry White	Jackie Cooper
Pa Kent	Glenn Ford
First Elder	Trevor Howard
Lois Lane	Margot Kidder
Non	Jack O'Halloran
Eve Teschmacher	Valerie Perrine
Vond-Ah	Maria Schell
General Zod	Terence Stamp
Ma Kent	Phyllis Thaxter
Lara	Susannah York
Young Clark Kent	Jeff East
Jimmy Olsen	Marc McClure
Ursa	Sarah Douglas
Second Elder	Harry Andrews

and Vass Anderson, John Hollis, James Garbutt, Michael Gover, David Neal, William Russell, Penelope Lee, John Stuart, Alan Cullen, Lee Quigley, Aaron Smolinski, Diane Sherry, Jeff Atcheson, Brad Flock, David Petrou, Billy J. Mitchell, Robert Henderson, Larry Lamb, James Brockington, John Cassady, John F. Parker, Antony Scott, Ray Evans, Su Shifrin, Miquel Brown, Vincent Marzello, Benjamin Feitelson, Lise Hilboldt, Leueen Willoughby, Jill Ingham, Pieter Stuyck, Rex Reed, Weston Gavin, Stephen Kahan, Ray Hassett, Randy Jurgenson, Matt Russo, Colin Skeaping, Bo Rucker, Paul Avery, David Maxt, George Harris II, Michael Harrigan, John Cording, Raymond Thompson, Oz Clarke, Rex Everhardt, Jayne Tottman, Frank Lazarus, Brian Protheroe, Lawrence Trimble, Robert Whelan, David Calder, Norwick Duff, Keith Alexander, Michael Ensign, Larry Hagman, Paul Tuerpe, Graham McPherson, David Yorston, Robert O'Neill, Robert MacLeod, John Ratzenberger, Alan Tilvern, Phil Brown, Bill Bailey, Burnell Tucker, Chief Tug Smith, Norman Warwick, Chuck Julian, Colin Etherington, Mark Wynter, Roy Stevens

© Warner Bros. 1978
Left: Marlon Brando, Terence Stamp, Jack O'Halloran, Sarah Douglas Top: Susannah York, Brando
1978 Academy Award for Special Visual Effects

Ned Beatty, Gene Hackman

Aaron Smolinski, Phyllis Thaxter, Glenn Ford

122

Margot Kidder, Christopher Reeve
Top: Reeve, Kidder, Jackie Cooper

Christopher Reeve

ICE CASTLES

(COLUMBIA) Executive Producer, Rosilyn Heller; Producer, John Kemeny; Director, Donald Wrye; Screenplay, Donald Wrye, Gary L. Baim; Story, Gary L. Baim; Co-Producer, S. Rodger Olenicoff; Photography, Bill Butler; Music, Marvin Hamlisch; Lyrics, Carole Bayer Sager; Sung by Melissa Manchester; Editors, Michael Kahn, Maury Winetrobe, Melvin Shapiro; Designer, Joel Schiller; Choreography, Brian Foley; Assistant Directors, Jerry Grandey, Cheryl Downey, Jonathan Zimmerman, William B. Venegas; Costumes, Richard Bruno; In Metrocolor; 113 minutes; Rated PG; December release.

CAST

Alexis Winston	Lynn-Holly Johnson
Nick Peterson	Robby Benson
Beulah Smith	Colleen Dewhurst
Marcus Winston	Tom Skerritt
Deborah Mackland	Jennifer Warren
Brian Dockett	David Huffman
Sandy	Diane Reilly
Doctor	Craig T. McMullen
Ceciel Monchet	Kelsey Ufford
Hockey Coach	Leonard Lilyholm
Choreographer	Brian Foley
French Coach	Jean-Claude Bleuze
Annette Brashlout	Teresa Willmus
X-ray Technician	Diana Holden
Skater	Michelle McLean
TV Producer	Carol Williams
Special Skating	Mary Schuster, Staci Loop
Stunts	Patti Elder, Jim Nickerson, Dee Ingalls

Right: Colleen Dewhurst, Tom Skerritt

Lynn-Holly Johnson

Robby Benson

THE LEGEND OF SEA WOLF (Cougar) Producer, Mino Loy; Director, Joseph Green; Based on Jack London's novel of the same title; Color by Gerry; Rated PG; No other credits available; January release. CAST: Chuck Connors, Barbara Bach

SCOTT JOPLIN (Universal) Executive Producer, Rob Cohen; Producer, Stan Hough; Director, Jeremy Paul Kagan; Associate Producer, Janet Hubbard; Screenplay, Christopher Knopf; Photography, David M. Walsh; Music, Scott Joplin; Performed by Richard Hyman; Art Director, William M. Hiney; Editor, Patrick Kennedy; Costumes, Bernard Johnson; Choreographer, Michael Peters; Assistant Directors, Jon C. Andersen, Joe Nayfack; In Technicolor; 92 minutes; Rated PG; January release. CAST: Billy Dee Williams (Scott), Clifton Davis (Chauvin), Margaret Every (Belle), Eubie Blake (Will), Godfrey Cambridge (Tom), Seymour Cassel (Dr. Jaelki), DeWayne Jessie (John the Baptist), Mabel King (Madam Amy), Taj Mahal (Poor Alfred), Spo-De-Odee (Left Hand of God), Art Carney (John Stark)

BILLY JACK GOES TO WASHINGTON (Taylor-Laughlin) Producer, Frank Capra, Jr.; Executive Producer, Delores Taylor; Director, T. C. Frank (Tom Laughlin); Screenplay, Frank and Teresa Cristina (Tom Laughlin, Delores Taylor); From screenplay "Mr. Smith Goes to Washington" by Sidney Buchman; Based on stbry by Lewis R. Foster; Photography, Jack Merta; Music, Elmer Bernstein; Art Director, Hilyard Brown; In color; 155 minutes; January release. CAST: Tom Laughlin (Billy Jack), Delores Taylor (Jean), E. G. Marshall (Sen. Paine), Teresa Laughlin (Staff Worker), Sam Wanamaker (Bailey), Lucie Arnaz (Saunders), Dick Gautier (Gov. Hopper), Pat O'Brien (Vice President)

THE HAZING (Miraleste) Producers, Douglas Curtis, Bruce Shelly; Director, Douglas Curtis; Screenplay, Bruce Shelly, David Ketchum; Music Ian Freebairn-Smith; A Robert Fridley-Dick Davis Production in color; 90 minutes; Rated PG; January release. CAST: Jeff East (Craig), Brad David (Rod), David Hayward (Carl), Charlie Martin Smith (Barney), Sandra Vacey (Dworskey), Kelly Moran (Wendy), Jim Joelson (Phil)

DARK SUNDAY (Intercontinental) Producer, Earl Owensby; Director, Jimmy Huston; Screenplay, Howard Lee; Music, Arthur Smith, Clay Smith; In color; Rated R; January release. CAST: Earl Owensby, Monique Proulx, Phillip Lanier, Ron Lampkin

WISHBONE CUTTER (Howco International) Produced, Directd and Written by Earl E. Smith; Executive Producer, Barbara Pryor; Co-Producer, Steve Lyon; Photography, James Roberson; Music, Jaime Mendoza-Nava; Editor, Tom Boutross; In color; Rated PG; January release. CAST: Joe Don Barker, Sondra Locke, Ted Neely, Joy Houck, Jr., Slim Pickens, Dennis Fimple, John Chandler, Linda Dano

RETURN TO BOGGY CREEK (777) Producer, Bob Gates; Director, Tom Moore; Screenplay, Dave Woody; In Technicolor; Rated G; January release. CAST Dawn Wells

HUGHES AND HARLOW: ANGELS IN HELL (PRO International) Producer-Director, Larry Buchanan; Screenplay, Lynn Shubert, Larry Buchanan; Photography, Nickolas Josef von Sternberg; Music, Jimmie Haskell; Executive Producer, William B. Silberkleit; In Color; 93 minutes; Rated R; January release. CAST: Victor Holchak (Howard Hughes), Lindsay Bloom (Jean Harlow), Royal Dano (Will Hays), Adam Roarke (Howard Hawks), David McLean, Adele Claire, Linda Cristal, Alberto Carrier, Patch McKenzie, Eric Holland, Clement St. George

THE PRIVATE FILES OF J. EDGAR HOOVER (American Internationa) Produced, Directed and Written by Larry Cohen; Photography, Paul Glickman; Editor, Christopher Lebenzon; Associate Producers, Arthur Mandelberg, Peter Sabiston; Assistant Director, Reid Freeman; Design, Cathy Davis; Costumes, Lewis Friedman; Music, Miklos Rozsa; A Larco Production in Movielab Color; 112 minutes; Rated PG; January release. CAST: Broderick Crawford (J. Edgar Hoover), Jose Ferrer (Lionel McCoy), Michael Parks (Robert F. Kennedy), Ronee Blakley (Carrie DeWitt), Celeste Holm (Florence Hollister), Rip Torn (Dwight Webb), Michael Sacks (Melvin Purvis), Dan Dailey (Clyde Tolson), Raymond St. Jacques (Martin Luther King, Jr.), Andrew Duggan (Lyndon B. Johnson), John Marley (Dave Hindley), Howard DaSilva (FDR), June Havoc (Hoover's mother), James Wainwright (Young Hoover), Lloyd Nolan (Att. Gen. Stone), Ellen Barber (FBI Secretary), Lloyd Gough (Walter Winchell), Brad Dexter (Alvin Karpas), Jennifer Lee (Ethel Brunette), George Plimpton (Quentin Reynolds), Jack Cassidy (Damon Runyon)

Chuck Connors
in "Sea Wolf"

RENALDO AND CLARA (Circuit) Direction and Screenplay, Bob Dylan; Photography, David Myers, Paul Goldsmith, Howard Alk, Michael Levine; Editors, Bob Dylan, Howard Alk; In color; 232 minutes; Rated R; January release. CAST: Bob Dylan (Renaldo), Sara Dylan (Clara), Joan Baez (Woman in White), Ronnie Hawkins (Bob Dylan), Ronee Blakley (Mrs. Dylan), Jack Elliott, Harry Dean Stanton, Bob Neuwirth, Helena Kalloaniotes, Allen Ginsberg, David Blue, Roger McGuinn, Sam Shepard, Arlo Guthrie, Roberta Flack

SASQUATCH, THE LEGEND OF BIGFOOT (North American Film Enterprises) Executive Producer, Ronald B. Olson; Director, Ed Ragozzini; Screenplay, Edward H. Hawkins; Based on story by Ronald B. Olson; Photography, John Fabian, Bill Farmer; Editors, Fabian and Farmer; In DeLuxe Color; 102 minutes; Rated G; January release. CAST: George Lauris (Chuck), Steve Boergadine (Hank), Jim Bradford (Barney), Ken Kenzle (Josh), William Emmons (Dr. Markham), Joe Morello (Techka Blackhawk)

RECORD CITY (American International) Producers, James T. Aubrey, Joe Byrne; Director, Dennis Steinmetz; Screenplay, Ron Friedman; Music, Freddie Perren; Photography, William M. Klages; Editor, Bill Breashears; Art Director, Gene MacAvoy; Costumes, Bill Whitten; In Movielab Color; 90 minutes; Rated PG; February release. CAST: Leonard Barr (Sickly Man), Ed Begley, Jr. (Pokey), Sorrell Booke (Coznowski), Dennis Bowen (Danny), Ruth Buzzi (Olga), Michael Callan (Eddie), Jack Carter (Manny), Rick Dees (Gordon), Kinky Friedman (Himself), Stuart Getz (Rupert), Alice Ghostley (Worried Wife), Frank Gorshin (Chameleon), Maria Grimm (Rita), Joe Higgins (Doyle), Ted Lange (Wiz), Alan Oppenheimer (Blindman), Isaac Ruiz (Macho), Harold Sakata (Gucci), Wendy Schall (Lorraine), Larry Storch (Deafman), Elliott Street (Hitch), Timothy Thomerson (Marty), Susan Tolsky (Goldie), Deborah White (Vivian)

TILL DEATH (Cougar) Producer-Director, Walter Stocker; Screenplay, Gregory Dana; In Color; Rated PG; February release. CAST: Keith Atkinson, Bert Freed, Belinda Balaski, Marshall Reed, Jonathan Cole, Keith Walker

Billy Dee Williams, Art Carney
in "Scott Joplin"

125

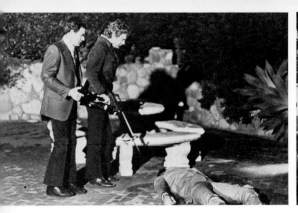

"Astral Factor"

Leif Garrett
in "Skateboard"

MIRRORS (First American) Producers, John T. Parker, Stirling Smith; Director, Noel Black; Screenplay, Sidney L. Stebel; Presented by J. B. Kelly; In color; 83 minutes; Rated PG; February release. CAST: Kitty Wynn (Marianne), Peter Donat (Dr. Godard), William Swetland (Hotel Owner), Mary-Robin Redd (Mrs. Godard), William Burns (Marianne's Husband)

THE ASTRAL FACTOR (Cougar) Producer, Earle Lyon; Director, John Floria; Screenplay, Arthur Pierce, Earle Lyon; Music, Bill Marx; Color by Getty; 91 minutes; Rated PG; February release. CAST: Frank Stell (Rodger), Robert Foxworth (Berret), Percy Rodriguez (Police Captain), Mark Slade (Holt), Elke Sommers (Chris), Stefanie Powers (Candy), Sue Lyon (Darlene), Leslie Parrish (Colleen), Mariana Hill (Bambi)

BEYOND AND BACK (Sunn Classic) Producer, Charles E. Sellier, Jr.; Director, James L. Conway; Screenplay, Stephen Lord; Based on book by Ralph Wilkerson; Music, Bob Summers; Photography, Henning Schellerup; Art Director, Charles Bennet; Assistant Directors, Jerry Fleck, Sam Baldoni; Editor, Kent Schafer; In technicolor; 93 minutes; Rated G; February release. CAST: Brad Crandall (Narrator), Vern Adix (Plato), Shelley Osterloh (Louisa May Alcott), Beverly Rowland (Mrs. Houdini), Linda Bishop, Janet Bylund, Richard Cannaday, Maxilyn Capell, Bill Carroll, David Chandler, Hyde Clayton, Elaine Daniels, Lori Davis, Stewart Falconer, James Fleming, Ian Flynn, Margaret Gibson, Mary Ethel Gregory, Myron Peter Griffen, John F. Hart, Barta Lee Heiner, Bruce Hertford, Carol Hertford, Donna K. W. Johnson, Rick Jury, Norman Keefer, Thomas Kelley, Diana Kozlowski, Charan Levitan, Marie Lillo, Anna Louise, Robert Macri, Anthony Mannino, James Montgomery, Alan Nash, Jan Noyes, Shelley Osterloh, Jean Stringam Oswald, Lucia Pappas, Kate Petley, Walt Price, H. E. D. Redford, Steve Riley, Bruce Robinson, Joe Robinson, Tony Romano, Larry Roupe, Beverly Rowland, Oscar Rowland, Stanley Russon, Michael Ruud, Malinda St. James, Craig Shipler, Craig Stephenson, Jim Strong, M. Scott Wilkinson

SKATEBOARD (Universal) Producers, Harry N. Blum, Richard A. Wolf; Assistant Producer, Roger Richman; Associate Producers, Susan Cohen, W. S. Tiger Warren; Director, George Gage; Screenplay, Richard A Wolf, George Gage; Story, Richard A. Wolf; Photography, Ross Kelsay; Editor, Robert Angus; Music, Mark Snow; Lyrics, Richard Sarstedt; Assistant Director, Richard Siegel; Costumes, Elizabeth Gage; In technicolor; 97 minutes; Rated PG; February release. CAST: Allen Garfield (Manny) Kathleen Lloyd (Millicent), Leif Garrett (Brad), Richard Van Der Wyk (Jason), Tony Alva (Tony), Steve Monahan (Peter), David Hyde (Dennis), Ellen Oneal (Jenny), Pam Kenneally (Randi), Anthony Carbone (Sol), Sylvester Words (Sol's Henchman), Gordon Jump (Harris), Pat Hitchcock (Mrs. Harris), Orson Bean (Himself), Joe Bratcher (Vito), Harvey Levine (U.E.O. Clerk), Thelma Pelish (Woman in motel), John Fox (Charlie), Damon Douglas (Scott), Marilyn Roberts (Waitress), David Carlile (Palmdale Announcer), Chuck Niles (Race Announcer), Raymond Kark (Gas Station Attendant), Owen Bush (Sign Painter), Eugene Elman (Maitre d'), Carol McGinnis (Script Girl), and Hubie Kerns, Reid Rondell, Tanya Russell, Randy Clark, Denise Dubarry, Jean Markell, Tom Padaca, Phil Settle, Sondra Theodore, Marylou York, Sabina Weber, Valerie Clark.

FINGERS (Brut) Producer, George Barrie; Direction and Screenplay, James Toback; Photography, Mike Chapman; Editor, Robert Lawrence; Design, Gene Rudolf; Costmes, Albert Wolsky; Assistant Director, Dan McCauley; In Eastmancolor; 90 minutes; Rated R; February release. CAST: Harvey Keitel (Jimmy), Tisa Farrow (Carol), Jim Brown (Deems), Michael V. Gazzo (Ben), Marian Seldes (Mother), Carole Francis (Christa), Georgette Muir (Anita), Danny Aiello (Butch), Dominick Chianese (Arthur), Anthony Siroco (Riccamonza), Tanya Roberts (Julie), Ed Marinaro (Gino), Zack Norman (Cop), Murray Mosten (Dr. Fry), Jane Elder (Esther), Lenny Montana (Luchino), Frank Pesche (Raymond)

**Richard Cannaday, Elizabeth Grand
Shelly Osterloh in "Beyond and Back"**

**Harvey Keitel, Jim Brown
in "Fingers"**

"Word Is Out"

Charlton Heston, Ronny Cox
in "Gray Lady Down"

WORD IS OUT (New Yorker) A Mariposa Film Group Production: Peter Adair, Nancy Adair, Veronica Selver, Andrew Brown, Robert Epstein, Lucie Massie Phenix; Producer, Peter Adair; In color; 124 minutes; Not rated; March release. A documentary on homosexuality in which 26 persons are interviewed.

GRAY LADY DOWN (Universal) Producer, Walter Mirisch; Director, David Greene; Screenplay, James Whittaker, Howard Sackler; Adaptation, Frank P. Rosenberg; Based on novel "Event 1000" by David Lavallee; Photography, Stevan Larner; Editor, Robert Swink; Music, Jerry Fielding; Designer, William Tuntke; Assistant Directors, Mack Bing, Pat Duffy, Michael Stanislavsky; In Panavision and Technicolor; 111 minutes; Rated PG; March release. CAST: Charlton Heston (Capt. Paul Blanchard), David Carradine (Capt. Gates), Stacy Keach (Capt. Bennett), Ned Beatty (Mickey), Stephen McHattie (Murphy), Ronny Cox (Cmdr. Samuelson), Dorian Harewood (Fowler), Rosemary Forsyth (Vickie), Hilly Hicks (Page), Charles Cioffi (Adm. Barnes), William Jordan (Waters), Jack Rader (Harkness), Anthony Ponzini (Caruso), Michael O'Keefe (Harris), Charlie Robinson (McAllister), Christopher Reeve (Phillips), Melendy Britt (Liz), David Wilson (Hanson), Robert Symonds (Sec of Navy), Lawrason Driscoll (Bloome)

MEAN DOG BLUES (American International) Producers, Charles A. Pratt, George Lefferts; Director, Mel Stuart; Screenplay, George Lefferts; Photography, Robert B. Hauser; Music, Fred Karlin; Editor, Houseley Stevenson; Art Director, J. S. Poplin; Assistant Director, Kenneth Swor; In DeLuxe Color; 108 minutes; Rated R; March release. CAST: Gregg Henry (Paul), George Kennedy (Capt. Kinsman), Kay Lenz (Linda), Scatman Crothers (Mudcat), Tina Louise (Donna), Felton Perry (Jake), Gregory Sierra (Jesus), James Wainwright (Sgt. Wacker), William Windom (Victor), Marc Alaimo (Guard), Edith Atwater (Linda's mother), James Boyd (Sonny), Edward Call (Road Gang Guard), John Daniels (Yakima), Christina Hart (Gloria)

KING OF THE HILL (Lone Star) No credits available; In color; Rated PG; March release. CAST: Jim Bohan, Jason Sommers, Robert Burton, Timm Daughtry, Jana Bellan

ACAPULCO GOLD (R. C. Riddell) Producers, Allan F. Bodoh, Bruce Cohn; Director, Burt Brinckerhoff; Executive Producer, Michael Leone; Screenplay, Don Enright, O'Brian Tomalin; In Color; Rated PG; March release. CAST: Marjoe Gortner, Robert Lansing, Ed Nelson, John Harkins, Randi Oakes, Lawrence Casey, Phil Hoover

THEIR ONLY CHANCE (Ellman) Direction and Screenplay, J. David Siddon; Producer, Larry Shapiro; Music, Al Capps; In color; 90 minutes; March release. CAST: Jock Mahoney, Steve Hoddy, Chris Jeffers, Mildred Watt

LUCIFER'S WOMEN (Constellation) Producer, Lou Sorkin; Director, Paul Aratow; Executive Producer, Edward H. Margolin; In Movielab Color; 88 minutes; Rated R; March release. CAST: Larry Hankin, Jane Brunel-Cohen, Emily Smith

CHECKERED FLAG OR CRASH (Universal) Producers, Fred Weintraub, Paul Heller; Director, Alan Gibson; Screenplay, Michael Allin; Title song, Norman Sachs, Mel Mandel; Sung by Harlan Sanders; In Technicolor; 95 minutes; Rated PG; March release. CAST: Joe Don Baker, Susan Sarandan, Alan Vint, Larry Hagmen, Parnelli Jones, Logan Clark, Dana House

BUFFALO RIDER (Starfire) Director, George Lauris; Music, Al Capps; Lyrics sung by Lane Caudell; A John Fabian-Dick Robinson Production; In color; Rated PG; March release. CAST: Rick Guinn, John Freeman, Priscilla Lauris, George Sager, Rich Scheeland

DOUBLES (Cinema World) Produced, Directed and Written By Bruce Wilson; Photography, P. Kip Anderson; Music, Jim Bredouw, Martin Lund; Editors, Art Coburn, Skeets McGrew; In Eastmancolor; 90 minutes; March release. CAST: Ted D'Arms (Dennis), Martin LaPlatney (Raymond/Randolph), Ann Bowden (Linda), Dean Meland (Dick), Peggy Nielsen (Sandra), Goen Mazen (Nick), Sally Pritchard (Carol), Niles Brewster (Bob)

Kay Lenz, Gregg Henry
in "Mean Dog Blues"

Joe Don Baker
in "Checkered Flag or Crash"

127

Cameron Mitchell, Wesley Eure
in "Toolbox Murders"

A. Martinez
in "Starbird"

THE TOOLBOX MURDERS (Cal-AM) Producer, Tony Didio; Associate Producers, Kenneth A. Yates, Jack Kindberg; Director, Dennis Donnelly; Assistant Directors, Ann Kindberg, Gary Lapoten; Story and Screenplay, Robert Easter, Ann Kindberg; Photography, Gary Graver; Editor, Skip Lusk; In color by EFI; 93 minutes; Rated R; March release. CAST: Cameron Mitchell (Kingsley), Pamelyn Ferdin (Laurie), Wesley Eure (Kent), Nicholas Beauvy (Joey), Aneta Coraut (Joanne), Tim Donnelly (Detective), Faith McSwain (Victim), Marciee Drake (Victim), Evelyn Guerrero (Butch), Mariane Walter (Victim)

LASERBLAST (Irwin Yablans) Producer, Charles Band; Director, Michael Rae; Screenplay, Franne Schacht, Frank Ray Perilli; Photography, Terry Bowen; Music, Joel Goldsmith, Richard Band; Effects, Dave Allen; In Technicolor; 85 minutes; Rated PG; March release. CAST: Kim Milford (Billy), Cheryl Smith (Cathy), Gianni Russo (Tony), Ron Masak (Sheriff), Dennis Burkley (Pete), Barry Cutler (Jesse), Mike Bobenko (Chuck), Eddie Deezen (Froggy), Keenan Wynn (Col. Farley), Roddy McDowall (Dr. Melon)

COACH (Crown International) Executive Producer, Newton P. Jacobs; Producer, Mark Tenser; Associate Producer, Will Zens; Director, Bud Townsend; Screenplay, Stephen Bruce Rose, Nancy Larson; Music, Anthony Harris; Assistant Directors, Mike Castle, Tikki Goldberg; Photography, Mike Murphy; Editor, Bob Gordon; Art Director, Ken Hergenroeder; In Metrocolor; 100 minutes; Rated PG; March release. CAST: Cathy Lee Crosby (Randy), Michael Biehn (Jack), Keenan Wynn (Fenton), Steve Nevil (Ralph), Channing Clarkson (Bradley), Jack David Walker (Ned), Meredith Baer (Janet), Myron McGill (Danny), Robyn Pohle (Candy), Kristien Greco (Darlene), Brent Huff (Kcith), Rosanne Katon (Sue), Lenka Novak (Marilyn), Otto Felix (Tom), Milt Oberman (Coach), Ron Wright (Gorman), Cindy Daly (Wanda), Derek Barton (Jack-Stunt Double), Bill McLean (Harold), Ted Dawson (Marvin), Tom Mahoney (Janitor)

THE ADVENTURES OF STARBIRD (Cougar) Producer, Dick Alexander; Director, Jack Hively; Screenplay, Alex Grunberg; Music, A. Martinez; In CFI-Eastman Color; 90 minutes; Rated G; April release. CAST: A. Martinez (Starbird), Don Haggarty (Hunter), Louise Fitch (Maddie), Skip Homeier (Ranger), Skeeter Vaughn (Grandfather)

DEATHSPORT (New World) Producer, Roger Corman; Directors, Henry Suso, Allan Arkush; Screenplay, Henry Suso, Donald Stewart; Story, Frances Doel; Photography, Gary Graver; Editor, Larry Bock; Music, Andrew Stein; Assistant Directors, Tom Jacobson, Jim Burnett; Art Director, Sharon Compton; Choreographer, George Fullwood; MGM Color; 90 minutes; Rated R; April release. CAST: David Carradine (Kaz Oshay), Claudia Jennings (Deneer), Richard Lynch (Ankar), William Smithers (Dr. Karl), Will Walker (Marcus), David McLean (Lord Zirpola), Jesse Vint (Polna), H. B. Haggerty (Jailer), John Himes (Tritan Pres.), Jim Galante (Tritan Guard), Peter Hooper (Bakkar), Brenda Venus (Adriann), Gene Hartline (Sgt.), Chris Howell (Officer), Valerie Rae Clark (Dancer)

THE GENTLEMAN TRAMP (Tinc) Producer, Bert Schneider; Written, Directed and Edited by Richard Patterson; Music, Charles Chaplin; Narrated by Walter Matthau; Passages read by Lord Laurence Olivier; Academy Award Citation read by Jack Lemmon; Associated Producer, Artie Ross; In black and white; 80 minutes; Rated G; April release. A feature film biography starring Charles Chaplin.

SWEATER GIRLS (Mirror) Producers, Gary Gibbs, Frank Rubin; Director, Don Jones; Screenplay, Don Jones, Neva Friedenn; Music, Richard Hieronymous; Photography, Ken Gibb; Executive Producer, Allan Elrod; In color; Rated R; April release. CAST: Harry Moses, Meegan King, Noelle North, Kate Sarchet, Carol Seflinger, Tamara Barkley, Julie Parsons, Michael Goodrow, William Kux, Jack O'Leary, Stephen Liss, Skip Lowell

NEW HOUSE ON THE LEFT (Central Park) Producer-Director, Evans Isle; In color; Rated R; April release. CAST: Kay Beal, Patty Edwards, Norma Knight, Delbert Moss, Richard Davis

David Carradine, Claudia Jennings
in "Deathsport"

Charles Chaplin
in "The Little Tramp"

"Goodbye Franklin High"

Sherri Coyle, William Nuckols, Jenni
Bardell in "Sunset Cove"

GOODBYE FRANKLIN HIGH (Cal-Am) Producer-Director, Mike MacFarland; Executive Producers, Joseph R. Laird, Kenneth J. Fisher; Associate Producers, Kenneth A. Yates, Kool Lusby; Screenplay, Stu Krieger; Songs written and performed by Lane Caudell; In color by CFI; 94 minutes; Rated PG; April release. CAST: Lane Caudell, Ann Dusenberry, Darby Hinton, Julie Adams, William Windom

HOT TOMORROWS (American Film Institute) Produced, Directed, Edited and Written by Martin Brest; Associate Producer-Photographer, Jacques Haitkin; Assistant Directors, Judy Horon, G. M. Cahill; Choreographer, Lloyd Gordon; In color; 73 minutes; Not rated; April release. CAST: Ken Lerner (Michael), Ray Sharkey (Louis), Herve Villechaize (Alberict), Victor Argo (Tony), George Memmoli (Man in mortuary), Donne Daniels (Night Embalmer), Rose Marshall (Tante Ethel), Paul Schumacher (Lecturer), Stan Laurel, Oliver Hardy, Marie Elfman, Danny Elfman (Singers), Dennis Madden (Bartender), Sondra Lowell (Polly), Marion Beeler (Waitress), Shelby Leverington (Hospital Receptionist), David Garfield (Dr. Stern), Vice Palmieri (Man in car), Janet Brandt (Old Woman in bus), Sonya Berman (Old Woman watching tv), Esther Cohen (Old Woman with postcard), Edith Gwinn (Old Woman in mortuary), Orson Welles (Voice of Parklawn Mortuary)

THE MARCH ON PARIS 1914 (Bauer International) Producer-Director, Walter Gutman; In black and white; 70 minutes; Not rated; April release. CAST: Jessie Holladay Duane, Wulf Gunther Brandes

SPEEDTRAP (First Artists-Intertamar) Producers, Howard Pine, Fred Mintz; Director, Earl Bellamy; Screenplay, Stuart A. Segal, Walter M. Spear; Based on story by Fred Mintz, Henry C. Parke; Photography, Dennis Dalzell; Editor, Michael Vejar; In color; 113 minutes; Rated PG; April release. CAST: Joe Don Baker (Pete), Tyne Daly (Nifty), Richard Jaeckel (Billy), Robert Loggia (Spillano), Morgan Woodward (Capt. Hogan), Lana Wood (New Blosom), Timothy Carey (Loomis), James Griffith (Wino)

SUNSET COVE (Cal-Am) Producer, Harry Hope; Executive Producers, Joseph R. Laird, Kenneth J. Fisher; Associate Producer, Kenneth A. Yates; Director, Al Adamson; Screenplay, Cash Maintenant, Budd Donnelly; Music, Bruce Stewart; Photography, Gary Graver; Editor, Ron Moler; In CFI Color; 87 minutes; Rated R; April release. CAST: Jay B. Larson (Dexter), Karen Fredrik (Joyce), John Carradine (Judge Winslow), John Durren (Kragg), Burr Schmidt (Mayor Nix), Ray Andrews (Mike), Steven Fisher (Chubby), Shirley Ann Broger (Mimi), Jane Ralston (Joanne), Mark Flynn (Bart), Will Walker (John)

THAT'S COUNTRY Producer, Henning Jacobsen; Director, Clark DaPrato; Executive Producer, Doug MacDonald; Host, Lorne Greene; April release. CAST: T. Tommy Cutrer, Jim Reeves, Ray Price, Kitty Wells, Marty Robbins, Ferlin Husky, Faron Young, Ernest Tubb, Bill Monroe and the Blue Grass Boys, Chet Atkins, Minnie Pearl, June Carter, Grandpa Jones, Carl Smith, Jimmy Dickens, Carter Family

THE REDEEMER (Dimension) Producer, Sheldon Tromberg; Director, Constantine S. Gochis; Screenplay, William Vernick; In color; 84 minutes; April release. CAST: Jeannetta Arnette, T. G. Finkbinder, Damien Knight, Nick Carter, Gyr Patterson, Nikki Barthen, Christopher Flint

DOUBLE NICKELS (Smokey) Producer-Director, Jack Vacek; Screenplay, Jack Vacek, Patrice Schubert; Executive Producer, John Vacek, Sr.; Photography, Tony Syslo, Ron Sawade; Associate Producer, Mick Brennan; In color; 89 minutes; Rated PG; April release. CAST: Jack Vacek (Smokey), Ed Abrams (Ed), Patrice Schubert (Jordan), George Cole (George), Heidi Schubert (Tami), Mick Brennan, Michael Cole, Les Taylor

WHERE'S WILLIE (Taurus) Producers, William H. White, Jorja A. Brown; Director, John Florea; Screenplay, Frank Koomen, Ann Koomen, Alan Cassidy; Story, William H. White; Music, Robert O. Ragland; In DeLux Color; Rated G; April release. CAST: Henry Darrow, Kate Woodville, Guy Madison, Marc Gilpin, Rock Montanio

Tyne Daly, Joe Don Baker
In "Speedtrap"

Danny and Marie Elfman
in "Hot Tomorrows"

129

Valerie Landsburg, Chick Vennera
in "Thank God It's Friday"

Frederic Forrest, Kathleen Lloyd
in "It Lives Again" © Warner Bros. 1978

BREAKFAST IN BED (William Haugse) Producer, Catherine Coulson; Directed, Written and Edited by William Haugse; Photography, Frederick Elmes; Music, Tom Grant; In Metrocolor; 56 minutes; Not rated; April release. CAST: Jenny Sullivan (Sara), John Ritter (Paul), V. Phipps-Wilson (Mimi), Mitchell Breit (Hairdresser), Timothy Near (Marcia), Buckline Beery (Man in car)

SNAPSHOT (First American) Eecutive Producer, Anthony Kramreither; Producer, John Hunter; Associate Producer, Samuel C. Jephcott; Director, Allan Eastman; Screenplay, Jim Henshaw, Allan Eastman; Photography, Robert Brooks; Music, Jove; A John B. Kelly Presentation; A Labyrinth-Burg Co-Production; In color; 84 minutes; Rated R; May release. CAST: Jim Henshaw (Cory), Susan Petrie (Annie), Susan Hogan (Linda), Peter Jobin, Allan Migicovsky (David)

THANK GOD IT'S FRIDAY (Columbia) Executive Producer, Neil Bogart; Producer, Rob Cohen; Director, Robert Klane; Screenplay, Barry Armyan Bernstein; Photography, James Crabe; Editor, Richard Halsey; A Motown-Casablanca Production; In color; 100 minutes; Rated PG; May release. CAST: Valerie Landsburg (Frannie), Terri Nunn (Jeannie), Chick Vennera (Marv), Donna Summer (Nicole), Ray Vitte (Bobby), Mark Lonow (Dave), Andrea Howard (Sue), Jeff Goldblum (Tony), Robin Menker (Maddy), Debra Winger (Jennifer), John Friedrich (Ken), Paul Jabara (Carl), Marya Small (Jackie), Chuck Sacci (Gus), Hilary Beane (Shirley), DeWayne Jessie (Floyd), The Commodres

BIG WEDNESDAY (Warner Bros.) Producer, Buzz Feitshans; Director, John Milius; Screenplay, John Milius, Dennis Aaberg; Executive Producers, Alex Rose, Tamara Asseyev; Photography, Bruce Surtees; Designer, Charles Rosen; Editors, Robert L. Wolfe, Tim O'Meara; Music, Basil Poledouris; Assistant Directors, Richard Hashimoto, Bill Scott, Victor Hsu; Art Director, Dean Mitzner; In Dolby Stereo, Panavision and Metrocolor; 126 minutes; Rated PG; May release. CAST: Jan-Michael Vincent (Matt), William Katt (Jack), Gary Busey (Leroy), Patti D'Arbanville (Sally), Lee Purcell (Peggy), Sam Melville (Bear)

IT LIVES AGAIN (Warner Bros.) Produced, Directed and Written by Larry Cohen; Based on characters created in film "It's Alive"; Music, Bernard Herrmann; Associate Producer, William Wellman, Jr.; Photography, Fenton Hamilton; Editors, Curt Burch, Louis Friedman, Carol O'Blath; Assistant Director, Reid Freeman; In Technicolor; 91 minutes; Rated R; May release. CAST: Frederic Forrest (Eugene Scott), Kathleen Lloyd (Judy Scott), John P. Ryan (Frank Davis), John Marley (Mallory), Andrew Duggan (Dr. Perry), Eddie Constantine (Dr. Forest), James Dixon (Det. Perkins)

YOUNGBLOOD (American International) Producers, Nick Grillo, Alan Riche; Director, Noel Nosseck; Screenplay, Paul Carter Harrison; Photography, Robbie Greenberg; Editor, Frank Morriss; Associate Producer, Hal DeWindt; Assistant Director, Bill Kerr; Art Director, James Dultz; Original Music written and performed by War; In CFI and Movielab Color; 92 minutes; Rated R; May release. CAST: Lawrence-Hilton Jacobs (Rommel), Bryan O'Dell (Youngblood), Ren Woods (Sybil), Tony Allen (Hustler), Vince Cannon (Corelli), Art Evans (Junkie), Jeff Hollis (Pusher), Dave Pendleton (Reggie), Ron Trice (Bummie), Sheila Wills (Joan), Ralph Farquhar (Geronimo), Herbert Rice (Durango), Lionel Smith (Chaka), Maurice Sneed (Skeeter-Jeeter), Ann Weldon (Mrs. Gordon), Isabel Cooley (School Principal), Bernie Weissman (Bodyguard)

TOWING (United International) Producer, Frederick A. Smith; Executive Producers, Alan Gelband, Bob Greenberg; Direction and Screenplay, Maura Smith; Photography, Hal Schullman; Music, Martin Rubinstein; Editor, Bernard F. Caputo; In color; 85 minutes; Rated PG; May release. CAST: Jennifer Ashley (Jean), Sue Lyon (Lynn), Bobby DiCicco (Tony), Joe Mantegna (Chris), J. J. Johnston (Butch), Audry Neenan (Irate Lady), Steve Kampman (Irate Man), Don DePollo (Pizza Man), Nan Mason (Nan), Mike Nusbaum (Phil), Susanne Smith (Lois), Jake Stockwell (Tow Truck Driver), Lee Stein (Mayor), Sandy Halpin (Waitress), Bob Wallace (Reporter)

Gary Busey, Jan-Michael Vincent, William Katt
in "Big Wednesday" © Warner Bros. 1978

Lawrence-Hilton Jacobs, Bryan O'Dell
in "Youngblood"

**Niles McMaster, Linda Miller
in "Alice Sweet Alice"**

**Joe Brooks, Shelley Hack
in "If Ever I See You Again"**

ALICE, SWEET ALICE (Allied Artists) formerly "Communion"; Producer, Richard K. Rosenberg; Director, Alfred Sole; Screenplay, Rosemary Ritvo, Alfred Sole; Photography, John Friberg, Chuck Hall; Music, Stephen Lawrence; Editor, Edward Salier; In Technicolor; 108 minutes; Rated R; May release. CAST: Paula Sheppard (Alice), Brooke Shields (Karen), Linda Miller (Catherine), Jane Lowry (Aunt Annie), Alphonso DeNoble (Alphonso), Rudolph Willrich (Father Tom), Mildred Clinton (Mrs. Tredoni), Niles McMaster (Dom Spages), Michael Hardstark (Detective), Gary Allen (Uncle), Tom Signorelli (Brenner), Louisa Horton (Psychiatrist), Antonino Rocco (Funeral Attendant), Lillian Roth (Pathologist)

THE ALIEN FACTOR (Cinemagic) Direction and Screenplay, Donald M. Dohler; Photography, Britt McDonough; Editors, Don Dohler, Dave Ellis; Music, Kenneth Walker; Assistant Director, Anthony Malanowski; In color; 80 minutes; May release. CAST: Don Leifert (Ben), Tom Griffith (Sheriff), Richard Dyszel (Mayor), Mary Mertens (Edie), Richard Geiwitz (Pete), George Stover (Steven), Eleanor Herman (Mary Jane), Anne Frith (Ruth), Christopher Gummer (Clay), Johnny Walker (Rex)

METAMORPHOSES (Sanrio) Producers, Terry Ogisu, Hiro Tsugawa; Executive Producer, Shintaro Tsuji; Produced, Directed and Written by Takashi; Based on material from Ovid's "Metamorphoses"; Photography, Bill Millar; Animation Editor, Barbara Ottinger; Music, Bob Randles; In Technicolor; 89 minutes; Rated PG; May release. A feature length animated film.

LOVE AND THE MIDNIGHT AUTO SUPPLY (Producers Capital) Produced, Directed and Written by James Polakof; Executive Producer, Beverley Johnson; Photography, Lawrence Raimond; Editor, Irving Rosenblum; Art Director, Perry Ferguson II; Music, Ed Bofas; In Movielab Color; 93 Minutes; Rated PG; May release. CAST: Michael Parks (Duke), Linda Cristal (Annie), Scott Jacoby (Justin), Bill Adler (Ramon), Colleen Camp (Billie Jean), Monica Gayle (Kathy), Sedena Spivey (Violet), George McCalister (Peter), John Ireland (Tony), Rory Calhoun (Len), Rod Cameron (Sheriff), Burt Freed (Mayor)

IF EVER I SEE YOU AGAIN (Columbia) Producer-Director, Joe Brooks; Screenplay, Joe Brooks, Martin Davidson; Music, Joe Brooks; Songs sung by Jamie Carr, Bill Deane, Big Hill Singers; Associate Producer, Edwin T. Morgan; Photography, Adam Holender; Editor, Rich Shaine; Assistant Directors, Jim Maniolas, David Worf, Don Greenholz; In Technicolor; 105 minutes; Rated PG; May release. CAST: Joe Brooks (Bob), Shelley Hack (Jennifer), Jimmy Breslin (Mario), Jerry Keller (Steve), George Plimpton (Laurence), Michael Decker (Young Bob), Julie Ann Gordon (Young Jennifer), Danielle Brisebois (Amy), Branch Emerson (Jonathan), Shannon Bolin (Elsa), Bob Kaliban (Supervisor), Len Gochman (Executive), Susan Rubenstein (Copywriter), Steve Hiott (Art Director), Gordon Ramsey (Larry), Vinnie Bell, Eric Weisberg (Guitarists), Dan Resin (Supervisor), John Nalpern (Executive), Malcolm Addey (Engineer), Caroline Mignini (Laura), Faye Dannick (Housemother), Sal Rapaglia (Chauffeur), Marvin Lichterman (Doctor), Joe Leon (Sosnick), Ed Kovins (Foster), Edwin T. Morgan (Passenger), Jimmy Kelly (Janitor), Joy Bond (Karen), Wendy Raebeck (Carol), Sue Jett (Nurse), Bob Lifton (Pretzel Buyer), Howard Weingrow (Commissioner), Robin Siegal (Renee), Simone Schachter, Tom Okon, Liza Moran, Peter Billingsley (Children)

MALIBU BEACH (Crown International) Executive Producer, Newton P. Jacobs; Producer, Marilyn J. Tenser; Director, Robert J. Rosenthal; Screenplay, Celia Susan Cotelo, Robert J. Rosenthal; Associate Producer, Richard Franchot; Photography, Jamie Anderson; Editor, Robert Barrere; Assistant Directors, Gerald T. Olson, Bruce E. Fritzberg; Art Director, Fred Chriss; Costumes, Diana Daniels; A Marimark Production in DeLuxe Color; 93 minutes; Rated R; May release. CAST: Kim Lankford (Dina), James Daughton (Bobby), Susan Player Jarreau (Sally), Michael Luther (Paul), Stephen Oliver (Dugan), Flora Plumb (Ms. Plicket), Roger Lawrence Pierce (Claude), Sherry Lee Marks (Margie), Tara Strohmeier (Glorianna), Rory Stevens (Charlie), Parris Clifton Buckner, Bruce Kimball, Bill Adler, Jim Kester, Diana Herbert, Walter Maslow, Marty Rogalny, Tom Mahoney, James Oliver, David Clover, Nathan Roth, Jacqueline Jacobs

**George Stover
in "The Alien Factor"**

**Michael Parks
in "Love and the Midnight Auto Supply"** 131

Alice Ghostley, Zalman King
in "Blue Sunshine"

"Here Come the Tigers"

BLUE SUNSHINE (Cinema Shares) Producer, George Manasse: Direction and Screenplay, Jeff Lieberman; Executive Producers, Edgar Lansbury, Joseph Beruh; Music, Charles Gross; In Movielab Color; 97 minutes; Rated R; May release. CAST: Zalman King, Deborah Winters, Mark Goddard, Robert Walden, Charles Siebert, Ann Cooper, Ray Young, Alice Ghostley, Stefan Gierasch, Bill Cameron, Richard Crystal

HI-RIDERS (Dimension) Producer, Mike Macfarland; Direction and Screenplay, Greydon Clark; Music, Gerald Lee; Songs performed by Coyote and The Pack; Executive Producer, Ronald Daniel; In color; Rated R; May release. CAST: Mel Ferrer, Stephen McNally, Darby Hinton, Neville Brand, Ralph Meeker, Diane Peterson

OUR WINNING SEASON (American International) Producer, Joe Roth; Executive Producer, Samuel Z. Arkoff; Director, Joseph Ruben; Screenplay, Nick Niciphor; Photography, Stephen Katz; Editor, Bill Butler; Music, Charles Fox; Art Director, Angelo Graham; Costumes, Jimmy George; Assistant Director, Ed Markley; In Movielab Color; 92 minutes; Rated PG; May release. Cast: Scott Jacoby (David), Deborah Benson (Alice), Dennis Quaid (Paul), Randy Herman (Jerry), Joe Penny (Dean), Jan Smithers (Cathy), P. J. Soles (Cindy), Robert Wahler (Burton), Wendy Rastatter (Susie), Damon Douglas (Miller), Joanna Cassidy (Sheila)

JENNIFER (American International) Producer, Steve Krantz; Director, Brice Mack; Screenplay, Kay Cousins Johnson; Story, Steve Krantz; Photography, Irv Goodnoff; Editor, Duane Hartzell; Associate Producer, Don Henderson; Assistant Directors, Cyrus I. Yavneh, Jim Inch; Title song written and sung by Porter Jordan; In CFI and Movielab Color; 90 minutes; Rated PG; May release. CAST: Lisa Pelikan (Jennifer), Bert Convy (Jeff), Nina Foch (Mrs. Calley), Amy Johnston (Sandra), John Gavin (Senator Tremayne), Jeff Corey (Luke), Louise Hoven (Jane), Wesley Eure (Pit), Florida Friebus (Miss Tooker), Georganne LaPiere (DeDee)

HERE COME THE TIGERS (American International) Producers, Sean S. Cunningham, Stephen Miner; Director, Seans S. Cunningham; Screenplay, Arch McCoy; Photography, Barry Abrams; Music, Harry Manfredini; Editor, Stephen Miner; Art Director, Susan E. Cunningham; Assistant Producer, Cindy Veazey; Assistant Director, Nancy Hart; In Movielab color; Rated PG; May release. CAST: Richard Lincoln (Eddie), James Zvanut (Burt), Samantha Grey (Betty), Manny Lieberman (Umpire), William Caldwell (Kreeger), Fred Lincoln (Aesop), Xavier Rodrigo (Buster), Kathy Bell (Patty), Noel John Cunningham (Peanuts), Sean P. Griffin (Art), Max McClellan (The Bod), Kevin Moore (Eaglescout), Lance Norwood (Ralphy), Ted Oyama (Umeki), Michael Pastore (Fingers), Philip Scuderi (Danny), David Schmalholz (Bionic Mouth), Nancy Willis (Sharyn), Andy Weeks (Scoop), Todd Weeks (Timmy)

MAG WHEELS (Peter Perry) Producer, Colleen Meeker; Direction and Screenplay, Bethel Buckalew; Exective Producers, George Barris, Irwin Schaeffer; In Movielab Color; Rated R; May release. CAST: Shelley Horner, John McLaughlin, Phoebe Schmidt, Steven Rose, Verkema Flower

THE GREAT SMOKEY ROADBLOCK (Dimension) Producer, Allan F. Bodoh; Executive Producer, Michael Leone; Direction and Screenplay, John Leone; Photography, Ed Brown, Sr.; Music, Craig Safan; In color; 100 minutes; Rated PG; June release. CAST: Henry Fonda (Elegant John), Eileen Brennan (Penelope), Robert Englund (Beebo), John Byner (Disk Jockey), Austin Pendelton (Guido), Susan Sarandan (Ginny), Melanie Mayron (Lulu), Marya Small (Alice), Leigh French (Glinda), Dana House (Celeste), Gary Sandy, Johnnie Collins III, Valerie Curtin, Bibi Osterwald

GOOD GUYS WEAR BLACK (Mar Vista) Producer, Allan F. Bodoh; Executive Producer, Michael Leone; Director, Ted Post; Screenplay, Bruce Cohn, Mark Medoff; Story, Joseph Fraley; Music, Craig Safan; In color; 96 minutes; June release. CAST: Chuck Norris, Anne Archer, Lloyd Haynes, Dana Andrews, Jim Backus, James Franciscus

Amy Johnston, Lisa Pelikan, Louise Hoven
in "Jennifer"

Chuck Norris
in "Good Guys Wear Black"

Joanna Pettet, Richard Crenna, Milton Selzer
in "Evil"

THE EVIL (New World) Executive Producers, Paul A. Joseph, Malcolm Levinthal; Producer, Ed Carlin; Director, Gus Trikonis; Screenplay, Donald G. Thompson; Music, Johnny Harris; Photography, Mario DiLeo; Editor, Jack Kirshner; Assistant Directors, Scott Adam, Dan Steinbrocker; Art Director, Peter Jamison; A Rangoon Production in Movie Lab Color; A Roger Corman Presentation; 90 minutes; Rated R; June release. CAST: Richard Crenna (C.J.), Joanna Pettet (Caroline), Andrew Prine (Raymond), Cassie Yates (Mary), Lynne Moody (Felicia), Victor Buono (Devil), George O'Hanlon, Jr. (Pete), Mary Louise Weller (Laurie), Robert Viharo (Dwight), Milton Selzer (Realtor), Ed Bakey (Sam), Galen Thompson (Vargas), Emory Souza (Demon)

STARHOPS (First American) Executive Producers, Daniel Grodnik, Robert Sharpe; Co-Executive Producer, Jack Rose; Producers, John B. Kelly, Robert D. Krintzman; Director, Barbara Peeters; Screenplay, Stephanie Rothman; In color; 82 minutes; Rated PG; June release. CAST: Dorothy Buhrman (Danielle), Sterling Frazier (Cupcake), Jillian Kesner (Angel), Peter Paul Liapis (Ron), Anthony Mannino (Kong), Paul Ryan (Norman), Al Hobson (Carter)

ZERO TO SIXTY (First Artists) formerly "Repo"; Producer, Katherine Brown; Director, Don Weis; Screenplay, W. Lyle Richardson; Story, Peg Shirley, Judith Bustany; Assistant Directors, Mack Bing, Kate Tilley; Photography, Don Birnkrant; Art Director, Jim Newport; In color; Rated PG; June release. CAST: Darren McGavin (Mike), Denise Nickerson (Larry), Joan Collins (Gloria), Dick Martin (Attorney), Sylvia Miles (Flo), Hudson Brothers (Repo Crew)

THE GREAT BRAIN (Osmond) Director, Sidney Levin; Screenplay, Alan Cassidy; Based on book by John D. Fitzgerald; Theme Song sung by Donny Osmond; A Richard Bickerton Film; In DeLuxe Color; Rated G; June release. CAST: Jimmy Osmond, Pat Delaney, Fran Ryan, Cliff Osmond, Arthur Roberts, Lynn Benesch, Len Birman

Nanette Fabray, Barbara Eden
in "Harper Valley P.T.A."

HARPER VALLEY P.T.A. (April Fools) Executive Producer, Phil Borack; Producer, George Edwards; Director, Richard Bennett; Music, Nelson Riddle; Assistant Directors, Tom McCrory, Steve Siporin; Screenplay, George Edwards, Barry Schneider; Story, George Edwards; Art Director Costume Designer, Tom Rasmussen; Photography, Willy Kurant; Editor, Michael Economu; Title song by Tom T. Hall, sung by Jeannie C. Riley; In color; 93 minutes; Rated PG; June release. CAST: Barbara Eden (Stella), Ronny Cox (Willis), Nanette Fabray (Alice), Susan Swift (Dee), Louis Nye (Kirby), Pat Paulsen (Otis), John Fiedler (Bobby), Audrey Christie (Flora), DeVara Marcus (Holly), Irene Yah Ling Sun (Myrna), Louise Foley (Mavis), Clint Howard (Corley), Jan Teige, Laura Teige (Reily Twins), Pitt Herbert (Henry), Faye Dewitt (Willa Mae), Molly Dodd (Olive), Ron Masak (Herbie), Amzie Strickland (Shirley), Brian Cook (Carlyle), Tobias Andersen (Barney), Bob Hastings (Skeeter), Arlene Stuart (Bertha), J. J. Barry (Nolan), Royce D. Applegate (Dutch), Whitey Hughes (Stunt Man)

TEXAS DETOUR (Cinema Shares International) Produced, Directed and Written by Hikmet Avedis; Executive Producer, Marlene Schmidt; In color; 92 minutes; Rated R; June release. CAST: Patrick Wayne, Mitch Vogel, Lindsay Bloom, R. G. Armstong, Priscilla Barnes, Anthony James, Michael Mullins, Cameron Mitchell, Kathy O'Dare, Gary Davis

CONVENTION GIRLS (EMC) Producer, Michael Moss; Director, Joseph Adler; Screenplay, T. Gertler; Executive Producer, C. Vernon Kane; Music, Lawrence S. Hurwit, David Frank; In color; Rated R; June release. CAST: Nancy Lawson, Ann Sward, Carol Linden, Roberta White

OUT OF THE DARKNESS (Dimension) Producer, Ross Hagen; Director, Lee Madden; Screenplay, Hubert Smith; A Larry Woolner Presentation; In color; 87 minutes; Rated PG; June release. CAST: Donald Pleasence, Nancy Kwan, Ross Hagen, Lesly Fine, Claire Hagen, Jennifer Rhodes

Darren McGavin, Dick Martin
in "Zero to Sixty"

Patrick Wayne, Priscilla Barnes
in "Texas Detour"

"Dracula's Dog"

**Clive Revill, Elliott Gould
in "Matilda"**

DRACULA'S DOG (Crown International) Producers, Albert Band, Frank Ray Perilli; Director, Albert Band; Screenplay, Frank Ray Perilli; Photography, Bruce Logan; Editor, Harry Keramidas; Music, Andrew Belling; In DeLuxe Color; 90 minutes; Rated R; June release. CAST: Michael Pataki (Michael Drake/Dracula), Reggie Nalder (Veidt-Smith), Jose Ferrer (Insp. Branco), Jan Shutan (Marla), Libbie Chase (Linda), John Levin (Steve), Cleo Harrington (Mrs. Parks), Simmy Bow, JoJo D'Amore (Fishermen)

THE BAD NEWS BEARS GO TO JAPAN (Paramount) Producer, Michael Ritchie; Director, John Berry; Screenplay, Bill Lancaster; Photography, Gene Polito; Editor, Richard A. Harris; Design, Walter Scott Herndon; Music, Paul Chihara; Assistant Director, Jerry Ziesmer; In Movielab Color; 91 minutes; Rated PG; June release. CAST: Tony Curtis (Marvin), Jackie Earle Haley (Kelly), Tomisaburo Wakayama (Coach), Hatsune Ishihara (Arika), George Wyner (Network Director), Lonny Chapman (Gambler), Matthew Douglas Anton (E.R.W. Tillyard III), Erin Blunt (Ahmad), George Gonzales (Miguel), Brett Marx (Jimmy), David Pollock (Rudy), David Stambaugh (Toby), Jeffrey Louis Starr (Mike), Scoody Thornton (Mustapha)

THE BILLION DOLLAR HOBO (International Picture Show) Producer, Lang Elliott; Executive Producers, Lloyd N. Adams, Jr., Dorrell McGowan; Director, Stuart E. McGowan; Screenplay, Stuart E. McGowan, Tim Conway, Roger Beatty; Photography, Irv Goodnoff; Music, Michael Leonard; In DeLuxe Color; 96 minutes; Rated G; June release. CAST: Tim Conway (Vernon), Will Geer (Choo Choo), Eric Weston (Steve), Sydney Lassick (Mitchell), John Myhers (Leonard), Frank Sivero (Ernie), Sharon Weber (Jen), Sheela Tessler (Rita), Victoria Carroll (Barbara)

HIGH-BALLIN' (American International) Executive Producers, Stanley Chase, William Hayward; Producer, John Slan; Director, Peter Carter; Screenplay, Paul Edwards; Photography, Rene Verzier; Art Director, Claude Bonniere; In Movielab Color; 100 minutes; Rated PG; June release. CAST: Peter Fonda (Rane), Jerry Reed (Duke), Helen Shaver (Pickup), Chris Wiggins (King Carroll), David Ferry (Harvey), Chris Langevin (Tanker)

MATILDA (American International) Executive Producer, Richard R. St. Johns; Producer, Albert S. Ruddy; Director, Daniel Mann; Screenplay, Albert S. Ruddy, Timothy Galfas; Based on book by Paul Gallico; Photography, Jack Woolf; Associate Producer, Paul Sapounakis; Editor, Allan A. Jacobs; Designer, Boris Levin; "When I'm with You, I'm Feeling Good" by Carol Connors and Ernie Sheldon, sung by Pat Boone and Debbie Boone; In MGM and Movielab Color; 105 minutes; Rated G; June release. CAST: Elliott Gould (Bernie), Robert Mitchum (Duke), Harry Guardino (Uncle Nono), Clive Revill (Billy), Karen Carlson (Kathleen), Roy Clark (Wild Bill), Lionel Stander (Pinky), Art Metrano (Gordon), Larry Pennell (Lee), Roberta Collins (Tanya), Lenny Montana (Mercanti), Frank Avianca (Renato), John Lennon (Ring Announcer), Don Dunphy (Ringside Announcer), George Latka (Referee), Mike Willesee (Australian Announcer)

DEATH DIMENSION (Movietime) Producer, Harry Hope; Director, Al Adamson; Screenplay, Harry Hope; Photography, Gary Graver; In color; Rated R; July release. CAST: Jim Kelly, George Lazenby, Bob Minor, Patch McKenzie, Aldo Ray, Harold Sakata, Terry Moore, Myron Bruce Lee, April Sommers

VAMPIRE HOOKERS (Capricorn Three) Producer, Robert E. Waters; Director, Cirio H. Santiago; Screenplay, Howard Cohen; Assistant Director, Leo Martinez; Music, Jaime Mendoza-Nava; In color; Rated R; July release. CAST: John Carradine, Bruce Fairbairn, Trey Wilson, Karen Stride, Lenka Novak, Katie Dolan, Lex Winter

MARTIN (Libra) Producer, Richard Rubinstein; Direction and Screenplay, George A. Romero; Photography, Michael Gornick; Music, Donald Rubinstein; Editor, George A. Romero; Special Effects, Tom Savini; Associate Producers, Patricia Bernesser, Ray Schamus; A Laurel Group Presentaion in color; 95 minutes; Rated R; July rlease. CAST: John Amplas (Martin), Lincoln Maazel (Cuda), Christine Forrest (Christina), Elyane Nadeau (Mrs. Santini), Tom Savani (Arthur), Sarah Venable (Housewife Victim), Fran Middleton (Train Victim), Al Levitsky (Lewis)

**Peter Fonda, Helen Shaver
in "High-Ballin' "**

**John Amplas
in "Martin"**

"The Mouse and His Child"

"Seniors"

THE MOUSE AND HIS CHILD (Sanrio) Producer, Walt de-Faria; Executive Producers, Warren Lockhart, Shintaro Tsuji; Directors, Fred Wolf, Chuck Swenson; Screenplay, Carol Mon-Pere from novel by Russell Hoban; Music, Roger Kellaway; Lyrics, Gene Lees; Assistant Producer, Judy Kauffman; In color; 83 minutes; Rated G; July release. A feature-length animated film featuring the voices of Peter Ustinov (Manny), Cloris Leachman (Euterpe), Sally Kellerman (Seal), Andy Devine (Frog), Alan Barzman (Mouse), Marcy Swenson (Mouse Child), Neville Brand (Iggy), Regis Cordic (Clock and Hawk), Joan Gerber (Elephant), Bob Holt (Muskrat), Maitzi Morgan (Startling and Teller), Frank Nelson (Crow), Cliff Norton (Crow), Cliff Osmond (Serpentina), Iris Rainer (Paper People), Bob Ridgely (Jack in the Box), Charles Woolf (Bluejay and Paper People)

THE SWARM (Warner Bros.) Producer-Director, Irwin Allen; Screenplay, Stirling Silliphant; Based on novel by Arthur Herzog; Photography, Fred J. Koenekamp; Designer, Stan Jolley; Music, Jerry Goldsmith; Editor, Harold F. Kress; Assistant Directors, Mike Salamunovich, Skip Burguine; Costumes, Paul Zastupnevich; In Panavision and Technicolor; 116 minutes; Rated PG; July release. CAST: Michael Caine (Brad), Katharine Ross (Helena), Richard Widmark (Gen. Slater), Richard Chamberlain (Dr. Hubbard), Olivia de Havilland (Maureen), Ben Johnson (Felix), Lee Grant (Anne), Jose Ferrer (Dr. Andrews), Patty Duke Astin (Rita), Slim Pickens (Jud), Bradford Dillman (Maj. Baker), Fred MacMurray (Clarence), Henry Fonda (Dr. Krim)

NIGHTMARE IN BLOOD (PFE) Produced and Written by John Stanley, Kenn Davis; Director, John Stanley; Photography, Charles Rudnick; Editor, Alfred Katzman; Assistant Director, Julie Staheli; In Techniscope and Technicolor; 90 minutes; Rated R; July release. CAST: Kerwin Mathews (Prince), Jerry Walter (Malakai), Dan Caldwell (Seabrook), Barrie Youngfellow (Cindy), John J. Cochran (Scotty), Ray K. Gorman (B.B.), Hy Pyke (Harris), Irving Israel (Ben-Halik), Drew Eshelman (Arlington), Morgan Upton (George), Justin Bishop (Unworth), Stan Ritchie (Marsdon), Charles Murphy (Flannery), Yvonne Young (Barbara), Mike Hitchcock (Driscoll), Erika Stanley (Girl)

THE SENIORS (Cinema Shares) Producers, Carter DeHaven, Stanley Shapiro; Director, Rod Amateau; Screenplay, Stanley Shapiro; Executive Producers, Ric R. Roman; Music, Pat Williams; Sung by Gene Cotton; Photography, Robert Jessup; Editor, Guy Scarpita; In color; Rated R; July release. CAST: Jeffrey Byron, Gary Imhoff, Dennis Quaid, Lou Richards, Priscilla Barnes, Rockey Flintermann, Edward Andrews, Ian Wolf, Robert Emhardt, Alan Hewitt, Lynn Cartwright, Woodrow Parfrey, Troy Hoskins, David Haney, Alan Reed

BUCKSTONE COUNTY PRISON (Film Ventures International) Producer, E. E. Owensby; Director, Jimmy Huston; Screenplay, Tom McIntyre; In DeLuxe Color; Rated R; 88 minutes; July release; Original title "Seabo." CAST: Earl Owensby, David Allan Coe, Donald "Red" Barry, Ed Parker, Leonard Dixon, Sunset Carson, Holly Conover, Rod Sacharnoski, Ron Lampkin

SLITHIS (Fabtrax) Producers, Stephen Traxle, Paul Fabian; Direction and Screenplay, Stephen Traxler; Photography, Robert Caramico; Music, Steve Zuckerman; A Dick Davis Production; Original title "Spawn of the Slithis"; In color; 86 minutes; Rated PG; July release. CAST: Alan Blanchard, Judy Motulsky, Mello Alexandria, Dennis Lee Falt, Win Condict, Hy Pyke, Don Cummins

STINGRAY (Avco Embassy) Direction and Screenpaly, Richard Taylor; Executive Producers, Donald R. Ham, Bill L. Bruce; In Technicolor; 99 minutes; Rated PG; August release. CAST: Christopher Mitchum, Les Lannom, William Watson, Sherry Jackson, Sondra Theodore, Cliff Emmich, Bert Hinchman, Richard Cosentino, Russell Bender

NURSE SHERRI (Independent International) Producer, Mark Sherwood; Director, Al Adamson; Screenplay, Michael Bockman, Gregg Tittinger; In Eastmancolor; Rated R; August release. CAST: Jill Jacobson, Geoffrey Land, Marilyn Joi, Mary Kay Pass, Prentiss Moulden, Clayton Foster

"Olivia DeHavilland in "The Swarm"
© Warner Bros. 1978

John Murphy, Chris Mitchum, Les Lannom, Sondra Theodore in "Stingray"

135

"Piranha"

Mel Ferrer, Lee Majors
in "The Norseman"

PIRANHA (New World) Producer, Jon Davison; Director, Joe Dante; Screenplay, John Sayles; Story, Richard Robinson, John Sayles; Executive Producers, Roger Corman, Jeff Schechtman; Co-Producer, Chako Van Leeuwen; Music, Pino Donaggio; Editors, Mark Goldblatt, Joe Dante; Photography, Jamie Anderson; Art Direction, Bill Mellin, Kerry Mellin; In color; 92 minutes; August release. CAST: Bradford Dillman (Paul), Heather Menzies (Maggie), Kevin McCarthy (Dr. Joak), Keenan Wynn (Jack), Dick Miller (Buck), Barbara Steele (Dr. Mengers), Belinda Balaski (Betsy), Melody Thomas (Laura), Bruce Gordon (Col. Waxman), Barry Brown (Trooper), Paul Bartel (Dumont), Shannon Collins (Suzie), Shawn Nelson (Whitney), Richard Deacon (Earl), Janie Squire (Barbara), Roger Richman (David), Bill Smillie (Jailer), Guich Koock (Pitchman), Jack Pauleson (In canoe), Eric Henshaw (Father in Canoe), Robert Vinson (Soldier), Virginia Dunnam (Girl), and Hill Farnsworth, Bruce Barbour, Robyn Ray, Mike Sullivan, Jack Cardwell, Roger Creed, Nick Palmisano, Bobby Sargent

THE MAGIC OF LASSIE (International Picture Show) Producers, Bonita Granville Wrather, William Beaudine, Jr.; Director, Don Chaffey; Screenplay, Jean Holloway, Robert B. Sherman, Richard M. Sherman; Story and Music, Robert B. Sherman, Richard M. Sherman; In Dolby Stereo and color; 99 minutes; Rated G; August release. CAST: James Stewart, Mickey Rooney, Pernell Roberts, Stephanie Zimbalist, Michael Sharrett, Alice Faye, Gene Vans, The Mike Curb Congregation, Lassie

KILLER'S DELIGHT (Intercontinental) Producer-Director, Jeremy Hoenack; Screenplay, Maralyn Thoma; In color; Rated R; August release. CAST: James Luisi, Susan Sullivan, John Karlan, Martin Speer

THE FOX AFFAIR (Ruff) Producer-Director, Fereidun G. Jorjani; Screenplay Barry Victor; Executive Producer, Richard Power; Music, Olubiji Adetoye; Editor, Gary Gasgarth; A Panther Production in color; Rated R; August release. CAST: Kathryn Dodd, Robert Bosco, Yuri Alexis, Steve Lincoln, Sunny Collins, Russ MacDonald, Jacquelyn Bernstein, Young Eagle Kim

THE NORSEMAN (American International) Produced, Directed and Written by Charles B. Pierce; Music, Jaime Mendoza-Nava; Narrated by Jesse Pearson; Associate Producer, Tom Moore; Assistant Director, Dave Woody; Photography, Robert Bethard; Designers, John Ball, Henry Peterson; A Samuel Z. Arkoff Presentation of a Fawcett-Majors Production in Panavison and color; 90 minutes; Rated PG; September release. CAST: Lee Majors (Thorvald), Cornel Wilde (Ragnar), Mel Ferrer (King Eurich), Jack Elam (Death Dreamer), Chris Connelly (Rolf), Kathleen Freeman (Indian), Denny Miller (Rauric), Seaman Glass (Gunnar), Jimmy Clem (Olaf), Susie Coelho (Winnetta), Jerry Daniels (Kiwonga), Deacon Jones (Thrall), Bill Lawler (Bjorn) and Fred Biletnikoff, David Kent, Frank Anderson, Curtis Jordan, Glen Hollis, John Welsh, Kevin Myers, Anthony Vitale, Cecil Kent, Steve Denny, Mike Kaminsky, Eric Crandall, Sandy Sanders, Ron Britt, Bob Hewlett, Gary Roy, Bill Twofeathers, Cyrus Strongshield, Mike Gallagher, Mike Rivera, Mike Vincent, Greg Rivera, Mark Wiles, Rick Merino, Wayne Harht, Joe Lopez

ONE MAN JURY (Cal-Am Artists) Producers, Theodor Bodnar, Steve Bono; Direction and Screenplay, Charles Martin; Executive Producers, Joseph R. Laird, Kenneth J. Fisher; Music, Morton Stevens; Assistant Directors, John Barnwell, John Neukum; In color by CFI; 98 minutes; Rated R; September release. CAST: Jack Palance (Wade), Christopher Mitchum (Blake), Pamela Shoop (Wendy), Cara Williams (Nancy), Joe Spinell (Mike), Jeff McCracken (Billy Joe), Alexandra Hay (Tessie), Angel Tompkins (Kitty), Andy Romano (Chickie), Tom Pedi (Angie), Chuck Bergansky (Kayo), Anthony Sirico (Charlie), Richard Foronjy (Al), Patrick Wright (Kinky), Frank Pesce (Freddie), Dick Yarmy (Customer), Don "Red" Barry (Murphy), James Bacon (Reporter), Kirk Scott (Cole), Royal Dano (Bartender), John Blythe Barrymore (Policeman), Elizabeth Kerr (Maid), Alfred T. Williams (Detective), John E. Neukum, Jr. (Cop), Lindsay Workman (Judge), George Deaton, Alex Hakobian (Pool Players), Myrna Dell (Landlady), Geraldine Smith (Barmaid), Mike Mazurki (Handler), Hany Ghorra (Floorman), Betty Hager, Sampa Tacorda (Chip Girls)

Jack Palance
in "One Man Jury"

Karen Lamm, Tim Matheson, Lee Purcell
in "Almost Summer"

ALMOST SUMMER (Universal) Executive Producer, Steve Tisch; Producer, Rob Cohen; Director, Martin Davidson; Screenplay, Judith Berg, Sandra Berg, Martin Davidson, Marc Reid Rubel; Associate Producer, Anthony R. Clark; Photography, Stevan Larner; Editor, Lynzee Klingman; Art Director, William M. Hiney; Music, Charles Lloyd, Ron Altbach; Title Song, Brian Wilson; Assistant Directors, Gary Daigler, Peter Burrell; Costumes, Sandra Davidson; A Motown Production in Technicolor; Rated PG; 88 minutes; September release. CAST: Bruno Kirby (Bobby), Lee Purcell (Christine), John Friedrich (Darryl), Didi Conn (Donna), Thomas Carter (Dean), Tim Matheson (Kevin), Petronia Paley (Nicole), David Wilson (Duane), Sherry Hursey (Lori), Harvey Lewis (Stanley), Karen Lamm (Felicia), Judith Nugent-Hart (Susie), Denise Denise (Gwen), Catherine Lee Smith (Bonnie), John Kirby (Larry), Allen G. Norman (Scratch), Byron Stewart (Scottie), Merie Earle (Mrs. Jenkins), Bill Bogert (Albrecht), Kres Mersky (Miss Margulies), Michael Stearns (Police), Don-Jack Rosseau (Upshaw), Yvette Sylvander (Stacy), Yvonne Sylvander (Tracy), Robert Resnick (Grant), Kurt G. Andon (Bkier), Gene LeBell (Coach), Conrad Palmisano (Assistant Coach), Donna Wilkes (Meredith) Sunny Johnson (Debbie), Jill Gold (Gail), Todd Hoffman (Sonny), Bryan Beardsly, Ty Page, Mark Bowden (Skateboarders)

TEAM-MATES (Independent International) Producer, Samuel M. Sherman; Director, Steven Jacobson; Screenplay, Jennifer Lawson; Music, Robert Rapson; Executive Producer, Dan Q. Kennis; In Technicolor; 84 minutes; Rated R; September release. CAST: Karen Corrado, Max Goff, Christopher Seppe, Ivy Sinclair, Michael Goldfinger, Richard Ciotti, Debbie Novak, Scott Sparks, G. E. Harris, David Sawyer

FAMILY ENFORCER (First American) Executive Producer, Peter S. Davis; Producer, William N. Panzer; Direction and Screenplay, Ralph DeVito; Photography, Bob Ballin; Music, Media Counterpoint; A John B. Kelly Presentation in color; 82 minutes; Rated R; September release. CAST: Joseph Cortese (Jerry), Lou Criscuola (Anthony), Joseph Pesci (Joe), Anne Johns (Paula), Keith Davis (Marley)

TINTORERA (United Film) Producer, Gerald Green; Director; Rene Cardona, Jr.; Based on novel by Ramon Bravo; Music, Basil Poledouris; In color; A Hemdale Leisure Corporation and Conacine Production; 91 minutes; Rated R; September release. CAST: Susan George (Gabriella), Fiona Lewis, Jennifer Ashley, Hugo Stiglitz (Esteban), Andres Garcia (Miguel)

DEATH FORCE (Caprican Three) Producer, Robert E. Waters; Director, Cirio H. Santiago; Screenplay, Howard Cohen; Music, Jaime Mendoza-Nava; A Cosa Nueva Production; In color; Rated R; September release. CAST: James Iglehart, Carmen Argenziano, Leon Isaac, Jayne Kennedy, Roberto Gonzales

LAND OF NO RETURN (International Picture Show) Producer-Director, Kent Bateman; Screenplay, Kent Bateman, Frank Ray Perilli; Based on book "Challenge to Survive" by Donn Davison; In DeLuxe Color; Rated G; September release. CAST: William Shatner, Mel Torme

CHEERLEADERS' BEACH PARTY (Cannon) Producers, Dennis Murphy, Alex E. Goitein; Director, Alex E. Goitein; Story and Screenplay, Chuck Vincent; In color; Rated R; September release. CAST: Stephanie Hastings, Linda Jenson, Mary Lou Loredan, Denise Upson, Max Goff

SCALPEL (AVCO Embassy) Originally "False Face"; Producers, Joseph Weintraub, John Grissmer; Direction and Screenplay, John Grissmer; Story, Joseph Weintraub; Photography, Edward Lachman, Jr.; Music, Robert Cobert; Editor, Joseph Weintraub; In Movielab Color; 95 minutes; Rated PG; September release. CAST: Robert Lansing (Phillip), Judith Chapman (Heather/Jane), Arlen Dean Snyder (Uncle Bradley), David Scarroll (Robert), Sandy Martin (Sandy), Bruce Atkins (Plumber)

BULLY (Maturo-Image) Producers, Sam Maturo, Mel Marshall; Director, Peter H. Hunt; Screenplay, Jerome Alden; Photography, Ken Pailus; Editor, Terry Green; Design, John Conklin; In color; 120 minutes; rated PG; September release. CAST: James Whitmore as Theodore Roosevelt in his one man theatre performance.

TOO HOT TO HANDLE (Derio Productions) Producer, Ralph T. Desiderio; Director, Don Schain; Screenplay, J. Michael Sherman, Don Buday; Music, Hugo Montenegro; In Metrocolor; Rated R; October release. CAST: Cheri Caffaro, Aharon Ipale, Corinne Calvet, John Van Dreelan, Vic Diaz, Vic Silayan, Subas Herrero

FRENCH QUARTER (Crown International) Producer-Director, Dennis Kane; Executive Producer, Herb Scheiderman; Screenplay, Barney Cohen, Dennis Kane; Associate Producer, Tony Alatis; Photography, Jerry Kalogeratos; Music, Dick Hyman; Editors, Ed Fricke, George Norris; Costumes, Ellen Mirojnick; Choreographer, Donnis Hunnicutt; In Movielab Color; 101 minutes; Rated R; October release. CAST: Bruce Davison (Kid Ross/Insp. Sordik), Virginia Mayo (Countess Piazza/Ida), Lindsay Bloom (Big Butt/Policewoman), Lance LeGault (Tom/Burt), Ann Michelle (Coke-Eyed Laura/Policewoman), Alisha Fontain (Trudy/Christine), Vernel Bagneris (Jelly Roll/Policeman), Rebecca Allen (Bricktop/Girl in Square), Laura Mish Owens (Ice Box Jose/Girl in Square), Anna Filamento (Mme. Papaloos/Mme. Beaudine), William Simms (Aaron Harris/Pimp), Stocker Fontelieu (Dr. Miles/Old Man), Stanley Reyes (Bellocq/-Drunk), Ronald Bolden (Satchelmouth/Shoeshine Boy), Sylvia "Kuumba" Williams (Wisterie/Cleaning Woman), Dino Head (Lady Lil/Stripper), Don Hood (Detective/Policeman)

HALLOWEEN (Compass International) Executive Producer, Irwin Yablans; Producer, Debra Hill; Director, John Carpenter; Screenplay, John Carpenter, Debra Hill; Music, John Carpenter; Assistant Directors, Rick Wallace, Jack DeWolf; In Panavision and Metrocolor; 93 minutes; Rated R; October release. CAST: Donald Pleasence (Loomis), Jamie Lee Curits (Laurie), Nancy Loomis (Annie), P J Soles (Lynda), Charles Cyphers (Brackett), Kyle Richards (Lindsey), Brian Andrews (Tommy), John Michael Graham (Bob), Nancy Stephens (Marion), Arthur Malet (Graveyard Keeper), Mickey Yablans (Richie), Brent LePage (Lonnie), Adam Hollander (Keith), Robert Phalen (Dr. Wynn), Tony Moran (Michael at 23), Will Sandin (Michael at 6), Sandy Johnson (Judith), David Kyle (Boy Friend), Peter Griffith (Laurie's father), Jim Windburn (Stunt), Nick Castle (The Shape)

ATTACK OF THE KILLER TOMATOES (NAI Entertainment) Producers, Steve Peace, John De Bello; Director, John De Bello; Screenplay, Costa Dillon, Steve Peace, John De Bello; Photography, John K. Culley; Music, Gordon Goodwin, Paul Sundfur; In CFI Color; 86 minutes; Rated PG; October release. CAST: David Miller, George Wilson, Sharon Taylor, Jack Riley

MUSTANG: THE HOUSE THAT JOE BUILT (RG Productions II) Produced, Directed and Photographed by Robert Guralnick; Executive Producer, William Walker; In color; 85 minutes; Rated R; October release. A documentary featuring Joe Conforte and the working girls of Mustang Ranch, a licensed brothel in Nevada.

KIDNAPPED CO-ED (Boxoffice International) Produced, Directed and Written by Frederick R. Friedel; Music, George Newman Shaw, John Willhelm; Executive Producer, Irwin Friedlander; In color; Rated R; October release. CAST: Jack Canon, Leslie Ann Rivers, Gladys Lavitan, Larry Lambeth, Jim Blankinship

HITCHHIKE TO HELL (Boxoffice International) Producer-Director, Irv Berwick; Screenplay, John Buckley; Executive Producers, Frances Adair, Joseph V. Agnello; In color; 87 minutes; Rated R; October release. CAST: Robert Gribbin (Howard), Russell Johnson (Capt. Shaw), John Harmon (Baldwin), Randy Echols (Lt. Davis), Dorothy Bennett, Jacquelyn Poseley, Mary Ellen Christie, Jane Ratliff, Beth Reis, Kippi Bell

GOIN' COCONUTS (Osmond) Producer, John Cutts; Director, Howard Morris; Screenplay, Raymond Harvey; Photography, Frank Phillips; Editor, Frank Bracht; Assistant Director, Bob Huddleston; In DeLuxe Color; 93 minutes; Rated PG; October release. CAST: Donny Osmond (Donny), Marie Osmond (Marie), Herbert Edelman (Sid), Kenneth Mars (Kruse), Chrystin Sinclaire (Tricia), Ted Cassidy (Mickey), Marc Lawrence (Webster), Khigh Dhiegh (Wong), Harold Sakata (Ito), Charles Walker (Jake), Danny Wells (Al), Jack Collins (Charlie), Tommy Fujiwara (Alecki)

C. B. HUSTLERS (Rochelle) Producer-Director, Stuart Segall; Screenplay, John Alderman, John Goff; Story, Martin Gatsby; Executive Producer, Martin W. Greenwald; In color; 85 minutes; Rated R; November release. CAST: Edward Roehm, Jake Barnes, John Alderman, Valdesta, Tiffany Jones, Connie Markus, Ron Kelly

BLACKJACK (SES International) Produced, Directed and Written by John Evans; Music, Jack Ashford, Robert White; In DeLuxe Color; 104 minutes; Rated R; November release. CAST: Bill Smith (Andy), Tony Burton (Charles), Paris Earl (Ojenke), Damu King (Roy), Diane Sommerfield (Nancy), Angela May, Tom Scott

**Angel Tompkins, John Saxon
in "The Bees"**

**A. Martinez, Brian Keith
in "Joe Panther"**

THE BEES (New World) Produced, Directed, and Written by Alfredo Zacharias; Story, Mr. Zacharias; Executive Producer, Michel Zacharias; Associate Producer, Teri Schwartz; Photography, Leon Sanchez; Music, Richard Gillis, Editors, Mort Tubor, Sandy Nervig; Art Director, Jose Rodriguez Granada; Costumes, elan; Assistant Directors, Manuel Ortega, David Silvan; In color; 86 minutes; Rated PG; November release. CAST: John Saxon (John), Angel Tompkins (Sandra), John Carradine (Dr. Hummel), Claudio Brook (Dr. Miller), Alicia Encinas (Alicia), Julio Cesar (Julio), Armand Martin (Arthur), Jose Chavez Trowe (Father), George Bellanger (Undersecretary Brennan), Deloy White (Winkler), Roger Cudney (Blankeley), Julia Yallop (Model), Chad Hastings (Gray), Elizabeth Wallace (Secretary), Al Jones, Gray Johnson (Muggers), Whitey Hughes (Gentleman in park), David Silverkleit, Brian Hanna, Alfred Melhem (Boys), Don Maxwell (U. S. General), Eddie Alexander (Announcer), Walter Hanna (President), Bill Bordy (Newscaster)

DAY OF THE WOMAN (Cinemagic Pictures) Producer, Joseph Zbeda; Direction and Screenplay, Meir Zarchi; Assistant Directors, Michael Penland, Beriau Picard; Photography, Yuri Haviv; Editor, Meir Zarchi; In Eastmancolor; 90 minutes; Rated R; November release. CAST: Camille Keaton (Jennifer), Eron Tabor (Johnny), Richard Pace (Matthew), Anthony Nichols (Stanley), Gunter Kleeman (Andy), Alexis Magnotti (Attendant's Wife), Tammy Zarchi, Terry Zarchi (Children), Traci Ferrante (Waitress), Bill Tasgal (Porter), Isac Agami (Butcher), Ronit Haviv (Supermarket Girl)

THE SILENT WITNESS (Independent International) Producer-Director, David W. Rolfe; Screenplay, Ian Wilson, Henry Lincoln, David W. Rolfe; Executive Producers, Adam J. Otterbein, Peter M. Rinaldi; Photography, Bahram Monocheri; Editor, Peter Hollywood; A Screenpro Production; Narrator, Kenneth More; In color; Rated PG; November release. A documentary exploring the mystery of the Shroud of Turin, believed to be the cloth around Christ's body in the tomb.

SMOKEY AND THE GOODTIME OUTLAWS (Howco International) Producer, Tommy Amato; Director, Alex Grasshoff; Screenplay, Frank Dobbs, Bob Walsh; Story, Jesse Turner; Music, Mauro Bruno; Executive Producer, Jesse Turner; In color; Rated PG; November release. CAST: Jesse Turner, Dennis Fimple, Slim Pickens, Diane Sherrill, Marcie Barkin, Hope Summers, Don Sherman, Gailard Sartain, Sully Boyer, Archie Campbell, Mickey Gilley, Johnny Paycheck

JOE PANTHER (Cougar) Executive Producer, Dr. Leroy C. Taylor; Producer, Stewart H. Beveridge; Associate Producers, L. Jay Monk, Dale Benson; Screenplay, Dale Eunson; Based on novel by Zachary Ball; Director, Paul Krasny; Music, Fred Karlin; "The Time Has Come" by Fred Karlin, Norman Gimbel; Sung by England Dan and John Ford Coley; In color by CFI; 110 minutes; Rated G; December release. CAST: Brian Keith (Capt. Harper), Ricardo Montalban (Turtle George), Ray Tracey (Joe Panther), A. Martinez (Billy Tiger), Alan Feinstein, Cliff Osmond

THEY WENT THAT-A-WAY AND THAT-A-WAY (International Picture Show) Executive Producer, Lloyd N. Adams, Jr.; Producer, Lang Elliott; Directors, Edward Montagne, Stuart E. McGowan; Screenplay, Tim Conway; Photography, Jacques Haitkin; Music, Michael Leonard; Associate Producers, Eric Weston, Wanda Dell; In color; 95 minutes; Rated PG; December release. CAST: Tim Conway (Dewey), Chuck McCann (Wallace), Richard Kiel (Duke), Dub Taylor (Warden), Reni Santoni (Billy Jo), Lenny Montana (Brick), Ben Jones (Lugs), Timothy Blake (Margie), Hank Worden (Butch)

UNCLE JOE SHANNON (United Artists) Executive Producer, Gene Kirkwood; Producers, Irwin Winkler, Robert Chartoff; Director, Joseph C. Hanwright; Screenplay, Burt Young; Photography, Bill Butler; Editor, Don Zimmerman; Music, Bill Conti; Design, Bill Kenney; Costumes, Bobbie Mannix; Assistant Director, Brian E. Frankish; In color; 108 minutes; Rated PG; December release. CAST: Burt Young (Joe Shannon), Doug McKeon (Robbie), Madge Sinclair (Margaret), Jason Bernard (Goose), Bert Remsen (Braddock), Allan Rich (Dr. Clark)

**Camille Keaton
in "Day of the Woman"**

**Burt Young, Doug McKeon
in "Uncle Joe Shannon"**

RICHARD DREYFUSS in "The Goodbye Girl"
1977 ACADEMY AWARD FOR BEST ACTOR

ANNIE HALL

(UNITED ARTISTS) Producer, Charles H. Joffe; Director, Woody Allen; Screenplay, Woody Allen, Marshall Brickman; Executive Producer, Robert Greenhut; Associate Producer, Fred T. Gallo; Photography, Gordon Willis; Editors, Ralph Rosenblum, Wendy Greene Bricmont; A Jack Rollins-Charles H. Joffe Production; In color; 93 minutes; Rated PG; April release.

CAST

Alvy Singer	Woody Allen
Annie Hall	Diane Keaton
Rob	Tony Roberts
Allison	Carol Kane
Tony Lacey	Paul Simon
Mom Hall	Colleen Dewhurst
Robin	Janet Margolin
Pam	Shelley Duvall
Duane Hall	Christopher Walken
Dad Hall	Donald Symington
Grammy Hall	Helen Ludlam
Alvy's Dad	Mordecai Lawner
Alvy's Mom	Joan Newman
Alvy at 9	Jonathan Munk
Alvy's Aunt	Ruth Volner
Alvy's Uncle	Martin Rosenblatt
Joey Nichols	Hy Ansel
Aunt Tessie	Rashel Novikoff

Left: Woody Allen, Diane Keaton
1977 Academy Awards for Best Picture,
Best Actress (Diane Keaton), Best Director,
Best Original Screenplay

Woody Allen, Tony Roberts, Diane Keaton
1977 ACADEMY AWARD FOR BEST PICTURE AND BEST ACTRESS

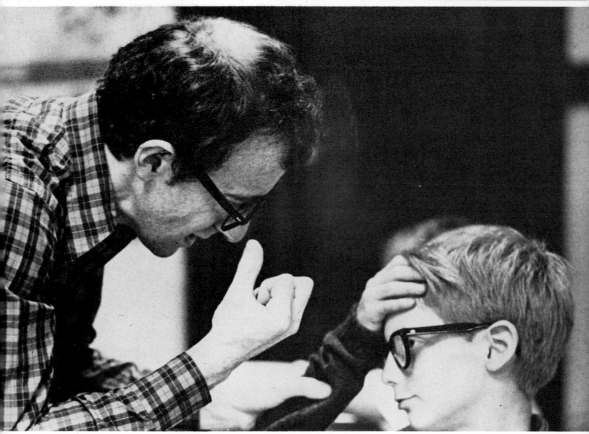

Woody Allen, Jonathan Munk
Top: Woody Allen, Diane Keaton

JASON ROBARDS
in "Julia"
1977 ACADEMY AWARD FOR BEST SUPPORTING ACTOR

VANESSA REDGRAVE
in "Julia"
1977 ACADEMY AWARD FOR BEST SUPPORTING ACTRESS

MADAME ROSA

(ATLANTIC) Executive Producers, Raymond Danon, Roland Girard, Jean Bolary; Production Executive, Ralph Baum; Direction and Screenplay, Moshe Mizrahi; Based on book by Emile Ajark; French with English subtitles; A Lira Film Production in color; 105 minutes; Rated PG; March release.

CAST

Madame Rosa	Simone Signoret
Mohammed (Momo)	Samy Ben Youb
Doctor	Claude Dauphin
Hamil	Gabriel Jabbour
Nadine	Michal Bat Adam
Ramon	Costa Gavros
Madame Lola	Stella Anicette
Yadir Youssef	Mohammed Zineth

Top: Samy Ben Youb

Samy Ben Youb, Simone Signoret
Above and Top: Simone Signoret

1977 ACADEMY AWARD FOR BEST FOREIGN LANGUAGE FILM

Claude Dauphin, Samy Ben Youb
Top: Simone Signoret, Samy Ben Youb

Simone Signoret

THE DEER HUNTER

(UNIVERSAL) Producers, Barry Spikings, Michael Deeley, Michael Cimino, John Peverall; Director, Michael Cimino; Screenplay, Deric Washburn; Story, Michael Cimino, Deric Washburn, Louis Garfinkle, Quinn K. Redeker; Photography, Vilmos Zsigmond; Associate Producers, Marion Rosenberg, Joann Carelli; Art Directors, Ron Hobbs, Kim Swados; Editor, Peter Zinner; Music, Stanley Myers; Assistant Directors, Charles Okun, Mike Grillo; In Dolby Stereo, Panavision and Technicolor; 183 minutes; Rated R; December release.

CAST

Michael	Robert DeNiro
Stan	John Cazale
Steven	John Savage
Nick	Christopher Walken
Linda	Meryl Streep
John	George Dzundza
Axel	Chuck Aspegren
Steven's Mother	Shirley Stoler
Angela	Rutanya Alda
Julien	Pierre Segui
Axel's Girl	Mady Kaplan
Bridesmaid	Amy Wright
Stan's Girl	Mary Ann Haenel
Linda's Father	Richard Kuss
Bandleader	Joe Grifasi
Wedding Man	Christopher Colombi, Jr.
Sad Looking Girl	Victoria Karnafel
Cold Old Man	Jack Scardino
Bingo Caller	Joe Strand
Helen	Henen Tomko
Sergeant	Paul D'Amato

and Dennis Watlington, Charlene Darrow, Jane Colette Disko, Michael Wollet, Robert Beard, Joe Dzizmba, Father Stephen Kopestonsky, John F. Buchmelter III, Frank Devore, Tom Becker, Lynn Kongkham, Dale Burroughs, Parris Hicks

Left: Robert DeNiro
1978 Academy Awards for Best Picture,
Best Supporting Actor (Christopher Walken),
Best Director, Best Film Editing, Best Sound

John Cazale, Chuck Aspegren, Christopher Walken, Robert DeNiro, John Savage

Meryl Streep, Robert DeNiro

rt DeNiro, John Savage Above: John Savage
arries Rutanya Alda Top: John Cazale, Chuck
spegren, Robert DeNiro, John Savage, Rutanya
Alda, Christopher Walken, Meryl Streep

Robert DeNiro
Above: Christopher Walken, DeNiro, John Savage

JANE FONDA
in "Coming Home"

1978 ACADEMY AWARD FOR BEST ACTRESS

JON VOIGHT
in "Coming Home"

1978 ACADEMY AWARD FOR BEST ACTOR

CHRISTOPHER WALKEN
in "The Deer Hunter"

1978 ACADEMY AWARD FOR BEST SUPPORTING ACTOR

MAGGIE SMITH
in "California Suite"

1978 ACADEMY AWARD FOR BEST SUPPORTING ACTRESS

GET OUT YOUR HANDKERCHIEFS

(NEW LINE CINEMA) Executive Producer, Paul Claudon; Direction and Screenplay, Bertrand Blier; French with English subtitles; Photography, Jean Penzer; Editor, Claudine Merlin; Music, Georges Delerue; Art Director, Eric Moulard; In color; 100 minutes; Not rated; December release.

CAST

Raoul	Gerard Depardieu
Stephane	Patrick Dewaere
Solange	Carol Laure
Christian Beloiel	Riton
Neighbor	Michel Serreaul
Mrs. Beloeil	Eleonore Hirt
Passerby	Sylvie Joly
Mr. Beloeil	Jean Rougerie

Left: Carol Laure, Riton

Gerard Depardieu, Carol Laure, Patrick Dewaere

1978 ACADEMY AWARD FOR BEST FOREIGN LANGUAGE FILM

THE DUELLISTS

(PARAMOUNT) Producer, David Putnam; Director, Ridley Scott; Screenplay, Gerald Vaughan-Hughes; Based on Joseph Conrad's story "The Duel"; Photography, Frank Tidy; Editor, Pamela Powers; Music, Howard Blake; In Color; 101 Minutes; Rated PG; January release.

CAST

D'Hubert	Keith Carradine
Feraud	Harvey Keitel
Fouche	Albert Finney
Colonel Reynard	Edward Fox
Adele	Cristina Raines
General Treillard	Robert Stephens
Jacquin	Tom Conti
Second Major	John McEnery
Laura	Diana Quick
Lacourbe	Alun Armstrong
Tall Second	Maurice Colbourne
Maid	Gay Hamilton
Leonie	Meg Wynn Owen
Mme. de Lionne	Jenny Runacre
Chevalier	Alan Webb

Top: Keith Carradine, Cristina Raines
Below: Harvey Keitel, Matthew Guiness, Keith Carradine

Harvey Keitel, Keith Carradine

161

MADO

(JOSEPH GREEN) Producer, Andre Genoves; Director, Claude Sautet; Screenplay, Claude Sautet, Claude Neron; Photography, Jean Boffety; Music, Philippe Sarde; Editor, Jacqueline Thiedot; Assistant Directors, Jacques Santi, Jean Sussfeld; In Eastmancolor; 130 minutes; In French with English sub-titles; Not rated; January release.

CAST

Simon Leotard	Michel Piccoli
Mado	Ottavia Piccolo
Helene	Romy Schneider
Pierre	Jacques Dutronc
Manecca	Charles Denner
Lepidon	Julien Guiomar
Barachet	Michel Aumont
Julien	Bernard Fresson
Vaudable	Claude Dauphin
Mathelin	Andre Falcon
Papa	Jean-Paul Moulinot
Lucienne	Denise Filiatrault
Maxime	Nicolas Vogel
Girbal	Jacques Richard
Antoine	Benoit Allemane
Juliette	Nathalie Baye
Alex	Jean-Denis Robert
Francis	Marc Chapiteau
William	David Tonelli
Roger	Daniel Russo
Married Man's Sister	Sabine Glaser
Crovetto	Dominique Zardi
Paul	Claude Neron

LANDSCAPE AFTER BATTLE

(NEW YORKER) Producers, Polish Corporation for Film Production; Director, Andrzej Wajda; Screenplay, Andrzej Wajda, Andrzej Brzozowski; Based on Stories by Tadeusz Borowski; Photography, Zygmunt Samosiuk; Music, Syzmunt Konieczny, Antonio Vivaldi, Frederic Chopin; Art Director, Jerzy Szeski; In color, 110 minutes; In Polish with English sub-titles; February release.

CAST

Tadeusz	Daniel Olbrychski
Nina	Stanislawa Celinska
Karol	Tadeusz Janczar
Officer	Mieczyslaw Stoor
Priest	Zygmunt Malanowicz
Tolek	Leszek Drogosz
Professor	Aleksander Bardini
Gypsy Man	Stefan Friedmann
Camp Commandant	Jerzy Zelnik

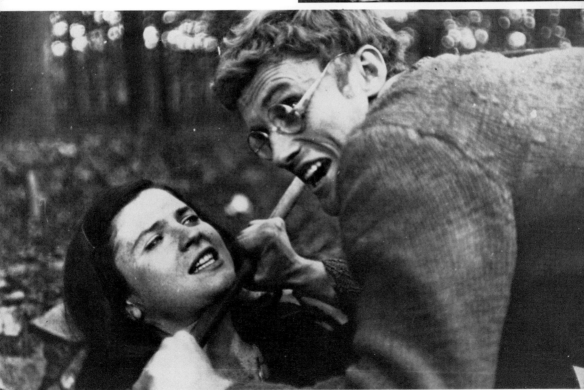

Stanislawa Celinska, Caniel Olbrychski

STARSHIP INVASIONS

(WARNER BROS.) Producers, Norman Glick, Ed Hunt, Ken Gord; Executive Producers, Earl A. Glick, Norman Glick; Direction and Screenplay, Ed Hunt; Editors, Millie Moore; Ruth Hope; Special Effects, Warren Keillor; Photography, Mark Irwin; Music, Gil Melle; Associate Producer, Trayton Adair; Assistant Producer, Holly Dale; Assistant Directors, Gary Flanagan, Don Brough; Art Director, Karen Bromley; In color; 89 minutes; Rated PG; February release.

CAST

Professor Duncan	Robert Vaughn
Captain Rameses	Christopher Lee
Anaxi	Daniel Pilon
Phi	Tiiu Leek
Betty	Helen Shaver
Malcolm	Henry Ramer
Gezeth	Victoria Johnson
Dorothy	Doreen Lipson

Left: Robert Vaughn

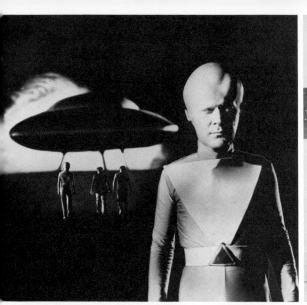

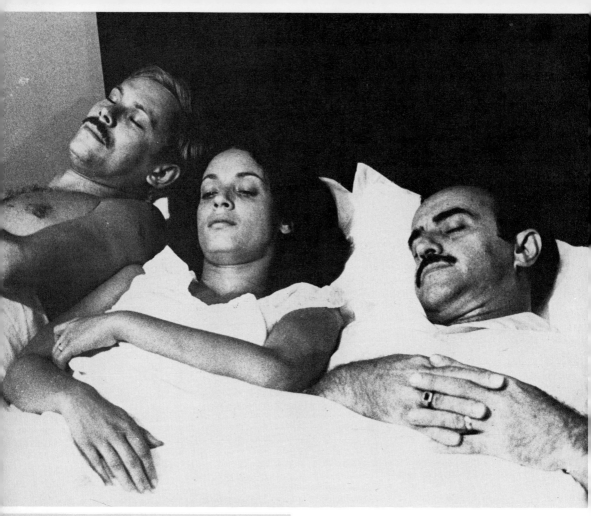

DONA FLOR AND HER TWO HUSBANDS

(NEW YORKER) Producers, Luiz Carlos Barreto, Newton Rique, Cia Serrador; Direction and Screenplay, Bruno Barreto; Based on novel by Jorge Amado; Photography, Maurilo Salles; Editor, Raimundo Higino; Art Director, Anisio Medeiros; Music, Chico Buarque; In color; Portugese with English subtitles; 106 minutes; Rated R; February release.

CAST

Dona Flor	Sonia Braga
Vadinho	Jose Wilker
Teodoro	Mauro Mendonca
Rozilda	Dinorah Brillanti
Mirandao	Nelson Xavier
Carlinhos	Arthur Costa Filho
Cazuzat	Rui Rezende
Arigof	Mario Gusmao

Jose Wilker, Sonia Braga
Top: Jose Wilker, Sonia Braga,
Mauro Mendonca

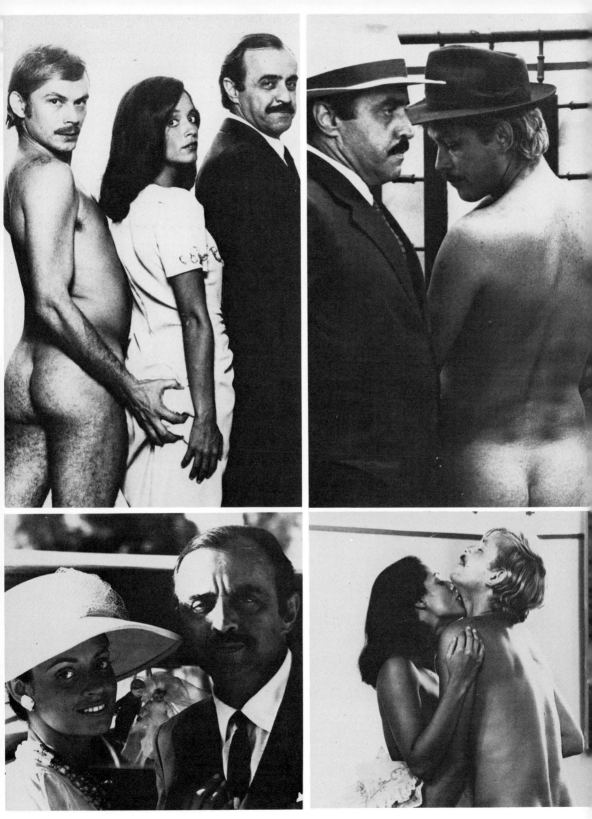

Sonia Braga, Mauro Mendonca

Sonia Braga, Jose Wilker

SUMMER PARADISE

(CINEMA 5) Producer, Ingmar Bergman; Director, Gunnel Linblom; Assistant Director, Ulla Ledin; Screenplay, Ulla Isaksson, Gunnel Lindblom; Based on novel by Ulla Isaksson; Photography, Tony Forsberg; Editor, Siv Lundren; Music, Georg Riedel; Art Director, Anna Asp; In Eastmancolor; 113 minutes; Not rated; March release.

CAST

Katha	Birgitta Valberg
Emma	Sif Ruud
Annika	Margaretha Bystrom
Sassa	Agnetta Ekmanner
Saga	Inga Landgre
Ingrid	Solveig Ternstrom
Alma	Dagny Lind
Wilhelm	Holger Lowenadler
Ture	Per Myrberg
Kiss	Goran Stangertz
Eva	Maria Blomkvist
Tomas	Pontius Gustafson
Arthur	Oscar Ljung
King	Tony Magnusson
Christina	Marianne Aminoff
Kajsa	Anna Borg
Andreas	Mats Helander
Carl-Henrik	Gosta Pruzelius

THE BIG SLEEP

(UNITED ARTISTS) Producers, Elliott Kastner, Michael Winner; Adapted and Directed by Michael Winner; Based on novel by Raymond Chandler; Photography, Robert Paynter; Editor, Freddie Wilson; Music, Jerry Fielding; Design, Harry Pottle; Art Director, John Graysmark; Costumes, Ron Beck; Assistant Director, Michael Dryhurst; In DeLuxe Color; 99 minutes; Rated R; March release.

CAST

Philip Marlowe	Robert Mitchum
Charlotte Sternwood	Sarah Miles
Lash Canino	Richard Boone
Camilla Sternwood	Candy Clark
Agnes Lozelle	Joan Collins
Joe Brody	Edward Fox
Inspector Carson	John Mills
Gen. Sternwood	James Stewart
Eddie Mars	Oliver Reed
Butler Norris	Harry Andrews
Harry Jones	Colin Blakely
Barker	Richard Todd
Mona Grant	Diana Quick
Inspector Gregory	James Donald
Arthur Geiger	John Justin
Karl Lundgren	Simon Turner
Owen Taylor	Martin Potter
Rusty Regan	David Savile
Lanny	Dudley Sutton
Lou	Don Henderson
Croupier	Nik Forster
Taxi Driver	Joe Ritchie
Reg	Patrick Durkin
Man in bookstore	Derek Deadman

Top: Robert Mitchum, Sarah Miles

Joan Collins, Robert Mitchum

Robert Mitchum, and Top with James Stewart
Above: Edward Fox, Candy Clark

Diana Quick, Richard Boone
Above: Sarah Miles, Oliver Reed

WE WILL ALL MEET IN PARADISE

(FIRST ARTISTS) La Gueville-Gaumont Co-Production; Associate Producers, Alain Poire, Yves Robert; Director, Ives Robert; Story, Jean-Loup Dabadie, Yves Robert; Screenplay, Jean-Loup Dabadie; Music, Vladimir Cosma; In Eastmancolor and Panavision; 110 minutes; Rated PG; March release.

CAST
Etienne Dorsay	Jean Rochefort
Bouly	Victor Lanoux
Simon	Guy Bedos
Daniel	Claude Brasseur
Marthe	Daniele Delorme
Mouchy	Marthe Villalonga
Bastion	Daniel Gelin

and Gaby Sylvia

Right: Claude Brasseur

Guy Bedos, Jean Rochefort, Victor Lanoux, Claude Brasseur

THE AMSTERDAM KILL

(COLUMBIA) Executive Producer, Raymond Chow; Producer, Andre Morgan; Director, Robert Clouse; Screenplay, Robert Clouse, Gregory Teifer; Story, Gregory Teifer; Photography, Alan Hume; Music, Hal Schaefer; Editors, Allan Holzman, Gina Brown; Assistant Directors, Louis Shektin, Chaplin Chang; Art Directors, John Blezard, K. S. Chen; A Golden Harvest Production in Panavision and Technicolor; 89 minutes; Rated R; March release.

CAST

Quinlan	Robert Mitchum
Odums	Bradford Dillman
Ridgeway	Richard Egan
Knight	Leslie Nielsen
Chung Wei	Keye Luke
Jimmy Wong	George Cheung
Assassin	Chan Sing

Right: Robert Mitchum

**Robert Mitchum, George Cheung
Above: Keye Luke, Robert Mitchum**

THE FIRST TIME

(EDP) Direction and Screenplay, Claude Berri; Production Executive, Ralph Baum; Photography, Jean Cesar Chiabaut; Art Director, Alexander Trauner; Editor, Dominique Daudon; Costumes, Mic Cheminal; Music, Rene Urtreger; In color; 85 minutes; Not rated; March release.

CAST

Claude	Alain Cohen
Claude's father	Charles Denner
Claude's mother	Zorica Lozic
Arlette	Delphine Levy
Rene	Claude Lubicki
Bernard	Philippe Teboul
Sammy	Jerome Loeb
Loulou	Bruno Resenker
Carole	Daniele Schneider
Bernadette	Maryse Raymond
Irene	Carine Riviere
Nathalie	Daniele Minazzoli
Robert	Roland Blanche
Cousin Leon	Joel Moskowitz

Left: Alain Cohen

Jerome Loeb, Daniele Minazzoli, Alain Cohen

Alain Cohen, Delphine Levy
Above: Charles Denner, Zorica Lozic

Lee Remick, Richard Burton

THE MEDUSA TOUCH

(WARNER BROS.) Producers, Anne V. Coates, Jack Gold; Executive Producer, Arnon Milchan; Associate Producer, Denis Holt; Director, Jack Gold; Screenplay, John Briley; From novel by Peter Van Greenaway; Music, Michael J. Lewis; Photography, Arthur Ibbetson; Art Director, Peter Mullins; Assistant Director, Derek Cracknell; Editor, Anne V. Coates; In Technicolor; 110 minutes; Rated PG; April release.

CAST

Morlar	Richard Burton
Brunel	Lino Ventura
Zonfeld	Lee Remick
Assistant Commissioner	Harry Andrews
Barrister	Alan Badel
Patricia	Marie-Christine Barrault
Parrish	Jeremy Brett
Fortune Teller	Michael Hordern
Dr. Johnson	Gordon Jackson
Publisher	Derek Jacobi
Pennington	Robert Lang

© Warner Bros. 1978

Lino Ventura

175

DEAR DETECTIVE

(CINEMA 5) Title changed to "Dear Inspector"; Producer, Alexandre Mnouchkine; Director, Philippe De Broca; Assistant Director, Jean-Claude Ventura; Screenplay, Philippe De Broca, Michel Audiard; Based on novel "Le Frelon" by Jean-Paul Rouland and Claude Olivier; Music, Georges Delerue; Photography, Jean-Paul Schwartz; Editor, Francoise Javet; In Eastmancolor; 105 minutes; Not rated; April release.

CAST

Lise Tanquerelle	Annie Girardot
Antoine Lemercier	Philippe Noiret
Cristine Vallier	Catherine Alric
Mr. Charmille	Hubert Deschamps
Simone (Mother)	Paulette Dubost
Inspector Dumas	Roger Dumas
Director of Criminal Division	Raymond Gerome
Commissioner Beretti	Guy Marchand
Suzanne (Aunt)	Simone Renant
Alexandre Mignonac	Georges Wilson
Catherine Tanquerelle	Armelle Pourriche
Cassard	Czarmiak
Picot	Maurine Illouz
Albert	Michel Norman
Prof. Pelletier	Georges Riquier
Dean Lavergne	Alain David

Annie Girardot
Top: Annie Girardot, Philippe Noiret

**Annie Girardot, and at
top with Philippe Noiret**

Annie Girardot

A GEISHA

(NEW YORKER) Director, Kenji Mizoguchi; Screenplay, Yoshikata Yoda; Story, Matsutaro Kawaguchi; Photography, Kazuo Miyagawa; Assistant Director, Mitsuo Hirotsu; Music, Ichiro Saito, Editor, Mitsuzo Miyata; Art Director, Kazumi Koike; 87 minutes; Not rated; May release.

CAST

Miyoharu	Michiyo Kogure
Eiko	Ayako Wakao
Kusada	Seizaburo Kawazy
Okimi	Chieko Naniwa
Sawamoto	Eitaro Shindo
Kanzaki	Mikio Koshiba
Saeki	Ichiro Sugai
Ogawa	Haruo Tanaka

INTERNATIONAL VELVET

(UNITED ARTISTS) Produced, Directed and Written by Bryan Forbes; Adapted from novel "National Velvet" by Enid Bagnold; Photography, Tony Imi; Editor, Timothy Gee; Music, Francis Lai; Design, Keith Wilson; Assistant Director, Philip Shaw; Costumes, John Furness, Dorothy Edwards, John Hilling; In Metrocolor; 125 minutes; Rated PG; July release.

CAST

Sarah Brown	Tatum O'Neal
John Seaton	Christopher Plummer
Capt. Johnson	Anthony Hopkins
Velvet Brown	Nanette Newman
Pilot	Peter Barkworth
Mr. Curtis	Dinsdale Landen
Beth	Sarah Bullen
Scott Saunders	Jeffrey Byron
Tim	Richard Warwick
Wilson	Daniel Abineri
Roger	Jason White
Mike	Martin Neil
Howard	Douglas Reith

Right: Tatum O'Neal, Anthony Hopkins

Christopher Plummer, Nanette Newman Above: Nanette Newman, Tatum O'Neal

Tatum O'Neal, Anthony Hopkins Above: Christopher Plummer, Nanette Newman, Tatum O'Neal, Jeffrey Byron

179

BREAD AND CHOCOLATE

(WORLD NORTHAL) Executive Producer, Turi Vasile; Director, Franco Brusati; Screenplay, Franco Brusati, Iaia Fiastri, Nino Manfredi; Based on story by Mr. Brusati; Photography, Luciano Tovali; Editor, Mario Morra; Music, Daniel Patrucci; In Italian and German with English subtitles; In color; 111 minutes; Not rated; July release.

CAST

Nino	Nino Manfredi
Elena	Anna Karina
Italian Industrialist	Johnny Dorelli
Commis	Paolo Turco
Old Man	Ugo d'Alessio
Grigory	Federico Scrobogna
The Turk	Gianfranco Barra
Police Inspector	Giorgio Cerioni
Renzo	Max Delys
Rudiger	Francesco D'Adda
Boegli	Geoffrey Copplestone
Maitre	Umberto Raho
The Blonde	Nelide Giammarco

Left: Nino Manfredi

Nino Manfredi, Anna Karina

Nino Manfredi

VIVA ITALIA!

(CINEMA 5) Producers, Pio Angeletti, Adriano De Micheli; Directors, Mario Monicelli, Dino Risi, Ettore Scola; Story and Screenplay, Age, Scarpelle, Ruggero Maccari, Bernardino Zapponi; Photography, Tonino Delli Colli; Designer, Luciano Ricceri; Editor, Alberto Gallitti; Music, Armando Trovajoli; In color; 90 minutes; Not rated; July release.

CAST
1. "The Canary of Padana Valley" with Ugo Tognazzi and Orietta Berti
2. "Tantum Ergo" with Vittorio Gassman and Luigi Diberti
3. "Abduction of a Loved One" with Vittorio Gassman
4. "First Aid" with Alberto Sordi
5. "Pornodiva" with Eros Pagni and Fiona Florence
6. "Like a Queen" with Alberto Sordi and Emilia Fabi
7. "The Inn" with Vittorio Gassman and Ugo Tognazzi
8. "Without Words" with Ornella Muti and Yorgo Voyagis
9. "Funeral Elegy" with Alberto Sordi

A DREAM OF PASSION

(AVCO EMBASSY) Produced, Directed and Written by Jules Dassin; Photography, George Arvanitis; Music, Iannis Markopoulos; Editor, George Klotz; Sets and Costumes, Dionysis Fotopoulos; In Color; 110 minutes; Rated R; August release.

CAST

Maya/Medea	Melina Mercouri
Brenda	Ellen Burstyn
Kostas	Andreas Voutsinas
Maria	Despo Diamantidou
Dimitris/Jason	Dimitris Papamichael
Edward	Yannis Voglis
Ronny	Phedon Georgitsis
Margaret	Betty Valassi
Stathis	Andreas Filippides
Bible Student	Kostas Arzoglou
Diana	Irene Emirza
Manos	Panos Papaioannou
Kreon	Manos Katrakis
Lighting Man	Nilos Galiatsos
Soundman	Savvas Axiotis

and Litsa Vaidou, Olympia Papadouka, Anna Thomaidou, Freddie Germanos, Stefanos Vlachos, Alexis Solomos

Left: Melina Mercouri

Melina Mercouri, Ellen Burstyn

Melina Mercouri, Andreas Voutsinas Above:
Mercouri, Dimitris Papamichael Top:
Mercouri, Betty Valassi

Melina Mercouri, Ellen Burstyn
Above and Top: Ellen Burstyn

NEA: A NEW WOMAN

(LIBRA) Producer, Andre Genoves; Director, Nelly Kaplan; Screenplay, Nelly Kaplan, Jean Chapot; Photography, Andreas Winding; Editors, Helene Plemiannikov, Catherine Dubeau; From the novel by Emmanuelle Arsan; In Eastmancolor; 101 minutes; Rated R; August release.

CAST

Axel Thorpe	Samy Frey
Sybille Ashby	Anne Zacharias
Helen Ashby	Micheline Presle
Judith Ashby	Francoise Brion
Philip Ashby	Heinz Bennent
Anne	Ingrid Caven
Benito	Robert Freitag
Florence	Chantal Bronner
Raphael	Martin Provost

Top: Ann Zacharias, Sami Frey

Ann Zacharias

186

Micheline Presle, Francois Brion
Above: Sami Frey, Ann Zacharias

Heinz Bennent, Ann Zacharias (also Top)
Above: Sami Frey, Ingrid Caven

A SLAVE OF LOVE

(CINEMA 5) Produced by Mosfilm Studio; Director, Nikita Mikhalkov; Screenplay, Friedrikh Gorenstein, Andrei Mikhalkov-Konchalovsky; Music, Eduard Artemyev; Photography, Pavel Lebeshev; Designers, Alexander Adabashyan, Alexander Samulekin; In black and white and color; 94 minutes; Not rated; August release.

CAST

Olga	Elena Solovei
Victor	Rodion Nakhapetov
Kalyagin	Alexander Kalyagin
Yuzhakov	Oleg Basilashivili
Fedotov	Konstantin Grigoryev

Right: Elena Solovei

Elena Solovei
Above: Rodion Nakhapetov

Elena Solovei
Above: Rodion Nakhapetov

STEVIE

(FIRST ARTISTS) Producer-Director, Robert Enders; Screenplay, Hugh Whitemore, based on his play and the works of Stevie Smith; Photography, Freddie Young; Music, Patrick Gowers; Editor, Peter Tanner; Art Director, Bob Jones; Assistant Director, Ken Baker; In color; 102 minutes; September release.

CAST

Stevie Smith ....Glenda Jackson
Lion Aunt .... Mona Washbourne
Freddy .... Alec McCowen
The Man ....Trevor Howard

Right: Glenda Jackson, Mona Washbourne

Alec McCowen, Glenda Jackson
Above: Trevor Howard, Jackson

Glenda Jackson

WATERSHIP DOWN

(AVCO EMBASSY) Produced, Directed and Written by Martin Rosen; Based on novel of same title by Richard Adams; Director of Animation, Tony Guy; Editor, Terry Rawlings; Music, Angela Morley, Malcolm Williamson; Songs, Mike Batt; In Dolby Stereo and Technicolor; 92 minutes; Rated PG; September release.

The voices of:

John Hurt as Hazel
Richard Briers as Fiver
Michael Graham-Cox as Bigwig
John Bennett As Captain Holly
Simon Cadell as Blackberry
Roy Kinnear as Pipkin
Richard O'Callaghan as Dandelion
Terence Rigby as Silver
Sir Ralph Richardson as Chief Rabbit
Denholm Elliott as Cowslip
Zero Mostel as Kehaar
Mary Maddox as Clover
Hannah Gordon as Hyzenthlay
Lyn Farleigh as Cat
Harry Andrews as General Woundwort
Nigel Hawthorne as Campion
Clifton Jones as Blackavar
Michael Hordern as Narrator
Jose Ackland as Black Rabbit

PERCEVAL

(GAUMONT/NEW YORKER) Executive Producer, Barbet Schroeder; Director, Eric Rohmer; Screenplay, Eric Rohmer from novel by Chretien do Troyes; Art Director, Jean-Pierre Kohut-Svelko; Costumes, Jacques Schmidt; Photography, Nester Almendros; Music, Guy Robert; Editor, Cecile Decugis; Assistant Director, Guy Chalaud; In color; 137 minutes; October release.

CAST

Perceval	Fabrice Luchini
Gawain	Andre Dussolier
Blanchefleur	Arielle Dombasle
Fisher King	Michel Etchverry
King Arthur	Marc Eyraud
Queen Guenievre	Marie-Christine Barrault
Perceval's Mother	Pascale de Boysson
Damsel in the tent	Clementine Amouroux
Proud Lord of the Heath	Jacques le Carpentier
Red Knight	Antoine Baud
Damsel who laughs	Jocelyne Boisseau
Kay	Gerard Falconnetti
The Fool	Alain Serve
Yvonet	Daniel Tarrare
Gornemant of Gohort	Raoul Billerey
Anguingueron	Sylvain Levignac
Clamadieu of the Isles	Guy Delorme
Hideous Damsel	Coco Ducados
Sagremor	Gilles Raab
Guingambresil	Jean Boissery
Thiebaut of Tintaguel	Claude Jaeger
Thiebaut's elder daughter	Frederique Cerbonnet
Damsel with small sleeves	Anne-Laure Meury
King of Escavalon	Frederic Norbert
King's sister	Christine Lietot
Hermit	Hubert Gignoux

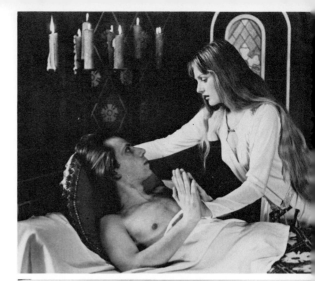

Top Right: Fabrice Luchini, Arielle Dombasle

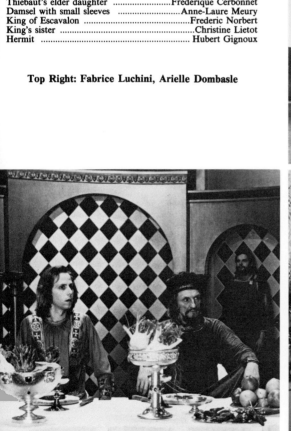

Fabrice Luchini, Michel Etchverry

Anne-Laure Meury

THE BOYS FROM BRAZIL

(20th CENTURY-FOX) Executive Producer, Robert Fryer; Producers, Martin Richards, Stanley O'Toole; Director, Franklin J. Schaffner; Screenplay, Heywood Gould; Based on novel by Ira Levin; Music, Jerry Goldsmith; Editor, Robert E. Swink; Designer, Gil Parrondo; Photography, Henri Decae; Art Director, Peter Lamont; Assistant Directors, Jose Lopez Roddro, Terry Churcher; Costumes, Anthony Mendleson; In DeLuxe Color and Panavision; 124 minutes; Rated R; October release.

CAST

Dr. Josef Mengele	Gregory Peck
Ezra Lieberman	Laurence Olivier
Eduard Seibert	James Mason
Esther Lieberman	Lilli Palmer
Frieda Maloney	Uta Hagen
Barry Kohler	Steven Guttenberg
Sidney Beynon	Denholm Elliott
Mrs. Doring	Rosemary Harris
Henry Wheelock	John Dehner
David Bennett	John Rubinstein
Mrs. Curry	Anne Meara
Jack Curry/Simon Harrington/Erich Doring/ Bobby Wheelock	Jeremy Black
Strasser	David Hurst
Prof. Bruckner	Bruno Ganz
Mundt	Walter Gotell
Harrington	Michael Gough
Lofquist	Wolfgang Preiss
Fassler	Joachim Hansen
Hessen	Guy Dumont
Trausteiner	Carl Duering
Nancy	Linda Hayden
Doring	Richard Marner
Gunther	Georg Marischka
Farnbach	Gunter Meisner
Mrs. Harrington	Prunella Scales
Ismael	Raul Faustino Saldanha
Kleist	Jurgen Anderson
Schmidt	David Brandon
Gertrud	Monica Gearson
Schwimmer	Wolf Kahler
Stroop	Mervyn Nelson
Berthe	Gerti Gordon

Left: Lilli Palmer, Laurence Olivier, John Rubinstein Top: Gregory Peck

Gregory Peck, James Mason

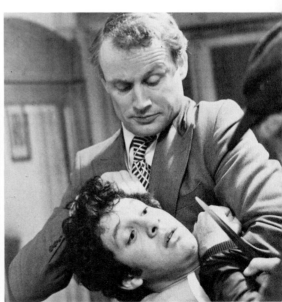

Steve Guttenberg is threatened

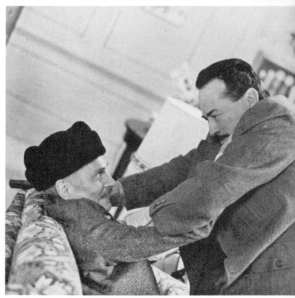

Laurence Olivier, Joachin Hansen
Uta Hagen Top: Laurence Olivier

Laurence Olivier, Gregory Peck Above: Anne
Meara, Jeremy Black, Olivier

VIOLETTE

(GAUMONT/NEW YORKER) Executive Producers, Eugene Lepicier, Denis Heroux; Director, Claude Chabrol; Screenplay, Odile Barski, Herve Bromberger, Frederic, Grendel; Adaptation and Dialogue, Odile Barski; From book by Jean-Marie Fitere; Music, Pierre Jansen; Photography, Jean Rabier; Editor, Yves Langlois; Art Director, Jacques Brizzio; Assistant Director, Philippe Delarbre; Costumes, Pierre Nourry; In Eastmancolor; 123 minutes; Rated R; October release.

CAST

Violette Noziere	Isabelle Huppert
Germaine Noziere	Stephane Audran
Baptiste Noziere	Jean Carmet
Jean Dabin	Jean-Francois Garreaud
Maddy	Lisa Langlois
Violette's Cellmate	Bernadette Lafont
The Judge	Guy Hoffman
Andre de Pinguet	Bernard Lajarrige
Mr. Emile	Jean Dalmain
Dr. Deron	Jean-Pierre Coffe
Zoe	Zoe Chauveau
Mr. Mayeul	Francois Maistre
First Student	Francois-Eric Gendron
Black Musician	Gregory Germain
Boy in cafe	Dominique Zardi
Willy	Maurice Vaudaux
Inspector Champs-de-Mars	Jean-Francois Dupas
Commissioner Guilleaume	Henri-Jacques Huet
Camus	Fabrice Luchini

Top: Isabelle Huppert, Jean Carmet,
Stephane Audran

Jean-Francois Garreaud, Isabelle Huppert

Isabelle Huppert, Jean-Francois Garreaud
Top: Jean Carmet, Huppert, Stephane Audran

Isabelle Huppert

AUTUMN SONATA

(NEW WORLD) Producer, Persona Film; Direction and Screenplay, Ingmar Bergman; Photography, Sven Nykvist; Designer, Anna Asp; Costumes, Inger Pehrsson; Editor, Sylvia Ingmarsdotter; Assistant Director, Peder Langenskiold; In Eastmancolor; 97 minutes; Rated PG; October release.

CAST

Charlotte	Ingrid Bergman
Eva	Liv Ullmann
Helena	Lena Nyman
Viktor	Halvar Bjork
Leonardo	Georg Lokkeberg
Professor	Knut Wigert
Nurse	Eva Von Hanno
Josef	Erland Josephson
Eva as a child	Linn Ullmann
Oncle Otto	Arne Bang-Hansen

Left: Ingrid Bergman, Linn Ullmann

Halvar Bjork, Liv Ullmann

Ingrid Bergman, Liv Ullmann
Top: Lena Nyman, Liv Ullmann

Shima Iwashita

BANISHED

(TOHO) Originally "Melody in Gray"; Producers, Kiyoshi Iwashita, Seikichi Iizumi; Director, Masahiro Shinoda; Screenplay, Keiji Hasebe, Masahiro Shinoda; Story, Tsutomu Minakami; Photography, Kazuo Miyagawa; Art Director, Kiyoshi Awazu; Music, Toru Takemitsu; Lyrics, Keiji Hasebe; In color; 109 minutes; Not rated; October release.

CAST

Orin .... Shima Iwashita
Tall Man .... Yoshio Harada
Teruyo .... Tomoko Naraoka
Charcoal Maker .... Shoji Tonoyama
Tsuketaro .... Toshiyuki Nishida
Hikosaburo .... Toru Abe

Erzsi Pasztor, Lajos Szabo

RAIN AND SHINE

(NEW YORKER) Director, Ferenc Andras; Screenplay, Ferenc Andras, Geza Beremenyi, Akos Kertesz; Photography, Lajos Koltai; In Eastmancolor; 98 minutes; Not rated; December release.

CAST

Kajtar, Sr. (grandfather) .... Imre Sarlai
Istvan Kajtar .... Lajos Szabo
Mrs. Kajtar .... Erzsi Paszter
Pityu, their son .... Zoltan Biro
Marika, their daughter .... Maria Fesus
Jolan, Kajtars's sister .... Ildiko Pecsi
Vetro, Jolan's boss .... Konstantin Anatol
Mrs. Vetro .... Eva Spanyik
Their Daughter .... Zsuzsa Szakacs

Imre Sarlai

Barbara Bach, Richard Kiel Above: Harrison
Ford, Carl Weathers, Michael Byrne, Edward Fox

FORCE 10 FROM NAVARONE

(AMERICAN INTERNATIONAL) Producer, Oliver A. Unger; Director, Guy Hamilton; Screenplay, Robin Chapman; Story, Carl Foreman; Based on novel by Alistair MacLean; Co-Producers, John R. Sloan, Anthony B. Unger; Photography, Chris Challis; Associate Producer, David Orton; Music, Ron Goodwin; Designer, Geoffrey Drake; Costumes, Emma Porteous; Assistant Director, Bert Batt; Editor, Ray Poulton; In Panavision and Technicolor; 118 minutes; Rated PG; December release.

CAST

Mallory	Robert Shaw
Barnsby	Harrison Ford
Miller	Edward Fox
Maritza	Barbara Bach
Lescovar	Franco Nero
Weaver	Carl Weathers
Drazac	Richard Kiel
Reynolds	Angus MacInnes
Schroeder	Michael Byrne
Petrovich	Alan Badel
Rogers	Christopher Malcolm
Salvone	Nick Ellsworth
Oberstein	Jonathan Blake
Bauer	Michael Sheard

Top: Franco Nero, Harrison Ford, Robert Shaw,
Edward Fox, Carl Weathers Below: Ford, Nero, Shaw

THE LAST WAVE

(WORLD NORTHAL) Producers, Hal McElroy, James McElroy; Director, Peter Weir; Screenplay, Peter Weir, Tony Morphett, Peter Popescu; Original Idea, Peter Weir; Photography, Russell Boyd; Editor, Max Lemon; Music, Charles Wain; Special Effects, Neil Angwin, Monty Fieguth; In color; 106 minutes; Rated PG; December release.

CAST

David Burton	Richard Chamberlain
Anne Burton	Olivia Hammett
Chris Lee	Gulpilil
Rev. Burton	Frederick Parslow
Dr. Whitburn	Vivean Gray
Charlie	Nanjiwarra Amagula
Gerry Lee	Walter Amagula
Larry	Roy Bara
Lindsey	Cedric Lalara
Jacko	Morris Lalara
Michael Zeadler	Peter Carroll
Billy Corman	Athol Compton
Judge	Hedley Cullen
Andrew Potter	Michael Duffield
Morgue Doctor	Wallas Eaton
Baby Sitter	Jo England
Policeman	John Frawley
Zeadler's Secretary	Jennifer de Greenlaw
Prosecutor	Richard Henderson
Publican	Merv Lilley
Morgue Clerk	John Meagher
Guido	Guido Rametta
Don Fishburn	Malcolm Robertson
Carl	Greg Rowe
Sophie Burton	Katrina Sedgwick
Grace Burton	Ingrid Weir

Right: Richard Chamberlain, Olivia Hammett
Top: Richard Chamberlain (C)

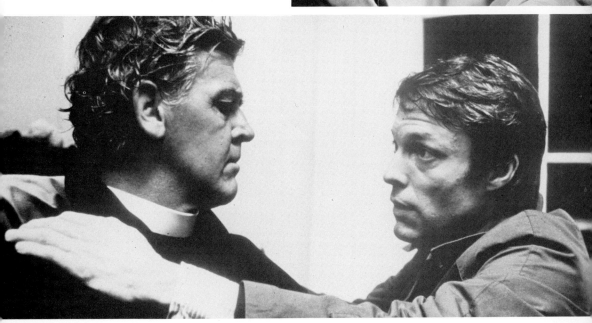

Frederick Parslow, Richard Chamberlain

"The Battle of Chile"

"Cantata de Chile"

THE BATTLE OF CHILE (Tricontinental) Director, Patricio Guzman; Production Manager, Federico Elton; Editor, Pedro Chaskel; Photography, Jorge Muller; Assistant Director, Jose Pino; In black and white; 191 minutes; Not rated; January release. An historical documentary on Chile.

CANTATA DE CHILE (Tricontinental) Direction and Screenplay, Humberto Solas; Collaborators, Patricio Manns, Manuel Payan, Orlando Rojas, Jorge Herrera; Assistant Directors, Orlando Rojas, Lazaro Buria; Photography, Jorge Herrera; Music, Leo Brouwer; Editor, Nelson Rodriguez; In color; Spanish with English sub-titles; Not rated; 119 minutes; January release. CAST: Nelson Villagra, Shenda Roman, Eric Heresmann, Alfredo Tornquist, Leonardo Perucci, Peggy Cordero

CARO MICHELE (Libra) Producer, Gianna Hecht Lucari; Director, Mario Monicelli; Screenplay, Suso Cecchi D'Amico, Tonino Guerra; Based on novel by Natalia Ginzburg; Photography, Tonino Delli Colli; Music, Nino Rota; A Rizzoli Film in Technicolor; 110 minutes; Not rated; Presented by Robert A. McNeil; January release. CAST: Mariangela Melato (Mara), Delphine Seyrig (Adriana), Aurore Clement (Angelica), Lou Castel (Osvaldo), Fabio Carpi (Colarosa), Marcella Michelangeli (Viola)

OPERATION THUNDERBOLT (Cinema Shares International) Producers, Menahem Golan, Yoram Globus; Director, Menahem Golan; Associate Producer, Rony Yacov; Art Director, Kuli Sandor; Screenplay, Clarke Reynolds; Photography, Adam Greenberg; Music, Dov Seltzer; Editor, Dov Henig; Assistant Directors, Riki Shelach, Shlomo Albert; Costumes, Rochelle Zaltzman; In color; 126 minutes; Rated PG; January release. CAST: Klaus Kinsky (Boese), Sybil Danning (Halima), Yitzhak Neeman (Jabbar), Yehoram Gaon (Jonathan), Assaf Dayan (Shuki), Ori Levy (Air Force Commander), Arik Lavi (Dan Shomron)

THE BEST WAY (Specialty) Director, Claude Miller; Screenplay, Luc Beraud, Claude Miller; Photography, Bruno Nytten; Editor, Jean-Bernard Bonis; In Eastmancolor; 90 minutes; January release. CAST: Patrick Dewaere (Marc), Patrick Bouchitey (Philippe), Christine Pascal (Chantel), Claude Pieplu (Father)

FLAT OUT (Variety) In Eastmancolor; Rated R; No other credits available; January release. CAST: Michel Norman, Yves Collignon, Christian Alers, Micheline Dax

NO PROBLEM! (Cine III) Director, Georges Lautner; Screenplay, Jean-Marie Poire; In Eastmancolor; 105 minutes; January release. CAST: Miou-Miou (Anita), Bernard Menez (Son), Jean Lefebvre (Father), Annie Duperey (Mistress), Pamela Moore (Emmanuelle), Henri Guibet (Friend), Renee Saint-Cyr (Doctor)

STRANGE THINGS HAPPEN AT NIGHT (Clark) No credits available; In Eastmancolor; Rated R; January release. CAST: Sandra Julien

TIGER FROM HONG KONG (Monarch) Producer, Chang Chien Shen; Director, Chang I; Presented by Allan Shackleton; In Technicolor; Rated R; January release. CAST: Chang I, Yueh Yang, Chang Feng, Lin Feng Chiao, Li Hung, Lung Fei

THE WAY OF THE WIND (R. C. Riddell) Produced and Written by Charles Tobias; Photography, Michael J. Dugan, Cal Naylor, Eduardo Admetilla, Donald S. Shoemaker, Charles Tobias; Music, John Bilezikjian; An RCR Product; In color; January release.

Klaus Kinsky, Sybil Danning
in "Operation Thunderbolt"

Mariangela Melato, Delphine Seyrig, Fabio
Carpi, Lou Castel in "Caro Michele"

"Ceddo"

Jacques Serres, Brigitte Fossey
in "Blue Country"

CEDDO (New Yorker Films) Direction and Screenplay, Ousmane Sembene; Photography, Georges Caristan; Editor, Florence Eymon; Music, Manu Dibango; In Eastmancolor; 120 minutes; In Wolof with English subtitles; February release. CAST: Tabara Ndiaye (Princess Dior), Moustapha Yade (Madior Fatim Fall), Ismaila Diagne (Kidnapper), Goure (The Imam), Makoura Dia (The King), Oumar Gueye (Jaraaf), Mamadou Doum (Prince Biram), Nar Modou Sene (Saxewar), Ousmane Camara (Diogomay), Ousmane Sembene (member of Ceddo)

CELINE AND JULIE GO BOATING (New Yorker Films) Director, Jacques Rivette; Executive Producer, Barbet Schroeder; Screenplay, Jacques Rivette, Eduardo de Gregorio, Juliet Berto, Dominique Labourier, Bulle Ogier, Merie-France Pisier; Photography, Jacques Renard, Michel Cenet; Editors, Nicole Lubtchansky, Chris Tullio Altan; Music, Jean-Marie Senia; Costumes, Pierre D'Alby, Jean-Luc Berne, Laurent Vicci; 193 minutes; Not rated; February release. CAST: Juliet Berto (Celine), Dominique Labourier (Julie), Bulle Ogier (Camille), Marie-France Pisier (Sophie), Barbet Schroeder (Olivier), Philippe Clevenot (Guilou), Marie-Therese Saussure (Poupie), Nathalie Asnar (Madlyn), Jean Douchet (Mn. Dede)

COUP DE GRACE (Cinema 5) Producer, Eberhard Junkersdorf; Director, Volker Schlondorff; Screenplay, Genevieve Dormann, Margarethe Von Trotta, Jutta Bruckner; Based on novel by Marguerite Yourcenar; Music, Stanley Myers; Photography, Luther; Art Director, Jurgen Kiebach; A Franco-German Co-Production by Argos-Films; 96 minutes; Not rated; February release. CAST: Margarethe von Trotta (Sophie), Matthias Habich (Erich), Rudiger Kirschstein (Konrad), Matthieu Carriere (Volkmar), Valeska Gert (Tante Praskovia), Marc Eyraud (Dr. Rugen), Frederik Zichy (Franz), Bruno Thost (Chopin), Henry Van Lyck (Borschikoff)

BLUE COUNTRY (Gaumont) Direction and Screenplay, Jean-Charles Tacchella; Photography, Edmond Sechan; Editor, Agnes Guillemot; Music, Gerard Anfosso; In Eastmancolor; 102 minutes; Rated PG; February release. CAST: Brigitte Fossey (Louise), Jacques Serres (Mathias), Ginette Garcin (Zoe), Armand Meffre (Moise), Ginette Mathieu (Manon), Roger Crouzet (Fernand), Albert Delpy (Armand)

MONTY PYTHON MEETS BEYOND THE FRINGE (New Line) Producer-Director, Roger Graef; In color; February release. CAST: John Cleese, Michael Palin, Graham Chapman, Carol Cleveland, Terry Gilliam, Terry Jones, Peter Cooke, Jonathan Miller, Alan Bennet

CATASTROPHE (New World) Producer-Director, Larry Savadove; Narrator, William Conrad; In color; Rated PG; February release. A documentary dealing with world disasters.

SMOOTH VELVET, RAW SILK (Dimension) Director, Brunello Rondi; Presented by Mickey Zide; In color; Rated R; February release. CAST: Laura Gemser, Annie Belle, Gabriele Tinti, Al Cliver, Susan Scott, Zigi Zanger

CONVOY BUDDIES (Film Ventures International) Producer-Director, Arthur Pitt; In DeLuxe Color; Rated PG; February release. CAST: Terrance Hall, Bob Spencer, Karen Blake

NIGHT OF THE ASKARI (Topar) Director, Juergen Goslar; Executive Producer, Barrie Saint-Clair; Screenplay, Juergen Goslar, Scot Finch; Based on novel by Daniel Carney; A Lord and Eichberg Film; Original title "Whispering Death"; In color; Rated R; February release. CAST: Christopher Lee (Bill), James Faulkner (Terrick), Trevor Howard (Johannes), Horst Frank (Whispering Death), Sybil Danning (Sally), Sascha Hehn (Peter), Sam Williams (Katchemu), Eric Schumann (Turner)

THE ENFORCER FROM DEATH ROW (Dinero) In color; Rated R; No other credits available; February release. CAST: Leo Fong, Darnell Garcia, Booker T. Anderson, Mariwin Roberts, Johnny Hammond

Dominique Labourier, Marie-France Pisier, Juliet Berto in "Celine and Julie Go Boating"

Horst Frank in "Night of the Askari"

Sophia Loren
in "Poopsie"

Barbara Bouchet
in "Death Rage"

SCHIZO (Niles International) Producer-Director, Peter Walker; Screenplay, David McGillivray; Photography, Peter Jessop; Music, Stanley Myers; Editor, Alan Brett; Presented by William J. Nagy and Maurice Smith; In Technicolor; 105 minutes; Rated R; February release. CAST: Lynne Frederick (Samantha), John Leyton (Alan), Stephanie Beacham (Beth), John Fraser (Leonard), Victoria Allum (Samantha as a child), Jack Watson (Haskin), Paul Alexander (Peter), Queenie Watts (Mrs. Wallace), Trisha Mortimer (Joy), John NcEnery (Stephens), Colin Jeavons (Commissioner), Raymond Bowers (Manager), Terry Duggan (Editor), Robert Mill (Maitre d'), Diana King (Mrs. Falconer), Lindsay Campbell (Falconer), Victor Winding (Sgt.), Pearl Hackney (Lady at seance), Primi Townsend (Secretary), Wendy Gilmore (Samantha's mother)

POOPSIE (Cougar) Producer, Carlo Ponti; Director, Georgio Capitani; Screenplay, Ernesto Gastaldi; In Technicolor; 91 minutes; Rated R; March release. CAST: Sophia Loren (Poopsie), Marcello Mastroianni (Charlie the Collar), Aldo Maccione (Chopin), Pierre Brice

WINIFRED WAGNER (Bauer International) Producer-Director, Hans-Jurgen Syberberg; In black and white; 104 minutes; March release. A documentary on Richard Wagner's English-born daughter-in-law and former manager of the Bayreuth Music Festival.

FURTIVOS (Empresa) Director, Jose Luis Borau; Screenplay, Manuel Gutierrez, Jose Luis Borau; Photography, Luis Cuadrado; Music, Vainica Doble; Editor, Ana Romer; In color; 88 minutes; March release. CAST: Lola Gaos, Ovidi Montilor, Alicia Sanchez, Ismael Merlo, Jose Luis Borau, Felipe Solano

THE LAST SURVIVOR (American International) Producer, Giorgio Carlo Rossi; Director, Ruggero Deodato; Screenplay, Tito Cardi Giafranco Clerici, Renzo Genta; Editor, Danielle Alabisco; Assistant Director, Stefano Rilla; In Movielab Color; 83 minutes; Rated R; March release. CAST: Massimo Foschi, Me-Me Lai, Ivan Rassimov, Sheik Renal Shker, Judy Rosly

DEATH RAGE (S. J. International) Producer, Umberto Lenzi; Director, Anthony Dawson; In color; March release; No other credits available. CAST: Yul Brynner, Massimo Ranieri, Barbara Bouchet, Martin Balsam, Giancarlo Sbragia

GOD'S GUN (Irwin Yablans) Producer, Menachem Golan; Director, Frank Kramer; Executive Producer, Yoram Globus; In color; Rated R; March release. CAST: Lee Van Cleef, Jack Palance, Richard Boone, Cody Palance, Robert Lipton, Sybil Danning, Leif Garrett

LOVE AT FIRST SIGHT (Movietime) Producer, Peter O'Brian; Direction and Screenplay, Rex Bromfield; Executive Producers, David Perlmutter, John Trent; Title song sung by Dionne Warwick; Music, Roy Payne; In color; 85 minutes; Rated PG; March release. CAST: Mary Ann McDonald (Shirley), Dan Aykroyd (Roy), Jane Mallett (Grandma), George Murray (Frank), Barry Morse (William), Mignon Elkins (Edna), Les Carlson (Stu), Grace Louis

THE CHOSEN (American International) Producer, Edmondo Amati; Director, Alberto De Martino; Screenplay, Sergio Donati, Aldo De Martino, Michael Robson; Photography, Enrico Menczer; Art Director, Umberto Betacca; Editor, Vincenzo Tomassi; Music, Ennio Morricone; In Technicolor; 102 minutes; Rated R; April release. CAST: Kirk Douglas (Caine), Agostine Belli (Sara), Simon Ward (Angel), Anthony Quayle (Prof. Griffith), Virginia McKenna (Eva), Alexander Knox (Meyer), Romolo Valli (Msgr. Charrier), Massimo Foschi (Assassin)

GISELLE (International TV Trading) Executive Producer, Fritz Buttenstedt; Director, Hugo Niebeling; Based on ballet by Adolphe Adam; Libretto, Vernoy de Saint-Georges, Theophile L. Gautier, Jean Coralli; Photography, Wolfgang Treu; Editor, Hugo Niebeling; Sets, Georges Wakhevitch, Oliver Smith; Costumes, Peter Hall, Jeanne Renucci-Wakhevitch; In color; 95 minutes; Not rated; April release. CAST: Carla Fracci (Giselle), Eric Bruhn (Albrecht), Bruce Marks (Hklarion), Toni Lander (Myrtha), Eleanor D'Antuono, Ted Kivitt (Peasants)

Lola Gaos, Ouidi Montllor, Alicia Sanchez
in "Furtivos (Poachers)"

Winifred Wagner

Judy Cornwell, Marty Feldman
in "Think Dirty"

"A Woman's Decision"

THE RUBBER GUN (Schuman-Katzka) Director, Allan Moyle; Screenplay, Steve Lack; Photography, Frank Vitale, Jim Lawrence; Editor, John Laing; Music, Lewis Furey; In color; 86 minutes; April release. CAST: Steve Lack (Steve), Pierre Robert (Pierre), Peter Brawley (Peter), Alain Moyle (Bozo), Pam Holmes (Pam)

THINK DIRTY (Quartet) Producer, Ned Sherrin; Director, Jim Clark; Screenplay, Marty Feldman; Associate Producer, Terry Glinwood; In color; 94 minutes; Rated R; April release. CAST: Marty Feldman, Shelley Berman, Judy Cornwell, Julie Ege

THE CHORUS GIRLS (Independent International) Producer, Joseph Frade; Director, Eugene Martin; In Techniscope and Technicolor; Rated R; April release. CAST: Marisol, Mel Ferrer, Sylvia Trent, Martha Miller

BLIND RAGE (Trans World) Director, Efren C. Pinion; In color; Rated R; April release. CAST: D'Urville Martin, Leo Fong, Tony Ferrer, Fred Williamson, Dick Adair, Darnell Garcia, Charlie Davao, Leila Hermosa

A WOMAN'S DECISION (Tinc) Producer, Film Polski; Direction and Screenplay, Krzysztof Zanussi; Photography, Slawomir Idziak; Music, Wojciech Kilar; Art Director, Tadeusz Wybult; In Eastmancolor; 99 minutes; May release. CAST: Maja Komorowska (Marta), Piotr Fronczewski (Her husband), Marek Piwowski (Jacek), Halina Mikolajska, Zofia Mrozowska, Barbara Wrzeninska, Mariusz Dmochowski, Chip Taylor

ANGOLA: VICTORY OF HOPE (Tricontinental) Director, Jose Massip; Music, Roberto Valera; In color; 72 minutes; May release. A documentary on the people of Angola.

BLACK RIVER (Tricontinental) Director, Manuel Perez; Story and Screenplay, Manuel Perez, Victor Cassaus, Daniel Diaz Torres; Photography, Jorge Herrera; Editor, Gloria Arguelles; Music, Juan Marquez; In color; 135 minutes; Spanish with English subtitles; May release. A tense, complex and critical period of the class struggle in the Escambray mountain range in Cuba.

THE BOUNTY-HUNTER (Tricontinental) Director, Sergio Giral; Screenplay, Sergio Giral, Jorge Sotolongo; Photography, Paul Rodriguez; Editor, Nelson Rodriguez; Music, Leo Brouwer; In color; 95 minutes; Spanish with English subtitles; Not rated; May release. CAST: Reynaldo Miravalles, Adolfo Llaurado, Samuel Claxton, Omar Valdes, Salvador Wood

DAYS OF WATER (Tricontinental) Director, Manuel Octavio Gomez; Screenplay, Manuel Octavio Gomez, Bernabe Hernandez, Julio Garcia Espinosa; Photography, Jorge Herrera; Editor, Nelson Rodriguez; Music, Leo Brouwer; In color; 110 minutes; Spanish with English subtitles; Not rated; May release. CAST: Idalia Anreus (Antonia), Raul Pomares (Lino), Adolfo Llaurado (Felipe), Mario Balmaseda (Toni)

THE LAST SUPPER (Tricontinental) Producers, Santiago Llapur, Camilo Vives; Director, Tomas Gutierrez Alea; Screenplay, Tomas Gonzalez, Maria Eugenia Haya, Tomas Gutierrez Alea; Photography, Mario Garcia Joya; Editor, Nelson Rodriguez; Music, Leo Brouwer; In color; 110 minutes; Spanish with English subtitles; Not rated; May release. CAST: Nelson Villagra, Silvano Rey, Luis Alberto Garcia, Jose Antonio Rodriguez, Samuel Claxton, Mario Balmaseda

ONE WAY OR ANOTHER (Tricontinental) Director, Sara Gomez Yara; Screenplay, Sara Gomez Yara, Tomas Gonzalez Perez; Photography, Luis Garcia; Editor, Ivan Arocha; Music, Sergio Vitier; Song, Sara Gonzalez; In black and white; 78 minutes; Spanish with English subtitles; Not rated; May release. A documentary about Miraflores, a housing development built in 1962.

SPEAR OF THE NATION (Tricontinental) Director, Rigoberto Lopez; Producer, Orlando de la Huerta; Screenplay, Rigoberto Lopez, Jorge Giannoni; Photography, Patricio Castilla; Editor, Dulce Maria Villaron; Music, Mario Apello; In color; 55 minutes; Spanish with English subtitles; Not rated; May release. A documentary on the history of the system of apartheid, and the racist regimes imposed by white minorities.

"Black River"

Nelson Villagra (L)
in "The Last Supper"

Mario Wood (R)
in "The Teacher"

Raquel Welch
in "Restless"

THE TEACHER (Tricontinental) Direction and Story, Octavio Cortazar; Screenplay, Luis R. Noguera; Costumes, Eduardo Arocha; Photography, Pablo Martinez; Editor, Roberto Bravo; Music, Sergio Vitier; In color; 113 minutes; Not rated; Spanish with English subtitles; May release. CAST: Patricio Wood, Salvador Wood, Rene de la Cruz, Luis Alberto Ramirez, Luis Rielo, Mario Balmaseda

SECRETS (Lone Star) Producer, John Hanson; Director, Philip Saville; Screenplay, Rosemary Davies; Story, Philip Saville; Photography, Nic Knowland, Harry Hart; Editor, Tony Woollard; Music, Mike Gibbs; In color; 92 minutes; Rated R; May release. CAST: Jacqueline Bisset (Jacky), Per Oscarsson (Raoul), Shirley Knight Hopkins (Beatrice), Robert Powell (Allan), Tarka Kings (Josy), Martin C. Thurley (Raymond), Stephen Martin (Dominique)

WARLORDS OF ATLANTIS (Columbia) Producer, John Dark; Director, Kevin Connor; Screenplay, Brian Hayles; Photography, Alan Hume; Editor, Bill Blunden; Art Director, Jack Maxsted; Designer, Elliot Scott; Music, Mike Vickers; In Technicolor; 96 minutes; Rated PG; May release. CAST: Doug McClure (Greg), Peter Gilmore (Charles), Shane Rimmer (Daniels), Lea Brodie (Delphine), Michael Gothard (Atmir), Hal Galili (Grogan), John Ratzenberger (Fenn), Derry Power (Jacko), Donald Bisset (Aitken), Ashley Knight (Sandy), Robert Brown (Briggs), Cyd Charisse (Atsil), Daniel Massey (Atraxon)

THE HILLS HAVE EYES (Vanguard) Producer, Peter Locke; Direction and Screenplay, Wes Craven; Photography, Eric Sadrinen; Art Director, Robert Burns; Music, Don Peake; In color; 89 minutes; Rated R; May release. CAST: Susan Lanier (Brenda), Robert Houston (Bobby), Virginia Vincent (Ethel), Russ Grieve (Bob), Dee Wallace (Lynne), Martin Speer (Doug), Brenda Marinoff (Katie), Flora (Beauty), Stricker (Beast), James Whitworth (Jupiter), Cordy Clark (Mama), Janus Blythe (Ruby), Michael Berryman (Pluto), Lance Gordon (Mars), Arthur King (Mercury), John Steadman (Fred)

RESTLESS (Joseph Brenner) Originally "The Beloved"; Producers, Patrick Curtis, Yorgo Pan Cosmatos; Direction and Screenplay, Yorgo Pan Cosmatos; Music, Yannis Markopoulos; Photography, Marcello Gatti; In Technicolor; 75 minutes; Rated R; May release. CAST: Raquel Welch (Elena), Richard Johnson (Orestes), Jack Hawkins, Flora Robson, Frank Wolf, Renato Romano

DRAGON SISTER (Cinema Shares International) Director, Ho Chang; A First Films Production; In color; Rated R; May release. CAST: Kam Kang, Shang Kuaw Ling

THE TIGRESS (New World) Producer, Julian Parnell; Director, Jean Lafleur; Screenplay, Marven McGara; In color; Rated R; May release. CAST: Dyanne Thorne, Michel Morin, Tony Angelo, Terry Coady, Howard Mauer

HONG KONG STRONGMAN (Cinema Shares International) A First Films Production; In color; Rated R; May release. CAST: Bruce Liang

FREE SPIRIT (Joseph Brenner) Producer, Sally Shuter; Executive Producer, Julian Wintle; Associate Producer, Basil Rayburn; Director, James Hill; Screenplay, James Hill; Based on novel "The Ballad of the Belstone Fox" by David Rook; Music, Laurie Johnson; Editor, Peter Tanner; Art Director, Hazel Peiser; In Todd–A035 and color; 88 minutes; Not rated; May release. CAST: Eric Porter (Asher), Rachel Roberts (Cathie), Jeremy Kemp (Kendrick), Bill Travers (Tod), Dennis Waterman (Stephen), Heather Wright (Jenny)

PIROSMANI Produced by Gruzia Film Studio; Director, Georgy Shengelaya; Screenplay, Georgy Shengelaya, Erlom Ackvledlani; Photography, Constantin Apryatin; Editor, M. Karalashvill; Music, V. Kukhlanidze; 85 minutes; Not rated; May release. CAST: Avtandil Varazi (Niko Pirosmanashvi)

"The Hills Have Eyes"

Eric Porter
in "Free Spirit"

**Jean-Pierre Aumont, Valerie Lagrange
in "Cat and Mouse"**

**Prunella Ransome, Lewis Fiander
in "Island of the Damned"**

CAT AND MOUSE (Quartet) Produced, Directed, and Written by Claude Lelouch; French with English subtitles; Photography, Jean Collomb; Music, Francis Lai; Presented by Robert A. McNeil; In color; 107 minutes; Rated PG; May release. CAST: Michele Morgan (Madame Richard), Serge Reggiani (Inspector Lechat), Philippe Leotard (His Assistant), Jean-Pierre Aumont (M. Richard), Valerie Legrange (Valerie)

THE CHESS PLAYERS (Creative Films) Producer, Siresh Jinda; Direction, Music and Screenplay, Satyajit Ray; In English and Hindi with English subtitles; Photography, Soumendu Roy; Editor, Dulal Dutta; In color; 135 minutes; Not rated; May release. CAST: Richard Attenborough (Gen. Outram), Sanjeev Kumar (Mirza Saljad Ali), Saeed Jaffrey (Mir Roshan Ali), Shabana Azmi (Mirza's Wife), Amzad Khan (Mawah Wajid Ali Shah), Tom Alter (Adviser)

BONJOUR AMOUR (Atlantic) Producers, Catherine Winter, Gisele Rebillon; Director, Roger Andrieux; Screenplay, Roger Andrieux, Jean Marie Besnard; Music, Maxime Le Forestier; Photography, Ramon Suarez; In color; 90 minutes; Not rated; June release. CAST: Pascal Meynier (Marc), Guilhaine Dubos (Martine), Michel Galabru (Marc's father), Alix Mahieux (Marc's mother), Francoise Prevost (Martine's mother), Bruno Raffaeli (Christian)

SERVANT AND MISTRESS (New Line Cinema) Director, Bruno Gatillon; Screenplay, Frantz-Andre Burghuet, Dominique Fabre; Executive Producer, Gilbert de Goldschmidt; Assistant Directors, Denis Mazars, Elena Racheva; Photography, Etienne Szabo; Editor, Georges Klotz; Music, Jean-Marie Benjamin; Costumes, Daniel Droeghmans; French with English subtitles; 90 minutes; Not rated; June release. CAST: Victor Lanoux (Jerome), Andrea Ferreol (Maria), Evelyne Buyle (Christine), Gabriel Cattand (Charles), David Pontreomli (Dancer), Jean Rougerie (Chef)

THE ISLAND OF THE DAMNED (American International) Executive Producer, Manuel Salvador; Director, Narciso Ibanez Serrador; Screenplay, Luis Penafiel; Based on novel "El Juego" by J. J. Plans; Photography, Jose Luis Alcaine; Music, Waldo De Los Rios; A Penta Films Production in Movielab Color; Rated R; June release. CAST: Lewis Fiander (Tom), Prunella Ransome (Evelyn)

ALL THINGS BRIGHT AND BEAUTIFUL (World Northal) Originally "It Shouldn't Happen to a Vet"; Executive Producer, David Susskind; Producer, Margaret Matheson; Director, Eric Till; Screenplay, Alan Plater; Based on books by James Herriot; Associate Producers, Cecil Ford, Roy Stevens; Music, Laurie Johnson; Photography, Arthur Ibbetson; Designer, Geoffrey Drake; Editor, Thom Noble; Assistant Director, Colin Brewer; In color; 94 minutes; Rated G; June release. CAST: John Alderson (Hames), Colin Blakely (Siegfried), Lisa Harrow (Helen), Bill Maynard (Hinchcliffe), Paul Shelley (Richard), Richard Pearson (Granville), Rosemary Martin (Mrs. Dalby), Raymond Francis (Col. Bosworth), John Barrett (Crump), Philip Stone (Jack), Clifford Kershaw (Kendall), Kevin Moreton (William), Liz Smith (Mrs. Dodds), Leslie Sarony (Kirby), Gwen Nelson (Mrs. Kirby), Juliet Cooke (Jean), Stacy Davies (Harry), Christine Hargreaves (Mrs. Butterworth), May Warden (Mrs. Tompkins), Richard Griffiths (Sam), Ian Hastings (Jackson)

THE PUNK ROCK MOVIE (Cinematic) Producers, Peter Clifton, Notting Hill Studios; Direction and Photography, Don Letts; Associate Producers, Andrew Czezdwski, Franz Schneider, Serafim Karalexis; Editor, John Hackney; In color; 86 minutes; Rated R; June release. CAST: Johnny Rotten and the Sex Pistols, The Clash, The Slits, Siouxsie & the Banshees, X-Ray Spec, Slaughter and the Dogs, Generation X, Subway Sect, Shane, Wayne County, Eater, Johnny Thunders & the Heartbreakers, Alternative TV

**Victor Lanoux, Andrea Ferreol
in "Servant and Mistress"**

**John Alderton, Lisa Harrow
in "All Things Bright and Beautiful"**

**Ann Michelle
in "Virgin Witch"**

**Umberto Orsini, Romy Schneider
in "A Woman at Her Window"**

AMUCK (Group 1) No credits available; In DeLuxe Color; Rated R; June release. CAST: Farley Granger, Barbara Bouchet

BRUCE VS THE BLACK DRAGON (Ark Films) An Insan Production; In color; Rated R; June release. CAST: Yang Zze, Chen Xing, Chiang Li, Gomi Chiba

EYEBALL (Joseph Brenner) Director, Umberto Lenzi; Executive Producer, Joseph Brenner; In color; 91 minutes; Rated R; June release. CAST: John Richardson, Martine Brochard, Ines Pelegrin, Silvia Solar, George Rigaud

THE VIRGIN WITCH (Joseph Brenner) Producer, Ralph Solomons; Director, Ray Austin; Screenplay, Klaus Vogel; Photography, Gerald Moss; Editor, Philip Barknel; Music, Ted Dicks; Assistant Director, Garth Haines; In color; 90 minutes; Rated R; June release. CAST: Ann Michelle (Christine), Patricia Haines (Sybil), Vicki Michelle (Betty), Keith Buckley (Johnny), James Chase (Peter), Neal Hallett (Gerald)

FACES OF LOVE (Gaumont/New Yorker) Executive Producers, Yves Peyrot, Yves Gasser; Associate Producer, Klaus Hellwig; Direction and Screenplay, Michel Soutter; Photography, Renato Berta; Music, Arie Dzierlatka; Editor, Albert Jurgenson; French with English subtitles; In Eastmancolor; 91 minutes; July release. CAST: Jean-Louis Trintignant (Victor), Delphine Seyrig (Julie), Lea Massari (Cecilia), Valerie Mairesse (Esther), Roger Jendly (Jean Vallee), Gabriel Arout (Russian Teacher), France Lambiotte (Young Mute), Francois Rochaix, Francois Berthet, Armen Godel

THE LAST CHALLENGE OF THE DRAGON (CineWorld) Producers, Alex Gouw, Chow Hiap Hou; Director, Steve Chan; Screenplay, Steve Chan, Kung Ming; Photography, Lee Man Kit; Editor, Hu Kie Chan; Music, Frankie Chan; In color; Rated R; 90 minutes; July release. CAST: Shi Chien (Godfather), Ou Yang So Fei (Son), Kuan Shan (Wong), Steve Chan (Addict Son), Chang Li (Accomplice), Chen Li Ji (Daughter), Anna Jones (Addict's girlfriend)

THE INHERITANCE (S. J. International) Producer, Gianni Hecht Lucari; Director, Mauro Bolognini; Screenplay, Ugo Pirro, Sergio Bazzini; Photography, Ennio Guarnieri; Art Director, Luigi Scaccianoce; Editor, Nino Baragli; Music, Ennio Morricone; In Eastmancolor; 121 minutes; Rated R; July release. CAST: Anthony Quinn (Gregorio), Fabio Testi (Mario), Dominique Sanda (Irene), Luigi Proietti (Pippo), Adriana Asti (Teta), Paolo Bonacelli (Paolo)

A WOMAN AT HER WINDOW (Cinema Shares) Director, Pierre Granier-Deferre; Screenplay, Jorge Semprun, Pierre Granier-Deferre; From novel by Pierre Drieu La Rochelle; Photography, Aldo Toni; Editor, Jean Ravel; Producer, Albina de Boisrouvray; In Eastmancolor; 110 minutes; Not rated; July release. CAST: Romy Schneider (Margot), Philippe Noiret (Raoul), Victor Lanoux (Michel), Umberto Orsini (Rico), Delia Boccardo (Dora), Gastone Moschin (Primoukis), Carl Mohner (Von Pahlen)

LET'S FACE IT, CEST LA VIE (KSP Entertainment) Producer, Rezi Kashfi; Direction and Screenplay, Samy Paval; In color; 98 minutes; July release. CAST: Martine Kelly, Richard Leduc, Neils Arestrup

BRUTAL JUSTICE (Aquarius) Direction and Screenplay, Bert Lenzi; Executive Producer, Terry Levene; Music, Maurice Sarli; In color; Rated R; July release. CAST: Arthur Kennedy, Tomas Milian, Rosemary Omaggio, Mike Merli

REPLAY (Quartet) Director, Michel Drach; Screenplay, Pierre Uytterhoven, Michel Drach; French with English subtitles; Based on book by Dominique St. Alban; Photography, Etienne Szabo; Music, Jacques Monty, Jean Louis d'Onorio; Editor, Francoise Bonnot; A Gaumont Presentation; 96 minutes; Not rated; July release. CAST: Marie-Jose Nat (Cecile), Victor Lanoux (Francois), Anne Lonnberg (Josepha), Vania Vilers (Bruno), Philippe March (Man on train), Marc Eyraud (Dr. Mercier), Albert Dray (Taxi Driver), Roland Blanche (Man in apartment)

**Delphine Seyrig (L), Roger Jendly (R)
in "Faces of Love"**

**Victor Lanoux, Marie Jose Nat
in "Replay"**

Fabrice Greco, Pierre Richard
in "The Toy"

THE TOY (Show Biz) Produced and Written by Francis Veber; Music, Vladimire Cosma; Executive Producer, Pierre Grunstein; Assistant Directors, Jean-Michel Carbonnaux, Pierre-Alain Cremieu; Photography, Etienne Becker; Costumes, Michele Marmande-Cerf; Art Director, Bernard Evein; French with English subtitles; Presented by Byron Lasky and Lee Weisel; Rated PG; August release. CAST: Pierre Richard, Jacques Francois, Michel Bouquet, Fabrice Greco, Daniel Ceccadli, Michel Aumont

THE DRAGON LIVES (Film Ventures) Producer, C. H. Wong; Director, Singloy Wang; Screenplay, Singloy Wang, Yi Kwan; Photography, Chen Wing, Li Wom Chung; Editor, Mike Harris; In color; 90 minutes; Rated R; August release. CAST: Bruce Li, Caryn White, Betty Chen, Ernest Curtis

RITUALS (Aquarius) Producer, Lawrence Dane; Director, Peter Crane; Screenplay, Ian Sutherland; Music, Hagood Hardy; An Astral Films Presentation; In color; 99 minutes; Rated R; August release. CAST: Hal Holbrook (Harry), Lawrence Dane (Mitzi), Robin Gammell (Martin), Ken James (Abel), Gary Reineke (D.J.)

LIN TSE-HSU: THE OPIUM WAR (Sino-American) Producer, Haiyen Film Studio; Director, Chen Chun-li; In color; 90 minutes; No other credits available; August release. CAST: Chao Tan (Commissioner), Kao Chen (Emperor), Haiao Tien (Chief Minister), Li Yung (Teng), Ten Nan (Kuan), Lian Shan (Customs Inspector), Otto Williams (British Consul), Gerald Tannenbaum (British Merchant), Chien Chien-li (Kuang), Wen Hsi-ying (Mai), Ching Yin (Mrs. Mai)

BLACKOUT (New World) Producers, Nicole Boisvert, Eddy Matalon, John Dunning; Executive Producers, Andre Link, Ivan Reitman, John Vidette; Director, Eddy Matalon; Screenplay, John C. Saxton; Photography, J. J. Tarbes; Music, Didier Vasseur; Editors, Debbie Karen, Michael Karen; In color; 89 minutes; Rated R; September release. CAST: Jim Mitchum (Dan), Robert Carradine (Christie), Belinda Montgomery (Annie), June Allyson (Mrs. Grant), Jean-Pierre Aumont (Henry Lee), Ray Milland (Mr. Stafford)

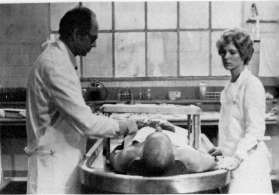

Mimsy Farmer (R)
in "Autopsy"

BLACK TRASH (Cinematic) Producer, Martin Wragge; Director, Chris Rowley; Screenplay, Bima Stagg; Photography, Fred Tammes; Executive Producer, Steven Brind; In color, Rated R; September release. CAST: Nigel Davenport, Ken Gampu, Peter Dyneley, Bima Stagg, Madala Mphahlele

THE EXECUTIONER (Trans Continental) Director, Turno Ishii; Screenplay, George Gonneau, A Toei Production; In color; Rated R; September release. CAST: Sonny Chiba

THE FRUIT IS RIPE (Espana) Director, Siggi Goetz; Photography, Heinz Hoelscher; Music, Gerhard Heinz; In Eastmancolor; 90 minutes; Rated R; September release. CAST: Betty Verges, Claus Richt, Olivia Pascal, Wolf Goldan, Corinne, Sabi Dorr

AUTOPSY (Joseph Brenner) Producer, Leonardo Pescarolo; Director, Armando Crispini; Photography, Carlo Carlini; In color; 125 minutes; Rated R; September release. CAST: Mimsy Farmer, Barry Primus, Ray Lovelock, Angela Goodwin

THE FAR SHORE (Bauer International) Producers, Joyce Wieland, Judy Steed; Director, Joyce Wieland; Executive Producer, Pierre Lamy; Screenplay, Bryan Barney; Story, Joyce Wieland; Photography, Richard Leiterman; Designer, Anne Pritchard; Music, Douglas Pringle; Editors, George Appelby, Brian French, Joyce Wieland, Judy Steed; A Far Shore Production in color; 104 minutes; October release. CAST: Frank Moore (Tom), Celine Lomez (Eulalie), Lawrence Benedict (Ross), Sean McCann (Cluny), Charlotte Blunt (Mary), Susan Petrie (Kate)

HIGH ROLLING IN A HOT CORVETTE (Martin) Producer, Tim Burstall; Director, Igor Auzins; Screenplay, Forest Redlich; Music, Sherbet; Photography, Dan Burstall; Art Director, Leslie Binns; Editor, Edward Queen-Mason; Associate Producer, Alan Finney; In color; 89 minutes; Rated PG; October release. CAST: Joseph Bottoms (Texas), Grigor Taylor (Alby), Judy David (Lynn), John Clayton (Arnold), Wendy Hughes (Barbie), Sandy McGregor (Susie), Simon Chilvers (Sideshow Boss), Gus Mercurio (Ernie), Robert Hewitt (Frank), Roger Ward (Lol), Peter Cummins (Busdriver)

Jim Mitchum, Robert Carradine
in "Blackout"

Frank Moore, Celine Lomez
in "The Far Shore"

Carla Gravina, George Coulouris, Alida
Valli in "The Tempter"

Bernard Lee, Leigh Lawson, Marika Rivera
in "It's Not the Size That Counts"

THE TEMPTER (Avco Embassy) Producer, Edmondo Amati; Director, Alberto DeMartino; Screenplay, Alberto De Martino, Vincenzo Mannino, Gianfranco Clerici; Music, Ennio Morricone; Photography, Aristide Massaccesi; Editor, Vincenzo Tomassi; Art Director, Umberto Bertacca; In color; 96 minutes; Rated R; October release. CAST: Carla Gravina (Ippolita), Mel Ferrer (Massimo), Arthur Kennedy (Bishop), George Coulouris (Father Mittner), Alida Valli (Irene), Anita Strindberg (Gretel), Mario Scaccia (Faith Healer), Umberto Orsini (Psychiatrist)

MESSAGE FROM SPACE (United Artists) Producers, Banjiro Uemura, Yoshinori Watanabe, Tan Takaiwa; Director, Kinji Fukasaku; Screenplay, Hiroo Matusda; Photography, Toro Nakajima; Music, Ken-Ichiro Morioka; Art Director, Tetsuzo Osawa; Photography, Nabaru Takanaski; In color; 105 minutes; Rated PG; October release. CAST: Vic Morrow (Gen. Garuda), Sonny Chiba (Hans), Philip Casnoff (Aaron), Peggy Lee Brennan (Meia), Sue Shiomi (Esmeralda), Tetsuro Tamba (Noguchi), Mikio Narita (Rockseia XII)

DESPAIR (New Line) Producer-Director, Rainer Werner Fassbinder; Screenplay, Tom Stoppard; Based on novel by Vladimir Nabokov; Photography, Michael Balhaus; Editors, Juliane Lorenz, Franz Walsch; Music, Peer Raben; Art Director, Rolf Zehetbauer; In Eastmancolor; 119 minutes; Not rated; October release. CAST: Dirk Bogarde (Hermann), Andrea Ferreol (Lydia), Volker Spengler (Ardalion), Klaus Lowitsch (Felix), Alexander Allerson (Mayer), Bernhard Wicki (Orlovius), Peter Kern (Muller), Gottfried John (Perebrodov), Roger Fritz (Inspector), Hark Bohm (Doctor)

SOUL BROTHERS OF KUNG FU (Cinema Shares International) Director, Hwa I. Hung; Producer, Eternal Film Company; In color; Rated R; October release. CAST: Bruce Li, Carl Scott, Jim James, Ku Feng, Kuan Lun

FORTRESS IN THE SUN (Independent) Director, George Rowe; In color; Rated R; October release. CAST: Nancy Kwan, Tony Ferrer, Fred Galang

COUNT DRACULA AND HIS VAMPIRE BRIDE (Dynamite Entertainment) Original title "Satanic Rites of Dracula"; Producer, Roy Skeggs; Director, Alan Gibson; Screenplay, Don Houghton; A Hammer Production; In color; 87 minutes; Rated R; October release. CAST: Christopher Lee, Peter Cushing, Michael Coles, William Franklyn, Freddie Jones, Joanna Lumley, Richard Vernon, Patrick Barr, Barbara Yu Ling, Richard Marrhews, Valerie Van Ost, Maggie Fitzgerald

THE FURIOUS MONK FROM SHAO-LIN (Cinema Shares International) Director, Hu Chang; Produced by First Film Organization; In color; Rated R; October release. CAST: Chen Sing, Lin Fun Chiao, Pei Ti, Kam Szu Yu

IT'S NOT THE SIZE THAT COUNTS (Joseph Brenner) Original title "Percy's Progress"; Producer, Betty E. Box; Director, Ralph Thomas; Screenplay, Sid Colin; In Eastmancolor; 90 minutes; Rated R; November release. CAST: Leigh Lawson (Percy), Elke Sommer (Helga), Denholm Elliott (Emmanuel), Vincent Price, Judy Geeson, George Coulouris, Harry H. Corbett, Adrienne Posta, Milo O'Shea

THE ADVENTURES OF PINOCCHIO (G.G. Communications) Director, Jesse Vogel; Screenplay, Albert D'Angelo; Based on novel by Carlo Collodi; Photography, Ralph Cenci; Music, Victor Thomas; Art Director, Earl Martin; Presented by N. W. Russo; In Movielab Color; Rated G; November release.

INDIAN SUMMER (Analysis) Director, Valerio Zurlini; Screenplay, Enrico Medioli, Valerio Zurlini; Photography, Dario DiPalma; Editor, Mario Morra; A Titanus Production; Rated R; November release. CAST: Alain Delon (Professor), Giancarlo Giannini (Narcotics Dealer), Sonya Petrova (Student)

THE BOTTOM LINE (Silverstein) Director, Georges Lautner; Screenplay, Francis Veber; Photography, Maurice Fellous; Editor, Michele David; In Eastmancolor; 96 minutes; Rated R; December release. CAST: Pierre Richard (Director), Miou-Miou (Friend), Jean-Pierre Marielle (Producer), Renee Saint-Cyr (Woman)

Carl Scott, Bruce Li
in "Soul Brothers of Kung Fu"

Sonya Petrova, Alain Delon
in "Indian Summer"

Basehart, Richard, 107, 215
Basilashivili, Oleg, 188
Baskette, James, 158
Bass, Emory, 56
Bast, William, 16
Bastin, Charles A., 56
Bateman, Kent, 137
Bates, Alan, 24, 25, 215
Bates, Kathy, 23
Batson, Susan, 20
Batt, Bert, 119, 202
Batt, Mike, 110, 190
Battaglia, Anthony, 8
Battle of Chile, The, 204
Baud, Antoine, 191
Bauer, Fred, 70
Bauert, Monika, 119
Baum, L. Frank, 92
Baum, Ralph, 148, 174
Baur, Lisa, 66
Baxley, Craig, 68
Baxter, Anne, 158, 215
Baxter, Jerry M., 44
Baxter, Keith, 215
Baxter, Les, 97
Baxter, Warner, 158
Bay, Frances, 68
Baye, Nathalie, 162
Bayer, Gary, 78
Bayless, Luster, 90
Bazzini, Sergio, 210
Beach, Jim, 70
Beach, Sarah, 116
Beacham, Stephanie, 206
Beagle, Peter S., 104
Beal, John, 215
Beal, Kay, 128
Bean, Orson, 126
Beane, Hilary, 130
Beard, Robert, 150
Beard, Stymie, 70
Beardsly, Bryan, 137
Beasley, Bill, 80
Beatles, The, 35
Beatty, Clarence, 102
Beatty, Ned, 107, 122, 127
Beatty, Robert, 215
Beatty, Roger, 134
Beatty, Warren, 6, 46, 47, 215
Beaudet, Deborah, 83
Beaudine, William, Jr., 136
Beaumont, Geoffrey, 212
Beauvy, Nicholas, 128
Bebermeyer, Pam, 66
Beck, Deborah, 78
Beck, John Fitzgerald, 94
Beck, Ron, 170
Beck, Stanley, 23
Becker, Etienne, 211
Becker, Tom, 150
Beckley, Tony, 60
Beckner, Rick, 80
Bedelia, Bonnie, 100
Bedi, Kabir, 215
Bedos, Guy, 172
Bee Gees, The, 62, 68
Beeler, Marian, 80, 81, 129
Beery, Buckline, 130
Beery, Noah, Jr., 215
Beery, Wallace, 158
Bees, The, 138
Beesley, Brad, 108
Beeson, Paul, 17
Begg, Jim, 52
Begley, Ed, 159
Begley, Ed Jr., 8, 12, 94, 125
Behn, Noel, 111
Bel Geddes, Barbara, 215
Belafonte, Harry, 215
Belasco, Leon, 215
Beliard, Francoise, 200
Belkin, Alan, 45
Bell, Bob, 199
Bell, Derrick, 92
Bell, Don, 18
Bell, Gene, 88
Bell, Kathy, 132
Bell, Kippi, 137
Bell, Tom, 215
Bell, Vinnie, 131
Bellamy, Earl, 129
Bellamy, Ralph, 215
Bellan, Jana, 127
Bellan, Joe, 68
Bellanger, George, 138
Bellaver, Harry, 12
Belle, Annie, 205
Beller, Kathleen, 16, 102, 215
Belleus, Dorene, 43
Belli, Agostine, 206
Belli, Laura, 212
Belling, Andrew, 134
Belmondo, Jean Paul, 215
Belson, Jerry, 40
Beltran, Alma, 20

Belushi, John, 66, 67, 94
Beluzzi, Maria Antonietta, 213
Benchley, Peter, 44
Bender, Bob, 75, 97
Bender, Russell, 135
Benedict, Dirk, 215
Benedict, Lawrence, 211
Benedict, Steven, 100
Benedict, William, 97
Benesch, Lynn, 133
Benham, Joan, 42
Ben-Hur, 159
Benjamin, Jean-Marie, 209
Benjamin, Richard, 20, 215
Bennent, Heinz, 186, 187
Bennet, Charles, 126
Bennett, Alan, 205
Bennett, Bruce, 215
Bennett, Dorothy, 137
Bennett, Jill, 215
Bennett, Joan, 215
Bennett, John, 42, 190
Bennett, Phillip, 56
Bennett, Richard, 133
Bennett, Richard Rodney, 111
Benoit, Ronald, 31
Benson, Dale, 138
Benson, Deborah, 18, 19, 132
Benson, James, 18
Benson, Norland, 76
Benson, Robby, 40, 41, 124, 215
Benton, Robert, 122
Beraud, Luc, 204
Beremenyi, Geza, 201
Berenguer, Andres, 213
Berenson, Marissa, 215
Berezin, Tania, 77
Berg, Judith, 137
Berg, Sandra, 137
Bergansky, Chuck, 136
Bergen, Candice, 7, 116, 117, 160, 215
Bergen, Edgar, 158, 232, 233
Bergen, Polly, 215
Berger, Helmut, 215
Berger, Peter E., 212
Berger, Senta, 215
Berger, William, 215
Bergerac, Jacques, 215
Bergman, Alan, 8
Bergman, Ingmar, 26, 168, 196
Bergman, Ingrid, 7, 158, 159, 196, 197, 215
Bergman, Marilyn, 8
Bergman, Rajah, 70
Berk, Howard, 212
Berle, Milton, 215
Berlin, Jeannie, 215
Berlinger, Warren, 215
Berman, Lester, 107
Berman, Martin, 64
Berman, Michael, 18
Berman, Shelley, 207
Berman, Sonya, 129
Bernard, Jason, 138
Bernardi, Herschel, 215
Bernath, Michele, 56
Bernay, Lynn, 212
Berne, Jean-Luc, 205
Bernesser, Patricia, 134
Bernhard, Harvey, 54
Berns, Wally, 56
Bernstein, Barry Armyan, 130
Bernstein, Elmer, 66, 96, 125
Bernstein, Jacquelyn, 136
Bernstein, Walter, 16
Berquist, Peter, 95
Berri, Claude, 174, 215
Berring, Douglas, 92
Berry, Chuck, 27
Berry, Jody, 70
Berry, John, 134
Berry, Ken, 52
Berryman, Michael, 208
Berta, Renato, 210
Bertacca, Umberto, 212
Berthet, Francois, 210
Berti, Orietta, 182
Berto, Juliet, 205, 215
Berton, Stuart I., 23
Beruh, Joseph, 132
Berwick, Irv, 137
Besch, Bibi, 212
Besnard, Jean Marie, 209
Best, James, 40, 72, 215
Best Way, The, 204
Best Years of Our Lives, The, 158
Betacca, Umberto, 206
Bethard, Robert, 136
Bethune, Ivy, 35
Betsy, The, 16

Betterfield, Paul, 38
Bettger, Lyle, 215
Betts, Richard, 31
Betz, Carl, 233
Beug, John, 80
Beveridge, Stewart H., 138
Beymer, Richard, 215
Beyond and Back, 126
Bickerton, Richard, 133
Bicycle Thief, The, 158
Biehn, Michael, 128
Big Country, The, 159
Big Fix, The, 100
Big Hill Singers, 131
Big Sleep, The, 170
Big Stick Up at Brink's, 111
Big Wednesday, 130
Biggs, Tex, 18
Bikel, Theodore, 215
Biletnikoff, Fred, 136
Bilezikjian, John, 204
Bille, Pam, 80
Billerey, Raoul, 191
Billingsley, Peter, 131
Billion Dollar Hobo, The, 134
Billy Jack Goes to Washington, 125
Bing, Mack, 127, 133
Bingenheimer, Rodney, 80
Binns, Edward, 116
Binns, Leslie, 211
Binyon, Claude, 233
Birch, Patricia, 26, 48, 62
Birkin, Jane, 84
Birman, Len, 133
Birnbaum, Bob, 8
Birney, David, 215
Birnkrant, Don, 133
Biro, Zoltan, 201
Bishop, Ed, 119
Bishop, Joey, 215
Bishop, Julie, 215
Bishop, Justin, 135
Bishop, Kelly, 24
Bishop, Larry, 100
Bishop, Linda, 126
Bishop, Stephen, 66
Bissell, Whit, 31
Bisset, Donald, 208
Bisset, Jacqueline, 7, 42, 91, 208, 215
Bixby, Bill, 215
Bjork, Halvar, 196
Blach, Leonard, 31
Black and White in Color, 159
Black, Eazy, 18
Black, Jeremy, 192, 193
Black, Karen, 50, 215
Black, Noel, 126
Black Orpheus, 159
Black River, 207
Black, Stephanie, 159
Black Trash, 211
Blackburn, Jeanne, 139
Black-Eyed Susan, 115
Blackjack, 137
Blackout, 211
Blacque, Taurean, 20
Blaine, Vivian, 215
Blair, Betsy, 215
Blair, Janet, 215
Blair, Linda, 215
Blake, Amanda, 215
Blake, Eubie, 125
Blake, Howard, 161
Blake, Jonathan, 202
Blake, Karen, 205
Blake, Robert, 215
Blake, Timothy, 138
Blake, Whitney, 16
Blake, Yvonne, 122
Blakely, Colin, 170, 209
Blakely, Susan, 215
Blakley, Ronee, 59, 125, 215
Blanchard, Alan, 135
Blanche, Roland, 174, 210
Blankinship, Jim, 137
Bleuze, Jean-Claude, 124
Blewitt, David, 70
Blezard, John, 173
Blier, Bertrand, 156
Blind Rage, 207
Bloch, Andrew, 100
Bloch, Walter, 97
Block, Larry, 46
Blodgett, Michael, 139
Blomkvist, Maria, 168
Blondell, Joan, 48, 215
Bloodbrothers, 96
Bloom, Claire, 215
Bloom, Jim, 53, 120
Bloom, John, 74, 108
Bloom, Lindsay, 125, 133, 137
Bloom, Verna, 66, 67
Blount, Lisa, 18

Blue Collar, 12
Blue Country, 205
Blue, David, 125
Blue Grass Boys, The, 129
Blue Sunshine, 130, 132
Blum, Harry N., 126
Blumenthal, Herman A., 16
Blunden, Bill, 208
Blunt, Charlotte, 211
Blunt, Erin, 134
Blyth, Ann, 215
Blythe, Janus, 208
Boa, Bruce, 36
Boam, Jeffrey, 23
Bobenko, Mike, 128
Boccardo, Delia, 210
Bochner, Hart, 215
Bock, Larry, 87, 128
Bockman, Michael, 135
Boddie, Aaron, 92
Bode, Ralf D., 82, 101
Bodnar, Theodor, 136
Bodoh, Allan F., 86, 127, 132
Boeke, Jim, 46
Boergadine, Steve, 125
Bofas, Ed, 131
Boffety, Jean, 162
Bogarde, Dirk, 211, 215
Bogart, Humphrey, 158
Bogart, Neil, 130
Bogart, Tiffany, 115
Bogert, Bill, 137
Bogert, William, 46
Boggs, Bill, 78
Boggs, Pete, 18
Bohan, Jim, 127
Bohm, Hark, 211
Boisseau, Jocelyne, 191
Boissery, Jean, 191
Boisvert, Nicole, 211
Boita, Peter, 17
Boland, Nora, 112
Bolary, Jean, 148
Bolden, Ronald, 137
Bole, Cliff, 18
Bolger, Ray, 215
Bolin, Shannon, 131
Bolkan, Florinda, 215
Bolling, Claude, 36, 112
Bolognini, Mauro, 210
Bolt, John, 42
Bonacelli, Paolo, 96, 210
Bonaduce, Danny, 53
Bonar, Ivan, 106
Bond, David, 20
Bond, Derek, 215
Bond, Joy, 131
Bond, Margery, 95
Bondi, Beulah, 215
Bonis, Jean-Bernard, 204
Bonjour Amour, 209
Bonner, Tom, 18
Bonnheim, Bruce, 66
Bonnie and Clyde, 159
Bonniere, Claude, 134
Bonnot, Francoise, 210
Bono, Steve, 158
Bonus, Shelley R., 118
Booke, Sorrell, 215
Boone, Debbie, 134
Boone, Pat, 134, 215
Boone, Richard, 170, 171, 206, 215
Booth, Maggie, 159
Booth, Margaret, 56
Booth, Shirley, 158, 215
Borack, Carl, 100
Borack, Phil, 133
Borau, Jose Luis, 206
Bordy, Bill, 138
Boretz, Alvin, 119
Borg, Anna, 168
Borgnine, Ernest, 30, 58, 159, 215
Born Again, 97
Born Yesterday, 158
Boromir, 104
Borowski, Tadeusz, 163
Borzage, Frank, 158
Bosco, Robert, 136
Boss, May R., 94
Bostwick, Barry, 102, 103, 140
Botana, Rene, 100
Botkin, Perry Jr., 94
Bottom Line, The, 212
Bottoms, James A., 32
Bottoms, Joseph, 211, 216
Bottoms, Timothy, 32, 216
Bouchet, Barbara, 206, 210
Bouchitey, Patrick, 204
Boulting, Ingrid, 216
Bounty-Hunter, The, 207
Bouquet, Michel, 211
Bourn, Mel, 64
Bourne, Mel, 43
Boutross, Tom, 125, 139
Bovee, Leslie, 216
Bow, Simmy, 134

Bowden, Ann, 127
Bowden, Mark, 137
Bowen, Dennis, 125
Bowen, Roger, 46
Bowen, Terry, 128
Bower, Antoinette, 212
Bowers, Raymond, 206
Bowker, Judi, 216
Bowman, Lee, 216
Box, Betty E., 212
Boyar, Sully, 116
Boyd, James, 127
Boyd, Russell, 203
Boyd, Tony, 96
Boyer, Charles, 158, 232, 233
Boyer, Sully, 158
Boyle, Michael, 112
Boyle, Peter, 39, 111, 216
Boyle, Robert F., 100
Boys from Brazil, The, 192
Boys in Company C, The, 18
Boys' Town, 158
Brabourne, John, 84
Bracht, Frank, 137
Bracken, Eddie, 216
Brackett, Charles, 159
Brackman, Jacob, 88
Braden, Harry, 37
Bradford, Jim, 125
Bradford, Richard, 94
Brady, Alice, 158
Brady, Scott, 216
Braga, Sonia, 166, 167
Braha, Herb, 116
Brana, Frank, 213
Brand, Amy, 95
Brand, Chris, 95
Brand, David, 95
Brand, Jenny, 95
Brand, Neville, 132, 135, 216
Brandes, Wulf Gunther, 129
Brando, Jocelyn, 102, 216
Brando, Marlon, 122, 159, 216
Brandon, David, 192
Brandon, John, 111
Brandon, Michael, 33
Brands, X, 87
Brandt, Brian, 18
Brandt, Janet, 33, 129
Brandt, Raymond, 100
Brandt, Victor, 35
Brannen, Ralph, 86
Brass Target, 119
Brasselle, Keefe, 216
Brasseur, Claude, 172
Bratcher, Joe, 126
Braun, Michael, 139
Bravo, Ramon, 137
Bravo, Roberto, 208
Brawley, Peter, 207
Brazzi, Rossano, 216
Bread and Chocolate, 180
Breakfast in Bed, 130
Brealond, Tony, 92
Breashears, Bill, 125
Bredouw, Jim, 127
Breen, Joseph, 159
Breit, Mitchell, 130
Brennan, Brian, 43
Brennan, Eileen, 33, 56, 132
Brennan, Mick, 129
Brennan, Peggy Lee, 211
Brennan, Walter, 158
Brenner, Albert, 10, 50, 112
Brenner, Joseph, 210
Brent, George, 97, 216
Breslin, Jimmy, 131
Brest, Martin, 129
Bretherton, David, 10
Brett, Alan, 206
Brett, Jeremy, 175
Brewer, Colin, 209
Brewster, Niles, 127
Brian, David, 216
Brice, Pierre, 206
Bricmont, Jeff, 107
Bricusse, Leslie, 139
Bridge on the River Kwai, The, 159
Bridges, Beau, 216
Bridges, James, 18
Bridges, Jeff, 82, 216
Bridges, Lloyd, 216
Bridges, Richard F., 107
Briemle, Ernst, 199
Briers, Richard, 190
Briley, John, 175
Brillanti, Dinorah, 166
Brinckerhoff, Burt, 127
Brind, Steven, 211
Bring, Bob, 22
Brinkman, Paul, 35
Brink's Job, The, 111
Brion, Francoise, 186, 187

Brisebois, Danielle, 115, 131
Britt, May, 216
Britt, Melendy, 127
Britt, Ron, 136
Brizzio, Jacques, 194
Broad, Anthony, 36
Broadway Melody, 158
Brochard, Martine, 210
Brockington, James, 122
Brocksmith, Roy, 115
Brodie, Don, 76
Brodie, Lea, 208
Brodie, Steve, 216
Broger, Shirley Ann, 129
Brolin, James, 50, 51, 216
Bromberger, Herve, 194
Bromfield, John, 216
Bromfield, Rex, 206
Bromley, Karen, 164
Bromley, Sydney, 17
Bronner, Chantal, 186
Bronson, Charles, 216
Brook, Claudio, 138
Brook, Sebastian, 102
Brooks, Claude, 92
Brooks, Dean, 97
Brooks, Joe, 130, 131
Brooks, Mel, 6
Brooks, Robert, 130
Brough, Don, 164
Brouwer, Leo, 207
Brown, Andrew, 127
Brown, Barry, 136, 233
Brown, David, 44
Brown, Ed Sr., 132
Brown, Edward R., 43
Brown, Georg Stanford, 216
Brown, Gina, 173
Brown, Hilyard, 72, 125
Brown, James, 216
Brown, Jim, 126, 216
Brown, Johnny, 92
Brown, Jophery, 68
Brown, Jorja A., 129
Brown, Judith, 20
Brown, Judith Hannah, 112
Brown, Katherine, 133
Brown, Miquel, 122
Brown, Phil, 36, 122
Brown, R. Hansel, 34
Brown, Robert, 208
Brown, Robert Jr., 54
Brown, Robert Latham, 32, 100
Brown, Speedy, 12
Brown, Tom, 216
Brown, William F., 92
Browne, Coral, 216
Browne, Leslie, 216
Browne, Peggy, 87
Broyles, Robert, 97
Bruce, Bill L., 135
Bruce, David, 216
Bruce, Virginia, 216
Bruce Vs the Black Dragon, 210
Bruck, Bella, 56
Bruckner, Jutta, 205
Bruhn, Erik, 206
Brunel-Cohen, Jane, 127
Bruno, Frank, 59
Bruno, Mauro, 138
Bruno, Richard, 46, 124
Bruns, Philip, 53
Brusati, Franco, 180
Brutal Justice, 210
Bryant, Lee, 50
Bryant, William, 32, 53
Brynner, Yul, 159, 206, 216
Brzozowski, Andrzej, 163
Buaraque, Chico, 166
Buchanan, Larry, 125
Buchholz, Horst, 216
Buchman, Sidney, 125
Buchmeister, John F. III, 150
Buckalew, Bethel, 132
Buckley, John, 137
Buckley, Keith, 210
Buckner, Parris Clifton, 131
Buckner, Susan, 48
Buckstone County Prison, 135
Buday, Don, 137
Budd, Roy, 199
Buetel, Jack, 216
Buffalo Rider, 127
Buffett, Jimmy, 33
Buford, Justin, 31
Buhrman, Dorothy, 133
Bujold, Genevieve, 10, 11, 216
Bull, Richard, 45
Bullen, Sarah, 179
Bully, 137
Bumstead, Henry, 20, 106
Bundy, Buzz, 87
Bunker, Edward, 23

Buono, Victor, 133, 216
Burch, Curt, 130
Burch, Lee, 71
Burghuet, Frantz-Andre, 209
Buria, Lazaro, 204
Burke, Art, 76
Burke, Paul, 216
Burkley, Dennis, 128
Burnett, Carol, 95, 216
Burnett, Jim, 128
Burnett, John F., 48, 118
Burns, Catherine, 216
Burns, George, 7, 62, 63, 159, 216
Burns, John Charles, 54
Burns, Patrick, 59
Burns, Ralph, 102
Burns, Robert, 208
Burns, Stephen, 31
Burns, William, 126
Burr, Raymond, 216
Burrell, Peter, 20, 33, 137
Burroughs, Dale, 150
Burstall, Dan, 211
Burstall, Tim, 211
Burstyn, Ellen, 106, 159, 184, 185, 216
Burton, Richard, 175, 199, 216
Burton, Robert, 127
Burton, Tony, 137
Busby, Gerald, 95
Busey, Gary, 23, 70, 130, 216
Bush, Owen, 126
Bushnell, Scott, 95
Bustany, Judith, 133
Butler, Bill, 48, 50, 54, 124, 132, 138
Butler, Eugene, 45
Butler, Michael, 44
Butler, Robert, 76
Butler, Ted, 92
Buttenstedt, Fritz, 206
Butterfield 8, 159
Butterflies Are Free, 159
Buttons, Red, 102, 103, 158, 159, 216
Butts, Steve, 12, 212
Buyle, Evelyne, 209
Buzby, Zane, 80
Buzzi, Ruth, 125, 216
Bygraves, Max, 216
Bylund, Janet, 126
Byner, John, 132
Byrne, Anne, 160
Byrne, Bobby, 12, 38, 40, 72
Byrne, Joe, 125
Byrne, Michael, 202
Byrnes, Burke, 45
Byrnes, Edd, 48, 216
Byrnes, Maureen, 94
Byron, Jeffrey, 135, 179
Bystrom, Margaretha, 168
Caan, James, 90, 216
Caan, Ronald, 90
Cabaret, 159
Cabot, Susan, 216
Cactus Flower, 159
Cadell, Simon, 190
Caesar, Harry, 31, 100
Caesar, Sid, 48, 56, 57, 216
Caffarel, Jose Maria, 213
Caffaro, Cheri, 137
Caffi, Juan Jose Garcia, 213
Cagney, James, 158, 216
Cagney, Jeanne, 216
Cahill, Barry, 23
Cahill, G. M., 129
Cain, Syd, 199
Cain, William B., 16
Caine, Michael, 36, 112, 135, 216
Caine, Richard, 97
Caine, Shakira, 216
Calder, David, 122
Caldwell, Dan, 135
Caldwell, Thomas, 31
Caldwell, William, 132
Calfa, Don, 68
Calhoun, Rory, 131, 216
California Suite, 112, 155, 159
Call, Edward, 35, 127
Callahan, Gene, 78, 96, 115
Callan, Michael, 125, 216
Calvert, Phyllis, 216
Calvet, Corinne, 137, 216
Calvin, John, 56
Camara, Ousmane, 205
Cambern, Donn, 40, 72
Cambridge, Godfrey, 125
Cameron, Bill, 132
Cameron, Rod, 131, 216
Camp, Colleen, 131, 216
Camp, Hamilton, 46
Camp, Steve, 70

Campanella, Frank, 46
Campbell, Archie, 138
Campbell, Glen, 216
Campbell, Lindsay, 206
Campbell, Ron, 18
Campbell, Stu, 44
Campbell, William, 32
Canale, Gianna Maria, 216
Canalito, Lee, 83
Canary of Padana Valley, The, 182
Candleshoe, 17
Cannaday, Richard, 126
Canning, James, 18
Cannold, Mitchell, 86
Cannon, Dyan, 46, 47, 60, 61, 216
Cannon, Vince, 130
Canon, Jack, 137
Canonero, Milena, 96
Canova, Judy, 216
Cantata de Chile, 204
Cantor, Eddie, 159
Cantrell, William, 106
Capell, Maxilyn, 126
Capers, Virginia, 216
Capitani, Georgio, 206
Capps, Al, 127
Capra, Frank, 158
Capra, Frank Jr., 97, 125
Capricorn One, 50
Captains Courageous, 158
Capucine, 216
Caputo, Bernard F., 130
Cara, Irene, 28
Carabella, Flora, 160
Caramico, Robert, 135
Caravans, 110
Carballo, Dick, 101
Carbone, Anthony, 126
Carbone, Tony, 87
Carbonnaux, Jean-Michel, 211
Card, Lamar, 139
Cardenas, Billy, 100
Cardi, Tito, 206
Cardiff, Jack, 30, 84
Cardinale, Claudia, 216
Cardona, Rene, Jr., 137
Cardwell, Jack, 136
Carelli, Joann, 150
Carenzo, Vito, 35
Carey, Harry Jr., 216
Carey, Macdonald, 216
Carey, Philip, 216
Carey, Richard, 59
Carey, Timothy, 129
Carfagno, Edward, 8
Caridi, Carmine, 56
Cariou, Len, 26
Caristan, Georges, 205
Carlile, David, 126
Carlin, Ed, 133
Carlini, Carlo, 211
Carlisle, John, 91
Carlson, Karen, 134
Carlson, Les, 206
Carlton, Mark, 86
Carlton, Roger, 87
Carmello, Paul, 70
Carmet, Jean, 194, 195
Carmichael, Hoagy, 216
Carmichael, Ian, 216
Carnacina, Stella, 212
Carne, Judy, 216
Carney, Art, 20, 21, 102, 125, 159, 216
Carney, Daniel, 199, 205
Carney, Fred, 16
Carney, Matt, 105
Caro Michele, 204
Caron, Leslie, 216
Carpenter, Carleton, 216
Carpenter, John, 78, 137
Carpenter, Linda, 45
Carpenter, Peter, 13
Carpenter, Thelma, 92
Carpenter, Willie, 92
Carpi, Fabio, 204
Carr, Allan, 48
Carr, Jamie, 131
Carr, Vikki, 216
Carradine, David, 127, 128, 216
Carradine, John, 129, 134, 138, 216
Carradine, Keith, 37, 161, 216
Carradine, Robert, 14, 15, 211, 216
Carreire, Jaime, 12
Carrel, Dany, 216
Carreras, Chris, 84
Carrere, Fernando, 58
Carrier, Alberto, 125
Carriere, Matthieu, 205
Carroll, Beeson, 82
Carroll, Bill, 126
Carroll, Diahann, 217
Carroll, Madeleine, 217

Carroll, Pat, 217
Carroll, Peter, 203
Carroll, Roberta Lee, 35
Carroll, Susette, 139
Carroll, Victoria, 134
Carroll, William, 52
Carson, John David, 217
Carson, Johnny, 217
Carson, Sunset, 135
Carsten, Peter, 212, 217
Carter Family, 129
Carter, Jack, 125
Carter, June, 129
Carter, Mel, 52
Carter, Nick, 129
Carter, Peter, 134
Carter, Thomas, 137
Cartwright, Lynn, 135
Cartwright, Veronica, 94, 120
Casablanca, 158
Casey, Chick, 83
Casey, Lawrence, 127
Casey, Warren, 48
Casey's Shadow, 31
Cash, Rosalind, 217
Casino, James J., 83, 102
Casnoff, Philip, 211
Cason, Barbara, 217
Cass, Dave, 76
Cass, Peggy, 217
Cassady, John, 122
Cassaus, Victor, 207
Cassavetes, John, 28, 119, 217
Cassel, Jean-Pierre, 91, 217
Cassel, Seymour, 58, 125
Cassidy, Alan, 129, 133
Cassidy, David, 217
Cassidy, Jack, 125
Cassidy, Joanna, 132, 217
Cassidy, Ted, 137
Castel, Lou, 204
Castellano, Richard, 217
Castilla, Patricio, 207
Castle, Mike, 128
Castle, Nick, 137
Cat and Mouse, 209
Cat Ballou, 159
Cat From Outer Space, The, 52
Catastrophe, 205
Catching, Bill, 87
Catching, Dottie, 87
Cathey, John, 87
Caton, Phil, 36
Cattand, Gabriel, 209
Caudell, Lane, 127, 129
Caulfield, Joan, 217
Causey, Jack, 17
Cavalcade, 158
Cavani, Liliana, 217
Caven, Ingrid, 186, 187
Cazale, John, 149, 150, 151, 233
C.B. Hustlers, 137
Ceccadli, Daniel, 211
Cedar, Jon, 75
Ceddo, 205
Ceder, Elayne Barbara, 27, 114
Celi, Adolfo, 217
Celine and Julie Go Boating, 205
Celinska, Stanislawa, 163
Cenci, Ralph, 212
Cenet, Michel, 205
Cerami, Armand, 112
Cerbonnet, Frederique, 191
Cerioni, Giorgio, 180
Cervera, Jorge Jr., 100
Cesar, John, 159
Cevetillo, Lou, 115
Chabrol, Claude, 194
Chaffey, Don, 136
Chakiris, George, 159, 217
Chalaud, Guy, 191
Chalk, Al, 27
Challenge to Survive, 137
Challis, Chris, 202
Chama, Sydney, 199
Chamberlain, Richard, 135, 203, 217
Chambers, John, 159
Chambliss, Woodrow, 62
Champ, The, 158
Champion, Gower, 217
Champion, Marge, 217
Chan, Frankie, 210
Chan, Hu Kie, 210
Chan, Madalena, 18
Chan, Steve, 210
Chandler, David, 126
Chandler, John, 125
Chandler, Raymond, 217
Chang, Chaplin, 173
Chang, Ho, 208
Chang, Hu, 211
Chang, I, 204
Channing, Carol, 217

Channing, Stockard, 48, 56, 217
Chapin, Ken, 24
Chapiteau, Marc, 162
Chaplin, Charles, 128, 158, 159
Chaplin, Geraldine, 95, 217
Chaplin, Sydney, 217
Chapman, David, 82
Chapman, Dianne Finn, 107
Chapman, Graham, 205
Chapman, Judith, 137
Chapman, Lonny, 134
Chapman, Michael, 38, 120
Chapman, Mike, 126
Chapman, Robin, 202
Chapot, Jean, 186
Charisse, Cyd, 208, 217
Charles, Annette, 48, 49
Charles, Charlie, 46
Charleston, 212, 213
Charlet, Sylviane, 105
Charly, 159
Charriere, Jean Jacques, 105
Chartoff, Robert, 90, 138
Chase, Chevy, 68, 69, 140, 217
Chase, Ilka, 233
Chase, James, 210
Chase, Libbie, 134
Chase, Stanley, 134
Chaskel, Pedro, 204
Chastain, Jane, 100
Chauveau, Zoe, 194
Cheap Detective, The, 56
Checkered Flag or Crash, 127
Cheerleaders' Beach Party, 137
Cheminal, Mic, 174
Chen, Betty, 211
Chen, K. S., 173
Chen, Kao, 211
Cher, 217
Chesnay, Patrick, 200
Chess Players, The, 209
Chester, Colby, 12
Chesterfields, The, 27
Cheung, George, 173
Chevalier, Maurice, 159
Chew, Richard, 94
Chiabaut, Jean Cesar, 174
Chianese, Dominick, 21
Chiao, Lin Feng, 204
Chiao, Lin Fun, 211
Chiari, Walter, 217
Chiba, Gomi, 210
Chiba, Sonny, 211
Chien, Shi, 210
Chien-li, Chien, 211
Chih, Chang I., 212
Chihara, Paul, 134
Chiles, Lois, 10, 84, 85
Chilvers, Simon, 211
Chin, Clint, 24
Chittel, Chris, 199
Chivers, Colin, 122
Chobanian, Arthur, 83
Chong, Tommy, 80, 81
Chopin, Frederic, 163
Chorus Girls, The, 207
Chosen, The, 206
Chow, Michael, 91
Chow, Raymond, 18, 173
Chrisafis, Chris, 199
Chriss, Fred, 131
Christian, Linda, 217
Christian, Robert, 217
Christie, Audrey, 133
Christie, Julie, 46, 47, 159, 217
Christie, Mary Ellen, 137
Christmas at Candleshoe, 17
Christopher, Bob, 70
Christopher, Dennis, 18, 95
Christopher, Jordan, 217
Chuck Banks' Big Band, 95
Chudy, Craig, 32
Chulay, Cornell, 56
Chulay, John C., 56
Chung, Li Wom, 211
Chun-li, Chen, 211
Churcher, Terry, 192
Churchill, Pat, 77
Churchill, Sarah, 217
Churchill, Ted, 139
Ciani, Leo, 43
Cilento, Diane, 217
Cimarron, 158
Cimino, Michael, 150, 159
Cioffi, Charles, 127
Ciotti, Richard, 137
Cipriani, Stelvio, 213
Ciral, Karen, 33
Cisy, Kacey, 8
Claire, Adele, 125
Clapton, Eric, 38, 217
Clark, Anthony R., 137

Clark, Candy, 170, 171
Clark, Cordy, 208
Clark, Dane, 217
Clark, Dennis Lynton, 90
Clark, Dick, 217
Clark, Greydon, 132
Clark, Jim, 207
Clark, Logan, 127
Clark, Mae, 217
Clark, Mary Kai, 18
Clark, Matt, 59
Clark, Petula, 217
Clark, Randy, 126
Clark, Ron, 60
Clark, Roy, 134
Clark, Susan, 217
Clark, Valerie, 126
Clark, Valerie Rae, 128
Clarke, Graham, 199
Clarke, Logan, 18
Clarke, Oz, 122
Clarke, Robin, 42
Clarke-Williams, Zoe, 43
Clarkson, Channing, 128
Clash, The, 209
Claudio, Andrea, 33
Claudon, Paul, 156
Claxton, Samuel, 207
Clayburgh, Jill, 7, 24, 25, 217
Clayton, Hyde, 126
Clayton, John, 211
Cleese, John, 205
Clem, Jimmy, 136
Clement, Aurore, 204
Clementelli, Silvio, 213
Clements, Stanley, 76, 217
Clennon, David, 86
Clerici, Gianfranco, 206, 212
Clery, Corinne, 217
Cleve, Corinne, 200
Cleve, Jenny, 200
Cleveland, Carlos, 92
Cleveland, Carol, 205
Clevenot, Philippe, 205
Clifford, Graeme, 39, 58
Clifton, Peter, 209
Clinton, Mildred, 131
Cliver, Al, 205
Clooney, Rosemary, 217
Cloquet, Ghislain, 139
Closely Watched Trains, 159
Clouse, Robert, 173, 212
Clover, David, 131
Clute, Sidney, 100
Clyde, Jeremy, 36
Coach, 128
Coady, Terry, 208
Coates, Anne V., 175
Cobert, Robert, 137
Coburn, Art, 127
Coburn, Charles, 158
Coburn, James, 217
Coca, Imogene, 13, 217
Cochran, John J., 135
Coco, James, 56, 212, 213, 217
Cody, Kathleen, 217
Coe, Barry, 44
Coe, David Allan, 135
Coelho, Susie, 136
Coffe, Jean-Pierre, 194
Coffin, Fred, 115
Cohen, Alain, 174
Cohen, Barney, 137
Cohen, Edward H., 70
Cohen, Esther, 129
Cohen, Howard, 134, 137
Cohen, Larry, 125, 130
Cohen, Michael, 18
Cohen, Rob, 92, 125, 130, 137
Cohen, Susan, 126
Cohn, Bruce, 127, 132
Colbert, Claudette, 158, 217
Colbourne, Maurice, 161
Cole, David, 68
Cole, George, 129, 217
Cole, Joe, 199
Cole, Jonathan, 125
Cole, King, 88
Cole, Michael, 129
Coleman, Cliff, 32, 58, 66, 83
Coles, Michael, 211
Coles, Stanley, 62
Coley, John Ford, 138
Colin, Sid, 212
Colla, Richard A., 71
Collazo-Levy, Dora, 116
Collentine, Barbara, 45
Colli, Tonino Delli, 182, 204
Collignon, Yves, 204
Collins, Jack, 137
Collins, Joan, 133, 170, 217
Collins, Johnnie III, 132

Collins, Roberta, 134
Collins, Shannon, 136
Collins, Sunny, 136
Collodi, Carlo, 212
Collomb, Jean, 209
Colman, Ronald, 158
Colombi, Christopher Jr., 150
Colombo, Alice, 160
Colombo, Harry, 160
Coma, 10
Combs, Gilbert, 66
Come and Get It, 158
Come Back, Little Sheba, 158
Comer, Anjanette, 217
Comes a Horseman, 90
Coming Home, 4, 14, 152, 153, 159
Commodores, The, 130
Communion, 131
Compton, Athol, 203
Compton, Fay, 233
Compton, Sharon, 87, 128
Conant, Oliver, 217
Conaway, Jeff, 48, 217
Condict, Win, 135
Conforte, Joe, 137
Conklin, John, 137
Conkling, Chris, 104
Conley, Renie, 110
Conn, Didi, 48, 137
Conn, Frank, 112
Connell, Jane, 13, 20
Connelly, Chris, 136
Connery, Sean, 217
Connor, Kevin, 208
Connors, Carol, 134
Connors, Chuck, 125, 217
Connors, Matt (Jim), 12
Connors, Mike, 217
Conover, Holly, 135
Conrad, Christopher, 97
Conrad, Joseph, 161
Conrad, Scott, 80
Conrad, Sid, 45
Conrad, William, 205, 217
Conried, Hans, 52
Considine, John, 95
Consoldone, Michael, 118
Constantine, Eddie, 130
Conte, Steve, 32
Conti, Bill, 24, 39, 83, 100, 101, 138
Conti, Tom, 161
Convention Girls, 133
Converse, Frank, 217
Convoy, 58
Convoy Buddies, 205
Convy, Bert, 132
Conway, James L., 126
Conway, Kevin, 39, 83
Conway, Tim, 134, 138, 217
Coogan, Jackie, 217
Cook, Brian, 133
Cook, David, 91
Cook, Elisha Jr., 217
Cook, Paul, 54
Cook, Peter, 205
Cook, Robin, 10
Cook, Roderick, 77
Cooke, Juliet, 209
Cooke, Malcolm, 84
Cooke, Sam, 66
Cool Hand Luke, 159
Cooley, Isabel, 130
Cooper, Alice, 62
Cooper, Ann, 132
Cooper, Ben, 217
Cooper, Gary, 158, 159
Cooper, Jackie, 122, 123, 217
Cooper, Maury, 16
Cooper, Merian C., 158
Coote, Robert, 217
Copplestone, Geoffrey, 159
Coppola, Francis Ford, 159
Coppola, Sam, 115
Coquette, 158
Coralli, Jean, 206
Corallo, Jesse, 86
Corbett, Gretchen, 32
Corbett, Harry H., 212
Corbett, Ray, 96
Corby, Ellen, 217
Corcoran, Donna, 217
Corcoran, Hugh, 75
Corcoran, John, 82
Corcoran, Kevin, 22, 76
Cord, Alex, 217
Corday, Mara, 217
Cordero, Peggy, 204
Cordic, Regis, 135
Cording, John, 122
Core, Traci, 92
Corey, Jeff, 132, 199, 217
Corinne, 211
Corlan, Anthony, 217
Corman, Gene, 39

Corman, Roger, 26, 87, 128, 133, 136
Cormier, Dean, 31
Cormier, Thelma, 31
Cornthwaite, Robert, 217
Cornwell, Judy, 207
Corona, Fidel, 59
Corrado, Karen, 137
Correll, Charles, 66
Corri, Adrienne, 217
Corsaut, Aneta, 128
Corso, John W., 83
Cortazar, Octavio, 208
Cortese, Valentina, 217
Cortese, Joseph, 137
Corvette Summer, 53
Cosby, Bill, 112, 113, 217
Cosentino, Richard, 135
Cosma, Vladimir, 172, 211
Cosmatos, Yorgo Pan, 208
Costello, Ward, 22
Coster, Nicolas, 100, 101, 217
Cotelo, Celia Susan, 131
Cotone, Mario, 213
Cotten, Joseph, 110, 217
Cotton, Gene, 135
Coulouris, George, 212
Coulson, Catherine, 130
Coulter, Allan, 107
Coulter, Jean, 44
Count Dracula and His Vampire Bride, 211
Country Girl, The, 159
Coup de Grace, 205
Courtenay, Tom, 217
Courtland, Jerome, 22, 217
Covan, Willie, 100
Coward, Noel, 158
Cox, Joel, 114
Cox, Ronny, 127, 133
Coyle, Sherri, 129
Coyne, Nancy Marlowe, 56
Coyote and The Pack, 132
Cozzi, Luigi, 213
Crabbe, Buster (Larry), 217
Crabe, James, 130
Cracknell, Derek, 175, 199
Craig, James, 217
Craig, Michael, 217
Crain, Jeanne, 217
Crandall, Brad, 126
Crandall, Eric, 136
Crane, Bob, 233
Crane, Peter, 211
Cranshaw, Pat, 62
Craven, Garth, 58
Craven, Wes, 208
Craver, William, 82
Crawford, Broderick, 125, 158, 217
Crawford, Joan, 158
Crawford, Nancy Voyles, 110
Creaghe, Joe, 80
Creaghe, June, 80
Credel, Curtis, 32
Creed, Roger, 136
Cremieu, Pierre-Alain, 211
Crenna, Richard, 130, 133, 217
Crichton, Michael, 10
Criscuola, Lou, 137
Crisp, Donald, 158
Crispini, Armando, 211
Cristal, Linda, 125, 131, 217
Cristina, Frank, 125
Cristina, Teresa, 125
Croce, Gerard, 105
Cromwell, James, 56
Cromwell, John, 95
Cronin, Kevin, 33
Crosby, Bing, 158
Crosby, Cathy Lee, 128
Crossed Swords, 30
Crothers, Scatman, 56, 127
Crouse, Lindsay, 217
Crouzet, Roger, 205
Crowe, Eileen, 233
Crowley, Pat, 218
Cruz, Brandon, 8
Crystal, Billy, 13, 218
Crystal, Richard, 132
Crystal, Ruby, 139
Cuadrado, Luis, 206
Cudney, Roger, 138
Cukor, George, 159
Cullen, Alan, 122
Cullen, Hedley, 203
Culley, John K., 137
Culliton, Joseph, 82
Cullum, John, 218
Culp, Robert, 218
Culver, Calvin, 218
Culver, Roland, 42
Cummings, Brian, 112
Cummings, Constance, 218
Cummings, Quinn, 218
Cummings, Robert, 218

Cummins, Don, 135
Cummins, Peggy, 218
Cummins, Peter, 211
Cunningham, John, 100
Cunningham, Noel John, 132
Cunningham, Sean S., 132
Cunningham, Susan E., 132
Curtin, Valerie, 45, 132
Curtis, Clive, 199
Curtis, Douglas, 125
Curtis, Ernest, 211
Curtis, Jamie Lee, 137
Curtis, Keene, 13, 46, 218
Curtis, Patrick, 208
Curtis, Tony, 75, 134, 218
Curtiz, Michael, 158
Cusack, Cyril, 218
Cushing, Peter, 211, 218
Cutell, Lou, 68
Cutler, Barry, 128
Cutler, Brian, 139
Cutrer, T. Tommy, 129
Cutts, John, 137
Cyphers, Charles, 137
Cyrano de Bergerac, 158
Czarmiak, 176
Czezdwski, Andrew, 209
Czmyr, Nick, 16
Dabadie, Jean-Loup, 172
D'Adda, Francesco, 180
Dahl, Arlene, 218
Dahlin, Bob, 95
Dahlmann, Jerry, 12
Daigler, Gary, 20, 68, 137
Dailey, Dan, 125, 232, 233
D'Alby, Pierre, 205
Dale, Holly, 164
Dale, Jim, 76
d'Alessio, Ugo, 180
Daley, Robert, 114
Dallas, Charlene, 107
Dallesandro, Joe, 218
Dalmain, Jean, 194
Dalton, Timothy, 218
Daltrey, Roger, 218
Daly, Cindy, 128
Daly, James, 233, 234
Daly, Tyne, 129, 218
Dalzell, Dennis, 129
Damamme, Rosalinde, 200
D'Amato, Paul, 150
D'Amico, Suso Cecchi, 204
Damien-Omen II, 54
Damone, Vic, 218
D'Amore, JoJo, 134
Dan, England, 138
Dana, Gregory, 125
Dane, Lawrence, 211
D'Angelo, Albert, 212
D'Angelo, Beverly, 114
Dangerous, 158
Dangler, Anita, 101
Daniel, Joshua, 66
Daniel, Ronald, 132
Daniels, Dennis, 139
Daniels, Diana, 131
Daniels, Diane, 16
Daniels, Donne, 129
Daniels, Elaine, 126
Daniels, Jerry, 136
Daniels, John, 127
Daniels, William, 8, 218
Danko, Rick, 38
Danner, Blythe, 218
Dannick, Faye, 131
Danning, Sybil, 30, 204, 205, 206
Dano, Linda, 204
Dano, Royal, 125, 136, 218
Danon, Raymond, 148
Danova, Cesare, 66, 67
Danson, Randy, 115
Dante, Joe, 136
Dante, Michael, 218
Dantine, Helmut, 218
Danton, Ray, 218
D'Antuono, Eleanor, 206
DaPrato, Clark, 129
D'Arbanville, Patti, 130
Darby, Kim, 8, 9, 218
Darcel, Denise, 218
Dark, John, 208
Dark Sunday, 125
Darke, Rebecca, 115
Darling, 159
D'Arms, Ted, 127
Darren, James, 218
Darrieux, Danielle, 218
Darrow, Charlene, 150
Darrow, Henry, 129
Darwell, Jane, 158
DaSilva, Howard, 125, 218
Dassin, Jules, 184
Daudon, Dominique, 174
Daughton, James, 66, 131
Dauphin, Claude, 148, 149, 162, 233, 234
Dautremay, Jean, 200

Davao, Charlie, 207
Davenport, Nigel, 211
Daves, Michael, 94
David, Alain, 176
David, Brad, 125
David, Clifford, 16
David, Judy, 211
David, Michele, 218
David, Thayer, 20, 234
Davidson, John, 218
Davidson, Martin, 131, 137
Davidson, Sandra, 137
Davies, Brian, 58
Davies, Rosemary, 208
Davies, Rupert, 218
Davies, Stacy, 209
Davis, Bette, 22, 84, 85, 158, 218
Davis, Brad, 96, 98, 99, 141
Davis, Cathy, 125
Davis, Chip, 58
Davis, Clifton, 125
Davis, Dick, 125, 135
Davis, Gary, 133
Davis, Jim, 90
Davis, Joanna, 213
Davis, Joy Shelton, 45
Davis, Keith, 137
Davis, Kenn, 135
Davis, Lori, 126
Davis, Ossie, 218
Davis, Peter S., 137
Davis, Richard, 128
Davis, Sammy, Jr., 139, 218
Davison, Bruce, 119, 137
Davison, Donn, 137
Davison, Jon, 136
Dawber, Pamela, 95
Dawson, Anthony, 206
Dawson, Ron, 12
Dawson, Ted, 128
Dawson, Tom, 31
Dax, Micheline, 204
Day, Dennis, 218
Day, Doris, 218
Day, Ernie, 60
Day for Night, 159
Day, Josette, 234
Day, Laraine, 218
Day of the Woman, 138
Dayan, Assaf, 204, 218
Days of Heaven, 88
Days of Water, 207
Dayton, June, 32
de Baer, Jean, 77
De Bello, John, 125
de Boisrouvray, Albina, 210
de Boysson, Pascale, 191
De Broca, Philippe, 176
De Cohen, Lisa, 26
De Dunoto, Agneso, 160
de Forest, Lee, 158
de Goldschmidt, Gilbert, 209
De Graot, James, 26
De Greenlaw, Jennifer, 203
de Gregorio, Eduardo, 205
de Havilland, Olivia, 134, 135, 158
de la Cruz, Rene, 208
de la Huerta, Orlando, 207
de la Madrid, Victor Gil, 116
De Laurentiis, Dino, 115
De Laurentiis, Federico, 115
de Leuw, Ray, 76
De Los Rios, Waldo, 209
De Marney, Derrick, 234
De Martino, Alberto, 206, 212
De Martino, Aldo, 206
De Micheli, Adriano, 182
de Ossio, Maria L., 71
De Palma, Brian, 28
De Rochemont, Louis, 234
de Saint-Georges, Vernoy, 206
Deacon, Richard, 136
Deadman, Derek, 170
Dean, Basil, 234
Dean, Felicity, 30
Dean, Jimmy, 218
Deane, Bill, 131
DeAngelis, Guido, 212
DeAngelis, Maurizio, 212
Dear Detective, 176
Dear Inspector, 176
Death Dimension, 134
Death Force, 137
Death on the Nile, 84
Death Rage, 206
Deathsport, 128
Deaton, George, 136
DeBell, Kristine, 35, 96
Decae, Henri, 192
DeCarlo, Yvonne, 218
Decker, Michael, 131
DeCroce, Fred, 212
Decugis, Cecile, 191

Dee, Frances, 218
Dee, Joey, 218
Dee, Ruby, 218
Dee, Sandra, 218
Deeley, Michael, 58, 150
Deer Hunter, The, 150, 154, 159
Dees, Rick, 125
Deezen, Eddie, 35, 48, 128
deParla, Walt, 135
DeFore, Don, 218
Deghy, Guy, 42
Degidon, Tom, 78
DeHaven, Carter, 135
DeHaven, Gloria, 218
Dehner, John, 192
DeJon, Denise, 92
Del Guidice, Daniele, 213
Del Ragno, John, 115
Del Rio, Dolores, 218
Delamain, Aimee, 91
Delaney, Gloria, 12
Delaney, Pat, 133
Delarbre, Philippe, 194
Delcher, Stephane, 105
Delerue, Georges, 156, 176
Del-Genio, Leni, 36
Delhomme, Sanders, 31
Delia, Russell P., 54
Dell, Gabriel, 218
Dell, Myrna, 136
Dell, Wanda, 138
Delle Aie, Michele, 213
Delon, Alain, 212, 218
Delorme, Daniele, 172, 218
Delorme, Guy, 191
Delpy, Albert, 205
DeLuise, Dom, 40, 41, 56, 57, 218
Delys, Max, 180
DeMaio, Nicole, 43
Demarest, William, 218
Dembo, Jack, 70
Demetrakes, Johanna, 43
DeMille, Cecil B., 158
Deming, Mark R., 95
Demongeot, Mylene, 218
Demora, Robert, 45
Deneuve, Catherine, 218
DeNiro, Robert, 7, 149, 150, 151, 159, 218
Denise, Denise, 137
Denison, John, 42
Denison, Michael, 218
Denissi, Mimi, 42
Denn, Marie, 45
Dennehy, Brian, 39, 68
Denner, Charles, 162, 174, 218
Denning, Katherine, 66
Dennis, Sandy, 159, 218
Denny, Steve, 155
DeNoble, Alphonso, 131
Deodato, Ruggero, 206
Depardieu, Gerard, 156, 157
DePollo, Don, 130
Derek, John, 218
Dern, Bruce, 14, 15, 59, 218
DeRogatis, Al, 46
Dersu Uzala, 159
DeSantis, Gregory J., 212
DeSautels, John, 78
Deschamps, Hubert, 176
Desiderio, Ralph T., 137
DeSimone, Roberto, 160
Despair, 211
Dessalles, Gerard, 200
DeTurenne, Gilles A., 75
Deville, Michel, 200
Devine, Andy, 135
Devine, Jim, 78
DeVito, Danny, 94
DeVito, Ralph, 137
Devore, Frank, 150
Dewaere, Patrick, 156, 157, 204
Dewhurst, Colleen, 124, 218
DeWindt, Hal, 130
DeWitt, Faye, 133
DeWolf, Jack, 137
Dexter, Anthony, 218
Dexter, Brad, 20, 125
Dey, Susan, 140
DeYoung, Cliff, 12, 218
DeYoung, Gypsi, 45
Dhiegh, Khigh, 137, 218
Di Giso, John Jr., 43
Di Re, Florence, 45
Dia, Makoura, 205
Diagne, Ismaila, 205
Diamantidou, Despo, 184
Diamond, Neil, 38
Diary of Anne Frank, The, 159
Diaz, Vic, 18, 137
Dibango, Manu, 205

Dibble, Daphne, 44
DiBenedetto, Tony, 43
Diberti, Luigi, 182
DiCicco, Bobby, 35, 130
Dickens, Jimmy, 129
Dickinson, Angie, 218
Dicks, Ted, 210
Dickson, Barbara, 110
Didio, Tony, 128
Die Sister, Die!, 139, 212
Diep, Phong, 86
Dietrich, Marlene, 218
Different Story, A, 45
DiGiuseppe, Enrico, 68
Dilbert, Frankl, 213
DiLeo, Mario, 133
Diller, Phyllis, 218
Dillman, Bradford, 135, 136, 173, 218
Dillon, Costa, 137
Dillon, Melinda, 99
Dimitri, Nick, 59
Dimster, Dennis, 71
Diogene, Franco, 96
DiPalma, Dario, 212
Disco Fever, 139
Discreet Charm of the Bourgeoisie, The, 159
Disko, Jane Colette, 150
Disney, Walt, 158
Disraeli, 158
Ditchburn, Anne, 101
Divine Lady, The, 158
Divorcee, The, 158
Dix, Belynda, 18
Dixon, James, 130
Dixon, Leonard, 135
Dixon, MacIntyre, 115
Dmochowski, Mariusz, 207
Dmytryk, Michael, 22
Dobbs, Frank, 138
Doble, Vainica, 206
Dobson, Tamara, 218
Dodd, Kathryn, 136
Dodd, Molly, 133
Doel, Frances, 87, 128
Dog Soldiers, 74
Doherty, Chuck, 18
Dohler, Donald M., 131
Dolan, Don, 33
Dolan, Katie, 134
Dolan, Maureen, 213
Dolan, Trent, 45
Dombasle, Arielle, 191
Dombek, James, 18
Domergue, Faith, 218
Dominguez, Berta, 30
Dona Flor and Her Two Husbands, 166
Donaggio, Pino, 136
Donahue, Troy, 218
Donald, James, 170
Donat, Lucas, 54
Donat, Peter, 39, 45, 126
Donat, Robert, 158
Donati, Sergio, 206
Donen, Stanley, 102
Donnell, Jeff, 218
Donnelly, Budd, 129
Donnelly, Dennis, 128
Donnelly, Jamie, 48
Donnelly, Ruth, 218
Donnelly, Terence A., 111
Donnelly, Terry, 24
Donnelly, Tim, 128
Donner, Richard, 152
d'Onorio, Jean Louis, 210
Donovan, Warde, 76
Donskov, Vladimir, 213
Dooley, Paul, 95
Dorelli, Johnny, 180
Dorin, Phoebe, 139
Dormann, Genevieve, 205
Dorr, Sabi, 211
Dors, Diana, 218
D'Orsay, Fifi, 218
Dossier 51, 200
Doubet, Steve, 70
Double Life, A, 158
Double Nickels, 129
Doubleday, Frank, 100
Doubles, 127
Douchet, Jean, 205
Doughty, Neal, 33
Douglas, Buddy, 112
Douglas, Damon, 126, 132
Douglas, Jerry, 87
Douglas, Kirk, 28, 206, 218
Douglas, Melvyn, 159, 218
Douglas, Michael, 10, 11, 218
Douglas, Sarah, 122
Douglas, Tom, 234
Doum, Mamadou, 205
Dourif, Brad, 78, 79, 218
Dowd, Judith, 54
Dowd, Nancy, 14
Down, Lesley-Anne, 16, 26, 218
Downey, Cheryl, 124

Downing, Frank, 10
Doyle, David, 50
Doyle, Richard, 10
Dr. Jekyll and Mr. Hyde, 158
Dr. John, 31, 38
Drach, Michel, 210
Dracula's Dog, 134
Dragon Lives, The, 211
Dragon Sister, 208
Drake, Betsy, 218
Drake, Charles, 218
Drake, Geoffrey, 202, 209
Drake, Marciee, 128
Drape, Colleen, 112
Dray, Albert, 210
Dream of Passion, A, 184
Drescher, Fran, 27
Dressler, Marie, 158
Drew, Ellen, 218
Dreyfuss, Richard, 6, 100, 143, 159, 219
Drier, Moosie, 27
Driscoll, Bobby, 158
Driscoll, Lawrason, 127
Drivas, Robert, 219
Driver, The, 59
Droeghmans, Daniel, 209
Drogosz, Leszek, 163
Dru, Joanne, 219
Dryhurst, Michael, 122, 170
Duane, Jessie Holladay, 129
Dubarry, Denise, 126
Dubbins, Don, 219
Dubeau, Catherine, 186
Dubin, Gary, 44
Dubos, Guilhaine, 209
Dubost, Paulette, 176
Dubrow, Donna R., 32
Dubs, Arthur, 139
Ducados, Coco, 191
Dudich, Robert, 31
Duell, William, 115
Duellists, The, 151
Duering, Carl, 192
Duff, Howard, 95, 219
Duff, Norwick, 122
Duffield, Michael, 203
Duffy, Pat, 127
Duffy, Patrick, 219
Dugan, Michael J., 204
Duggan, Andrew, 125, 130
Duggan, Terry, 206
DuHaime, Terri, 82
Dukakis, John, 44
Duke, Edward, 36
Duke, Patty, 159, 219
Dullea, Keir, 219
Dultz, James, 130
Dumas, Jebidiah R., 66
Dumas, Jennifer, 45
Dumas, Roger, 176
Dumont, Guy, 192
Dunaway, Faye, 7, 78, 79, 159, 219
Duncan, Andrew, 24
Duncan, Sandy, 52, 219
Dunlop, G. Thomas, 44
Dunlop, Lesley, 26
Dunmore, Beatrice, 92
Dunn, James, 158
Dunn, Stephen P., 12
Dunnam, Virginia, 136
Dunne, Irene, 219
Dunning, John, 211
Dunnock, Mildred, 219
Dunphy, Don, 134
Dupas, Jean-Francois, 194
Duperey, Anny, 204, 219
Dupray, Pierre, 105
Durante, Jimmy, 219
Durbin, Deanna, 158, 219
Durfee, Ross, 12
Durkin, Patrick, 170
Durning, Charles, 28, 42, 219
Durren, John, 129
Dusenberry, Ann, 44, 129
Dussart, Philippe, 200
Dussollier, Andre, 191, 219
Dutronc, Jacques, 162
Dutta, Dulal, 209
Duvall, Robert, 16, 219
Duvall, Shelley, 219
Dvorak, Ann, 219
Dvorska, Eva, 26
Dyer, Eddy C., 45
Dyer, Gary L., 56
Dylan, Bob, 88, 125
Dylan, Sara, 125
Dyneley, Peter, 211
Dyszel, Richard, 131
Dzierlatka, Arie, 210
Dzizmba, George, 150
Dzundza, George, 150

East of Eden, 159
Easter, Robert, 128
Eastman, Allan, 130
Easton, Joyce, 28, 100
Easton, Robert, 219
Eastwood, Clint, 6, 114, 219
Eater, 209
Eaton, Shirley, 219
Eaton, Wallas, 203
Eatwell, Brian, 62
Ebsen, Buddy, 219
Eby, Rick, 66
Eccles, Aimee, 83
Echols, Randy, 137
Eckemyr, Agneta, 219
Economu, Michael, 133
Edelman, Herbert, 112, 137
Eden, Barbara, 130, 133, 219
Edmonds, Mitchell, 78
Edwards, Blake, 60
Edwards, Dorothy, 159
Edwards, George, 133
Edwards, Henry, 62
Edwards, Patty, 128
Edwards, Paul, 134
Edwards, Vince, 219
Egan, Pat, 87
Egan, Richard, 173, 219
Ege, Julie, 207
Eggar, Samantha, 219
Eggenweiler, Robert, 95
8½, 159
Eikenberry, Jill, 24
Eilers, Sally, 234
Einbinder, Cory, 115
Eisenmann, Ike, 22
Ekberg, Anita, 219
Ekins, Bud, 66, 102
Ekland, Britt, 219
Ekmanner, Agnetta, 168
El Shenawi, Ahmed, 96
Elam, Jack, 76, 136
elan, 138
Elder, Jane, 126
Elder, Patti, 124
Eles, Sandor, 42
Elfman, Danny, 129
Elfman, Marie, 129
Elios, Tom, 24
Elizondo, Hector, 219
Elkins, Hillard, 139
Elkins, Mignon, 206
Elliott, David, 44
Elliott, Denholm, 190, 192, 212, 219
Elliott, Jack, 125
Elliott, Lang, 134, 138
Elliott, Patricia, 82
Elliott, Robert, 66
Elliott, Sam, 219
Ellis, Dave, 131
Ellis, David Graham, 213
Ellis, Joseph M., 13
Ellsworth, Nick, 202
Elman, Eugene, 126
Elmer Gantry, 159
Elmes, Frederick, 130
Elrod, Allan, 128
Elsom, Isobel, 219
Elton, Federico, 204
Ely, Ron, 219
Emde, Kathy Marie, 44
Emerson, Branch, 131
Emerson, Faye, 219
Emhardt, Robert, 135, 212
Emilfork, Daniel, 91
Emirza, Irene, 184
Emmich, Cliff, 135
Emmons, William, 125
Enberg, Dick, 46
Encinas, Alicia, 138
End of the World in Our Usual Bed in a Night Full of Rain, The, 160
End, The, 40
Enders, Robert, 189
Enforcer from Death Row, The, 205
England, Jo, 203
English, David, 36
Englund, Robert, 96, 132
Enright, Don, 127
Enserro, Michael, 219
Ensign, Michael, 96, 122
Epstein, Julius J., 20
Epstein, Phillip, 33
Epstein, Robert, 127
Erdman, Paul E., 36
Erdman, Richard, 219
Erhart, Thomas O. Jr., 54
Ericksen, Leon, 80
Erickson, C. O., 108
Erickson, Leif, 219
Ericson, John, 219
Erlichman, Martin, 10
Ermey, Lee, 219
Esemplare, Anthony, 43
Eshelman, Drew, 135

Esmond, Carl, 219
Espinosa, Julio Garcia, 207
Espinoza, James, 112
Estabrook, Howard, 234
Estrada, Angelina, 80
Eszterhas, Joe, 39
Etchverry, Michel, 191
Etherington, Colin, 122
Etting, Ruth, 234
Eunson, Dale, 138
Eure, Wesley, 128, 132
Evans, Art, 130
Evans, Dale, 138
Evans, Gene, 219
Evans, John, 137
Evans, Maurice, 219
Evans, Ray, 122
Evein, Bernard, 211
Event 1000, 127
Everett, Chad, 219
Everhardt, Rex, 122
Every, Margaret, 125
Every Which Way But Loose, 114
Evil, The, 130, 133
Ewell, Tom, 219
Ewen, Linda, 112
Executioner, The, 211
Eyeball, 210
Eyes of Laura Mars, 78
Eymon, Florence, 205
Eyraud, Marc, 191, 205, 210
Fabares, Shelley, 219
Fabi, Emilia, 182
Fabian, 139, 219
Fabian, John, 125, 127
Fabian, Paul, 135
Fabray, Nanette, 130, 133, 219
Fabre, Dominique, 209
Faces of Love, 210
Fagan, Ronald J., 27
Fairbairn, Bruce, 134
Fairbanks, Douglas, 158
Fairbanks, Douglas Jr., 219
Fairchild, June, 80
Falco, Mike, 36
Falcon, Andre, 162
Falconer, Stewart, 126
Falconnetti, Gerard, 191
Falk, Peter, 56, 57, 111, 219
False Face, 137
Falt, Dennis Lee, 135
Family Enforcer, 137
Far Shore, The, 211
Faracy, Stephanie, 46
Faraldo, Daniel, 101
Farentino, James, 219
Farentino, Tony, 82
Fargas, Antonio, 37
Fargo, James, 110, 114
Farina, Sandy, 62, 63, 219
Farleigh, Lyn, 190
Farley, Morgan, 46, 62
Farmer, Bill, 125
Farmer, Mimsy, 211
Farmer, Reginald H., 66
Farmer's Daughter, The, 158
Farnsworth, Hill, 136
Farnsworth, Richard, 90
Farquhar, Ralph, 130
Farr, Derek, 219
Farr, Felicia, 219
Farrel, John, 111
Farrell, Charles, 219
Farrell, Peggy, 116
Farris, John, 28
Farris, Mike, 18
Farrow, Mia, 84, 85, 87, 95, 219
Farrow, Tisa, 126
Fasciano, Richard, 42
Fassbinder, Rainer Werner, 211
Fast, Russ, 76
Fats, 108
Faulk, Norman, 31
Faulkner, Gay, 92
Faulkner, Graham, 219
Faulkner, James, 205
Fawcett-Majors, Farrah, 82, 219
Faye, Alice, 136, 219
Faye, Frances, 37
Fei, Lung, 204
Fei, Ou Yang So, 210
Feinstein, Alan, 138, 219
Feitelson, Benjamin, 122
Feitshans, Buzz, 130
Feldman, Edward S., 32
Feldman, Marty, 207
Feldon, Barbara, 219
Feldshuh, Tovah, 43
Felix, Otto, 80, 128
Fell, Norman, 13, 40
Fellous, Maurice, 212
Fellows, Edith, 219

Feng, Chang, 204
Feng, Ku, 211
Fenichel, Jay, 33
Fenn, Suzanne, 37
Fenton, Leslie, 234
Ferdin, Pamelyn, 128
Ferguson, Frank, 234
Ferguson, Perry II, 131
Ferrante, Traci, 138
Ferrell, Conchata, 219
Ferreol, Andrea, 209, 211, 213
Ferrer, Jose, 125, 134, 135, 158, 219
Ferrer, Mel, 132, 136, 207, 212, 219
Ferrer, Tony, 207, 211
Ferri, Marsha, 94
Ferris, Barbara, 219
Ferris, Melissa, 82
Ferry, David, 134
Ferzetti, Gabriele, 219
Fesus, Maria, 201
Fetet, Andre, 105
Feuer, Debra, 118
Fiander, Lewis, 209
Fiastri, Iaia, 180
Fiedler, John, 133
Fieguth, Monty, 203
Field, Carole H., 35
Field, Sally, 7, 40, 41, 72, 73, 219
Fielding, Athene, 42
Fielding, Jerry, 127, 170
Fields, Charlie, 16
Fields, Chip, 12
Figueroa, Ruben, 219
Filamento, Anna, 137
Filho, Arthur Costa, 166
Filiatrault, Denise, 162
Filippides, Andreas, 184
Fimple, Dennis, 94, 125, 138
Finch, Jon, 84, 85
Finch, Peter, 159
Finch, Scot, 205
Fine, Lesly, 133
Fine, Mort, 42
Fingers, 126
Finkbinder, T. G., 129
Finlay, Frank, 199
Finley, William, 28
Finney, Alan, 211
Finney, Albert, 161, 219
Finney, Jack, 120
Fiore, William J., 20
First Aid, 182
First Time, The, 174
Fiscoe, Martin, 35
Fisher, Carrie, 219
Fisher, Dave, 212
Fisher, Eddie, 219
Fisher, George, 102
Fisher, Kenneth J., 129, 136
Fisher, Steven, 56, 129
Fisk, Jack, 88, 102
F.I.S.T., 39
Fists of Bruce Lee, 212
Fitch, Louise, 128
Fitere, Jean-Marie, 194
Fitzgerald, Barry, 158
Fitzgerald, David, 95
Fitzgerald, Geraldine, 219
Fitzgerald, John D., 133
Fitzgerald, Maggie, 211
Flack, Roberta, 125
Flagg, Fannie, 13, 48
Flanagan, Gary, 164
Flanagan, Neil, 118
Flannery, Susan, 219
Flat Out, 204
Flavin, James, 219
Flaxman, John, 212
Fleck, Jerry, 126
Fleer, Alicia, 97
Fleischer, Richard, 30
Fleming, James, 126
Fleming, Lone, 213
Fleming, Marvin, 45
Fleming, Rhonda, 219
Fleming, Victor, 158
Flemyng, Robert, 219
Fletcher, Jack, 13
Fletcher, Louise, 56, 57, 159, 219
Flicker, Theodore J., 212
Flint, Christopher, 129
Flint, Derek, 45
Flintermann, Rockey, 135
Flippin, Lucy Lee, 8, 94
Flock, Brad, 122
Flora, 208
Florea, John, 129
Florence, Davone, 12
Florence, Fiona, 182
Flores, Rosa, 12
Flores, Stefano Satta, 91
Floria, John, 135
Flower, George "Buck", 139

Flower, Verkema, 132
Fluegel, Darlanne, 78
Fluellen, Joel, 31
Flynn, Ian, 126
Flynn, Mark, 129
FM, 33
Foch, Nina, 132, 219
Foley, Brian, 124
Foley, Louise, 133
Folsey, George Jr., 66
Fonda, Henry, 132, 135, 219
Fonda, Jane, 4, 6, 14, 15, 90, 112, 152, 159, 219
Fonda, Peter, 134, 219
Fondato, Marcello, 212
Fong, Benson, 116
Fong, Harold, 80
Fong, Leo, 205, 207
Fontain, Alisha, 137
Fontaine, Frank, 234
Fontaine, Joan, 158, 219
Fontelieu, Stocker, 137
For Whom the Bell Tolls, 158
Foran, Dick, 219
Forbes, Bryan, 179
Forbidden Games, 158
Force 10 from Navarone, 202
Ford, Cecil, 209
Ford, Daniel, 86
Ford, Fritz, 54
Ford, Glenn, 122, 219
Ford, Harrison, 202, 219
Ford, John, 158
Ford, Karen, 24
Foreman, Carl, 202
Forest, Mark, 220
Forman, Milos, 159
Formanez, Ulysses, 18
Foronjy, Richard, 136
Forrest, Christine, 134
Forrest, Frederic, 130
Forrest, Steve, 220
Forsberg, Tony, 168
Forslund, Constance, 107
Forster, Nik, 170
Forster, Robert, 87, 220
Forsyth, Rosemary, 127
Forsythe, Henderson, 42
Forsythe, John, 220
Fortescue, Kenneth, 91
Fortier, Robert, 95
Fortress in the Sun, 211
Fortune Cookie, The, 159
Foschi, Massimo, 206
Fosse, Bob, 159
Fosser, William B., 54
Fossey, Brigitte, 205
Foster, Barry, 199
Foster, Carole Tru, 32
Foster, Clayton, 135
Foster, Jodie, 17, 220
Foster, Lewis R., 125
Foster, Meg, 45
Fotopoulos, Dionysis, 184
Foul Play, 66
Fournel, Max, 105
Fowles, Glenys, 68
Fox Affair, The, 136
Fox, Charles, 68, 132
Fox, Dorothy, 92
Fox, Edward, 161, 170, 171, 202, 220
Fox, James, 220
Fox, John, 126
Fox, Marilyn, 35
Fox, Peter, 33
Foxworth, Robert, 54, 126, 220
Foxx, Redd, 220
Fracci, Carla, 206
Frade, Joseph, 207
Fraker, William A., 27, 46
Fraley, Joseph, 132
Frampton, Peter, 62, 63
Franchot, Richard, 131
Franciosa, Anthony, 220
Francis, Anne, 97, 220
Francis, Arlene, 220
Francis, Carole, 126
Francis, Connie, 66, 220
Francis, Raymond, 220
Franciscus, James, 42, 132, 220
Francks, Don, 220
Franco, Larry J., 68
Francois, Jacques, 211
Frank, Charles, 8, 32
Frank, David, 45, 133
Frank, Horst, 205
Frank, T. C., 125
Franken, Steve, 87
Frankfather, William, 68
Frankish, Brian E., 138
Franklin, Dan, 12
Franklin, Pamela, 220
Franklin, Fred, 100

Franklyn, William, 211
Franks, Chloe, 26
Franz, Arthur, 220
Franz, Dennis, 95
Franz, Eduard, 220
Fraser, George MacDonald, 30
Fraser, John, 206
Fraser, Ronald, 199
Fraticelli, Franco, 160
Frawley, John, 203
Frazier, Sheila, 112, 113, 220
Frazier, Sterling, 133
Frederick, Lynne, 206
Frediani, Paolo, 112
Fredrick, Joel, 100
Free Soul, A, 158
Free Spirit, 208
Freebairn-Smith, Ian, 125
Freed, Bert, 125
Freed, Burt, 131
Freeman, Al Jr., 220
Freeman, Christine, 44
Freeman, John, 66, 127
Freeman, Kathleen, 136
Freeman, Mona, 220
Freeman, Reid, 125, 130
Freiburger, James, 45
Freitag, Robert, 186
Frelon, Le, 176
French, Brian, 211
French, Bruce, 96
French Connection, The, 159
French, Leigh, 132
French Quarter, 137
French, Robin, 12
French, Susan, 44
Fresson, Bernard, 162
Frey, Leonard, 220
Frey, Sami, 186, 187
Friberg, John, 131
Fricke, Ed, 137
Fridley, Robert, 125
Friebus, Florida, 132
Friedel, Frederick R., 137
Friedenn, Neva, 128
Friedhofer, Hugo, 212
Friedkin, William, 111, 159
Friedlander, Irwin, 13
Friedman, Hanny, 78
Friedman, Kinky, 125
Friedman, Lewis, 125
Friedman, Louis, 130
Friedman, Ron, 125
Friedman, Stephen, 96
Friedmann, Stefan, 163
Friedrich, John, 130, 137
Friel, Paula, 56
Fries, Bill, 58
Frith, Anne, 131
Fritz, Roger, 211
Fritzberg, Bruce E., 131
Frodo, 104
Froehlich, Bill, 71
From Here to Eternity, 159
Fronczewski, Piotr, 207
Fruit is Ripe, The, 211
Fryer, Robert, 192
Fuchs, Manny, 105
Fudge, Alan, 50
Fuentes, Ernie, 80
Fuhrman, Ben, 18
Fuhrman, Richard, 43
Fujikawa, Jerry, 52
Fujiwara, Tommy, 137
Fukasaku, Kinji, 211
Fuller, Penny, 220
Fullwood, George, 128
Funeral Elegy, 182
Funk, Terry, 83
Funny Girl, 159
Furey, Lewis, 207
Furey, Louis, 212
Furie, Sidney J., 18
Furious Monk from Shao-Lin, The, 211
Furneaux, Yvonne, 220
Furness, John, 179
Furst, Stephen, 66, 67
Furtivos, 206
Fury, The, 28
Gabel, Martin, 220
Gable, Clark, 158
Gabor, Eva, 220
Gabor, Zsa Zsa, 220
Gage, Elizabeth, 126
Gage, George, 126
Gage, Loutz, 70
Gagliardi, Enzo, 20
Gailin, Bob, 139
Gaines, Leonard, 12
Galabru, Michel, 209
Galang, Fred, 211
Galante, Jim, 128
Gale, Bob, 35
Galfas, Timothy, 134

Galiatsos, Nilos, 184
Galik, Denise, 112, 113
Galili, Hal, 208
Gallagher, Mike, 136
Gallico, Paul, 134
Gallitti, Alberto, 182
Gallo, Fred, 18
Gallo, Lew, 56
Gam, Rita, 220
Gamble, Bill, 68
Gammell, Robin, 211
Gampu, Ken, 199, 211
Gandalf, 104
Ganz, Bruno, 192
Ganz, Isabelle, 200
Gaon, Yehoram, 204
Gaos, Lola, 206
Garber, Victor, 220
Garbo, Greta, 159, 220
Garbutt, James, 122
Garcia, Andres, 137
Garcia, Darnell, 205, 207
Garcia, Luis, 207
Garcia, Luis Alberto, 207
Garcia, Robert, 115
Garcin, Ginette, 205
Garden of the Finzi-continis, The, 159
Gardenia, Vincent, 46, 47, 220
Gardiner, Reginald, 220
Gardner, Ava, 220
Garfield, David, 129
Garfield, Julie, 115
Garfinkle, Louis, 150
Gariazzo, Mario, 212
Garland, Beverly, 220
Garland, Judy, 158
Garmes, Lee, 234
Garner, James, 220
Garner, Martin, 100
Garner, Peggy Ann, 95, 158, 220
Garr, Teri, 220
Garreaud, Jean-Francois, 194, 195
Garrett, Betty, 220
Garrett, Eliza, 66
Garrett, Leif, 126, 206
Garrett, Scott, 108
Garrison, Sean, 220
Garson, Greer, 158, 220
Gary, Lorraine, 44
Gasgarth, Gary, 136
Gaslight, 158
Gasser, Yves, 210
Gassman, Vittorio, 95, 182, 220
Gastaldi, Ernesto, 206
Gastoni, Lisa, 213
Gate of Hell, 159
Gates, Bob, 125
Gatillon, Bruno, 209
Gatsby, Martin, 137
Gatti, Marcello, 208
Gaudet, Liliane, 200
Gautier, Dick, 125
Gautier, Theophile L., 206
Gaven, Jean, 91
Gavigan, Gerry, 110
Gavin, John, 132, 220
Gavin, Weston, 122
Gavros, Costa, 148
Gayle, Monica, 131
Gaynor, Janet, 158, 159, 220
Gaynor, Mitzi, 220
Gazzara, Ben, 220
Gazzo, Michael V., 115, 126
Gearson, Monica, 192
Gee, Timothy, 179
Geer, Will, 134, 234
Geeson, Judy, 212, 220
Geisha, A, 178
Geiwitz, Richard, 131
Gelband, Alan, 130
Gelbart, Larry, 102
Gelin, Daniel, 172
Gellis, Danny, 100
Gemignani, Paul, 26
Gemser, Laura, 205
Gendron, Francois-Eric, 194
Generation X, 209
Genn, Leo, 234, 235
Genoves, Andre, 162, 186
Genta, Renzo, 206
Gentleman Tramp, The, 128
Gentleman's Agreement, 158
George, Bonnie, 42
George, Chief Dan, 220
George, Jimmy, 132
George, Susan, 137
George, Tanja, 136
Georgitsis, Phedon, 184
Gerard, Gil, 220
Gerber, Joan, 135
Gere, Richard, 88, 89, 96, 220

Germain, Gregory, 194
Germanos, Freddie, 184
Gerome, Raymond, 176
Gerringer, Robert, 115
Gerry, 125
Gert, Valeska, 205
Gertler, T., 133
Get Out Your Handkerchiefs, 156, 159
Getz, Stuart, 125
Gharib-Afshar, Parviz, 110
Gholson, Julie, 220
Ghorra, Hany, 136
Ghostley, Alice, 13, 48, 125, 130, 132
Giammarco, Nelide, 180
Gianfrancisco, Glen, 115
Giannini, Giancarlo, 160, 212, 220
Giannoni, Jorge, 207
Giant, 159
Gibb, Barry, 62
Gibb, Ken, 128
Gibb, Maurice, 62
Gibb, Robin, 62
Gibbons, Chris, 199
Gibbs, Gary, 128
Gibbs, Mike, 208
Gibbs, Tony, 39
Gibson, Alan, 127, 211
Gibson, John, 82
Gibson, Margaret, 126
Gielgud, John, 220
Gierasch, Stefan, 132
Gifford, G. Adam, 101
Gifford, Gloria, 112, 113
Gigi, 159
Gignoux, Hubert, 191
Gilbert, Lou, 235
Gilberti, Anthony, 43
Gilberti, Jennifer, 43
Gilford, Jack, 220
Gilley, Mickey, 138
Gilliam, Terry, 205
Gillis, Anne, 220
Gillis, Richard, 138
Gillmore, Margalo, 220
Gilmore, Peter, 208
Gilmore, Virginia, 220
Gilmore, Wendy, 206
Gilmour, Victor, 59
Gilpin, April, 44
Gilpin, Marc, 44, 129
Gilpin, Sally, 30
Gilroy, Frank D., 105
Gimbel, Norman, 68, 138
Gimpel, Sandy, 87
Ging, Jack, 212
Gingold, Hermione, 26, 220
Ginsberg, Allen, 125
Ginty, Robert, 14
Ginzburg, Natalia, 204
Giovagnoni, Gianni, 160
Giral, Sergio, 207
Girard, Roland, 148
Girardot, Annie, 176, 177
Girdler, William, 75
Girlfriends, 77
Giselle, 206
Gish, Lillian, 95, 159, 220
Gittes, Harry, 94
Gittler, Robert, 70
Giuffre, Gus, 34
Givney, Kathryn, 235
Glaser, Paul Michael, 220
Glaser, Sabine, 162, 200
Glass, Ron, 220
Glass, Seaman, 136
Glass, Sydney A., 12
Glattes, Wolfgang, 16, 91
Gleason, Jackie, 220
Glenn, Pierre-William, 87
Glick, Earl A., 164
Glick, Norman, 164
Glickman, Paul, 125
Glinwood, Terry, 207
Globus, Yoram, 204, 206
Glover, John, 82
Glover, William, 100
Go Tell the Spartans, 86
Gobel, George, 13
Gochis, Constantine S., 129
Gochman, Len, 131
Godar, Godfrey A., 18
Goddard, Mark, 132
Goddard, Paulette, 220
Godel, Armen, 210
Godfather Part II, The, 159
Godfather, The, 159
Godfrey, Arthur, 107
God's Gun, 206
Goetz, Siggi, 211
Goff, John, 137
Goff, John F., 70
Goff, Max, 137
Goin' Coconuts, 137
Goin' South, 94
Going My Way, 158
Goitein, Alex E., 137
Golan, Menahem, 204, 206

Gold, Bert, 33
Gold, Donald, 45
Gold, Jack, 175
Gold, Jill, 137
Goldan, Wolf, 211
Goldberg, Tikki, 128
Goldblatt, Mark, 136
Goldblum, Jeff, 120, 121, 130
Golden, Annie, 220
Goldfinger, Michael, 137
Goldman, William, 108
Goldoni, Lelia, 96, 120, 121
Goldsmith, Jerry, 10, 50, 54, 108, 135, 192
Goldsmith, Joel, 128
Goldsmith, Jonathan, 86
Goldsmith, Paul, 125
Goldstein, Bob, 20
Gollum, 104
Gomez, Manuel Octavio, 207
Gomez, Rita, 112
Gone with the Wind, 158
Gonneau, George, 211
Gonzales, George, 134
Gonzales, Roberto, 137
Gonzales-Gonzalez, Pedro, 220
Gonzalez, Armando, 56
Gonzalez, Sara, 207
Gonzalez, Tomas, 207
Good Earth, The, 158
Good Guys Wear Black, 130, 132
Goodbye Franklin High, 129
Goodbye Girl, The, 143, 159
Goodbye, Mr. Chips, 158
Goodman, David Zelag, 78
Goodman, Dody, 48
Goodnoff, Irv, 132, 134
Goodrow, Garry, 68
Goodrow, Michael, 128
Goodwin, Angela, 211
Goodwin, Gordon, 137
Goodwin, Richard, 84
Goodwin, Ron, 17, 202
Goorwitz, Allen, 111, 126, 220
Goplerud, Hal, 80
Gord, Ken, 164
Gordon, Bob, 128
Gordon, Bruce, 136
Gordon, Clarke, 46
Gordon, Fredi O., 83
Gordon, Gale, 220
Gordon, Gerti, 192
Gordon, Hannah, 190
Gordon, Julie Ann, 131
Gordon, Keith, 44
Gordon, Lance, 208
Gordon, Lawrence, 40, 59
Gordon, Lloyd, 129
Gordon, Margie, 100
Gordon, Ruth, 114, 159, 220
Gordon, Steve, 8
Gordy, Melvin G., 75
Gorenstein, Friedrikh, 188
Goring, Marius, 220
Gorman, Cliff, 24, 25, 220
Gorman, Ray K., 135
Gorney, Walter, 43
Gornick, Michael, 134
Gorshin, Frank, 125
Gortner, Marjoe, 127, 220
Goslar, Juergen, 205
Gossett, Louis, 220
Gotell, Walter, 192
Gothard, Michael, 208
Gottlieb, Carl, 44
Gottlieb, Morton, 106
Gough, Lloyd, 20, 125
Gough, Michael, 192
Gould, Elliott, 50, 51, 134, 220
Gould, Harold, 8, 220
Gould, Heywood, 192
Goulet, Robert, 220
Goure, 205
Gourson, Jeff, 18, 33
Gouw, Alex, 210
Gover, Michael, 122
Gowans, Kip, 26
Gowans, Mike, 36
Gowdy, Curt, 46
Gowers, Patrick, 189
Goya, Lydia, 83
Graduate, The, 159
Graef, Roger, 205
Graf, Allan, 59
Graham, Angelo, 39, 111, 132
Graham, Anita, 91
Graham, Gerrit, 37
Graham, John Michael, 137
Graham-Cox, Michael, 190
Grahame, Gloria, 158, 220

Granada, Jose Rodriguez, 138
Grand, Elizabeth, 126
Grand Hotel, 158
Grandey, Jerry, 38, 48, 124
Granger, Farley, 210, 220
Granger, Stewart, 199, 220
Granier-Deferre, Pierre, 210
Grant, Barra, 101
Grant, Cary, 159, 220
Grant, Kathryn, 220
Grant, Lee, 54, 135, 159, 220
Grant, Tom, 130
Granville, Bonita, 220
Grapes of Wrath, The, 158
Grappelli, Stephane, 115
Grasshoff, Alex, 138
Gratsos, Xenia, 212
Gratzer, Alan, 33
Grauman, Sid, 158
Graver, Gary, 128, 129, 134
Graves, Peter, 220
Gravina, Carla, 212
Gray, Charles, 36
Gray, Coleen, 220
Gray, Dobie, 31
Gray Lady Down, 127
Gray, Robert, 97
Gray, Vivean, 203
Graysmark, John, 170
Grayson, Kathryn, 220
Grayson, Kurt, 139
Grease, 48
Great Brain, The, 133
Great Georgia Bank Hoax, The, 107
Great Lie, The, 158
Great Smokey Roadblock, The, 132
Great Ziegfeld, The, 158
Greatest Show on Earth, The, 158
Greco, Fabrice, 211
Greco, Kristien, 128
Greek Tycoon, The, 42
Green, Gerald, 137
Green, Joseph, 125
Green, Maxine, 70
Green, Michael, 30
Green, Terry, 137
Green, Walon, 111, 139
Green, Walt, 72
Greenberg, Adam, 204
Greenberg, Bob, 130
Greenberg, Robbie, 130
Greene, Angela, 235
Greene, Bob, 37
Greene, David, 127
Greene, Ellen, 221
Greene, Lorne, 129, 220
Greene, Richard, 221
Greene, Stanley, 92
Greenfield, Howard, 82
Greenholz, Don, 131
Greenhut, Robert, 64
Greenlaw, Charles F., 122
Greenough, Rich, 66
Greenwald, Martin W., 137
Greenwood, Charlotte, 235
Greenwood, Joan, 221
Greer, Dan, 34
Greer, Jane, 221
Greer, Michael, 221
Gregorio, Rose, 78
Gregory, Mary Ethel, 126
Grendel, Frederic, 194
Grey, Joel, 159, 221
Grey, Samantha, 132
Grey, Virginia, 221
Gribbin, Robert, 137
Gribble, Bernard, 36
Griem, Helmut, 221
Grier, Rod, 70
Grier, Roosevelt, 13
Grieve, Russ, 208
Grifasi, Joe, 150
Griffen, Myron Peter, 126
Griffin, Jack, 20
Griffin, Peter, 70
Griffin, Sean P., 132
Griffis, Lynn, 56
Griffith, Andy, 221
Griffith, D. W., 158
Griffith, Hugh, 159, 221
Griffith, James, 129
Griffith, Kenneth, 199
Griffith, Kristin, 64, 65, 141
Griffith, Melanie, 221
Griffith, Peter, 137
Griffith, Tom, 131
Griffith, William, 44
Griffiths, Richard, 209
Grigoryev, Konstantin, 188
Grillo, Michael, 118
Grillo, Mike, 133
Grillo, Nick, 130
Grimes, Chester, 100
Grimes, Gary, 221

Grimes, Stephen, 23
Grimes, Tammy, 82, 139, 221
Grimm, Maria, 125
Grisman, David, 115
Grissmer, John, 137
Grizzard, George, 90, 221
Grodin, Charles, 46, 47, 221
Grodnik, Daniel, 133
Grody, Kathryn, 100
Groh, David, 221
Grooman, Stacy, 66
Grosbard, Ulu, 23
Gross, Charles, 132
Grossberg, Jack, 16
Grover, Cynthia, 44
Grow, Ron, 10
Grunberg, Alex, 128
Gruner, Mark, 44
Grunstein, Pierre, 211
Grusin, Dave, 46
Guard, Christopher, 26
Guardino, Harry, 134, 221
Guarnieri, Ennio, 210
Guber, Peter, 96
Gucciardo, Steve, 43
Gueramian, Behrooz, 110
Guerra, Tonino, 204
Guerrero, Chavo, 8
Guerrero, Evelyn, 128
Guess Who's Coming to Dinner, 159
Guest, Christopher, 77
Guest, Don, 12
Gueye, Oumar, 205
Guibet, Henri, 204
Guillemot, Agnes, 205
Guillermin, John, 84
Guiness, Matthew, 161
Guinn, Rick, 127
Guinness, Alec, 159, 221
Guiomar, Julien, 162
Guittard, Laurence, 26, 82
Gulkin, Harry, 212
Gulpilil, 203
Gummer, Christopher, 131
Gundlach, Robert, 78, 116
Gunn, Moses, 221
Guralnick, Robert, 137
Gusmao, Mario, 166
Gustafson, Pontius, 168
Guthrie, Arlo, 125
Gutierrez, Manuel, 206
Gutman, Walter, 129
Guttenberg, Steve, 192
Gutteridge, Lucy, 42
Guy, Tony, 190
Guyot, Raymonde, 200
Guzman, Pato, 24
Guzman, Patricio, 204
Gwenn, Edmund, 158
Gwillim, David, 221
Gwinn, Edith, 129

Haber, David, 59
Haber, David M., 50
Haber, Mark, 82
Habich, Matthias, 205
Hack, Shelley, 130, 131
Hackett, Buddy, 221
Hackett, Joan, 221
Hackman, Bob, 108
Hackman, Gene, 122, 159, 221
Hackney, John, 209
Hackney, Pearl, 206
Haddon, Dale, 221
Haenel, Mary Ann, 150
Hagen, Claire, 133
Hagen, Laurie, 56
Hagen, Ross, 133
Hagen, Uta, 192, 193
Hager, Betty, 136
Haggarty, Don, 128
Haggerty, H. B., 8, 128
Hagman, Larry, 122, 127, 221
Haid, Charles, 74, 116
Haines, Garth, 210
Haines, Patricia, 210
Haitkin, Jacques, 129, 138
Hakobian, Alex, 136
Hale, Barbara, 221
Haley, Jackie Earle, 134
Hall, Bruce, 33
Hall, Chuck, 131
Hall, Peter, 206
Hall, Sands, 82, 115
Hall, Terrance, 205
Hall, Tom T., 133
Hallam, Paul, 213
Hallas, Lisa, 59
Haller, Mike, 14
Hallett, Neal, 210
Halligan, Dick, 86
Halloween, 137
Halmi, Robert, 59
Halpin, Sandy, 130
Halsey, Richard, 130
Halty, Jim, 31, 66

Ham, Donald R., 135
Hambling, Gerry, 96
Hamburger, David, 72
Hamill, Mark, 53, 221
Hamilton, Fenton, 130
Hamilton, Gay, 161
Hamilton, George, 221
Hamilton, Guy, 202
Hamilton, Margaret, 221
Hamilton, Melody, 18
Hamilton, Murray, 31, 44
Hamilton, Neil, 221
Hamlet, 158
Hamlin, Harry, 102
Hamlisch, Marvin, 106, 124
Hammett, Olivia, 203
Hammond, Johnny, 205
Hampshire, Susan, 221
Hampton, James, 52
Hancock, John, 68
Haney, David, 135
Hankin, Larry, 127
Hanna, Brian, 138
Hanna, Walter, 138
Hannemann, Walter, 32
Hansen, Joachim, 192, 193
Hansen, Joshua, 45
Hanson, John, 208
Hanwright, Joseph C., 138
Happy, Clifford, 66, 102
Hapsas, Alex, 82
Harada, Yoshio, 198
Harari, Clement, 105
Hardin, Ty, 221
Harding, Ann, 221
Hardstark, Michael, 131
Hardy, Hagood, 211
Hardy, Oliver, 129
Hare, Will, 46
Harewood, Dorian, 127, 221
Harford, Betty, 18
Hargreaves, Christine, 209
Hargrove, Robert, 96
Harht, Wayne, 136
Harkins, John, 127
Harkness, Sam, 27
Harmon, John, 137
Harmon, Kelly, 112
Harmon, Mark, 90
Harper, Ken, 92
Harper, Valerie, 221
Harper Valley P.T.A., 130, 133
Harpman, Fred, 54
Harrigan, Michael, 122
Harrington, Cleo, 134
Harrington, Pat, 221
Harris, Anthony, 128
Harris, Barbara, 102, 221
Harris, Burtt, 92
Harris, Cassandra, 42
Harris, Emmylou, 38
Harris, G. E., 137
Harris, George II, 122
Harris, Greg, 44
Harris, Jack H., 78
Harris, Johnny, 133
Harris, Julie, 17, 221
Harris, Larnell, 97
Harris, Mike, 211
Harris, Richard, 199, 221
Harris, Richard A., 134
Harris, Rosemary, 192, 221
Harrison, Noel, 221
Harrison, Paul Carter, 130
Harrison, Rex, 30, 158, 159, 221
Harrow, Lisa, 209
Harry and Tonto, 159
Hart, Christina, 127
Hart, Harry, 208
Hart, John F., 126
Hart, Nancy, 132
Hart, Stephen, 108
Harte, Michael, 108
Hartley, Gene, 128
Hartman, David, 221
Hartman, Elizabeth, 221
Hartzell, Duane, 132
Harvey, 158
Harvey, Raymond, 137
Hasebe, Keiji, 198
Hashimoto, Richard, 130
Haskell, Jimmie, 125
Hasley, William, 59
Hasse, O. E., 235
Hassett, Marilyn, 32
Hassett, Ray, 122
Hastings, Bob, 133
Hastings, Chad, 138
Hastings, Ian, 209
Hastings, Stephanie, 137
Hatfield, John, 68
Hattinga, Ryno, 199
Haufrect, Alan, 10
Haugse, William, 130
Hauser, Robert B., 127
Haver, June, 221
Havers, Nigel, 91

Haviv, Ronit, 138
Haviv, Yuri, 138
Havoc, June, 125, 221
Hawker, John, 112
Hawkins, Anthony, 54
Hawkins, Edward H., 125
Hawkins, Jack, 208
hawkins, Robert, 16
Hawkins, Ronnie, 38, 125
Hawkins, Sadie, 16
Hawkins, Screamin' Jay, 27
Hawks, Howard, 159
Hawn, Goldie, 68, 69, 159, 221
Haworth, Ted, 82
Hawthorne, Nigel, 190
Hay, Alexandra, 136
Haya, Maria Eugenia, 207
Hayden, Crystal, 43
Hayden, Larry, 102
Hayden, Linda, 192, 221
Hayden, Robert, 43
Hayden, Sterling, 115, 221
Hayes, Billy, 96
Hayes, Dallas Edward, 78
Hayes, Helen, 17, 158, 159, 221
Hayles, Brian, 208
Haynes, Lloyd, 132
Hayward, David, 125
Hayward, Susan, 159
Hayward, William, 134
Hayworth, Rita, 221
Haze, Jonathan, 139
Hazelhurst, Wayne, 80
Hazing, The, 125
Head, Dino, 137
Head, Edith, 71, 100
Healey, Myron, 32
Heard, John, 221
Heatherton, Joey, 221
Heaven Can Wait, 46
Heckart, Eileen, 159, 221
Hedison, David, 221
Heflin, Marta, 95
Heflin, Van, 158
Hegierski, Kathleen, 68
Hegyes, Robert, 221
Hehn, Sascha, 205
Heiner, Barta Lee, 126
Heininger, Jan, 75
Heinz, Gerhard, 211
Heiress, The, 158
Heitzer, Don, 37
Helander, Mats, 168
Helland, Eric, 45
Heller, Paul, 127, 212
Heller, Rosilyn, 124
Hellman, Jerome, 14
Hellwig, Klaus, 210
Helm, Levon, 38
Helmick, Paul, 90
Hemingway, Carole, 75
Hemmings, David, 30, 221
Hemphill, Ray, 18
Henderson, Don, 71, 132, 170
Henderson, Marcia, 221
Henderson, Richard, 203
Henderson, Robert, 122
Hendrix, Gary, 112
Hendrix, Wanda, 221
Hendry, Gloria, 221
Henig, Dov, 204
Henner, Marilu, 96
Henreid, Paul, 221
Henriksen, Lance, 54
Henry, Buck, 46, 221
Henry, Gregg, 127
Henry, John, 102
Henshaw, Eric, 136
Henshaw, Jim, 130
Hepburn, Audrey, 159, 221
Hepburn, Katharine, 71, 158, 159, 221
Herald, Peter V., 68
Herbert, Diana, 131
Herbert, Percy, 199
Herbert, Pitt, 133
Hercules, Evan, 96
Herd, Richard, 39
Here Come the Tigers, 130, 132
Heresmann, Eric, 204
Hergenroeder, Ken, 128
Herman, Eleanor, 137
Hermosa, Leila, 207
Hernandez, Bernabe, 207
Hernandez, Wilfredo, 116
Herndon, Walter Scott, 72, 75, 134
Heroux, Denis, 194
Herrera, Jorge, 204, 207
Herrero, Subas, 137
Herring, Pembroke, 68
Herriot, James, 209
Herrmann, Bernard, 130
Herrmann, Edward, 16, 119

Herron, Robert, 102
Hershewe, Michael, 31, 96, 100
Hersholt, Jean, 158
Hertford, Bruce, 126
Hertford, Carol, 126
Herzog, Arthur, 135
Hessey, Russ, 120
Heston, Charlton, 30, 127, 159, 221
Hewitson, Michael, 35
Hewitt, Alan, 135
Hewitt, Robert, 211
Hewlett, Bob, 136
Heywood, Anne, 221
Hice, Fred, 66, 87
Hickey, Bill, 43
Hickman, Darryl, 221
Hickman, Dwayne, 221
Hicks, Chuck, 102
Hicks, Hilly, 86, 127
Hicks, Parris, 18, 150
Hieronymous, Richard, 128
Higgins, Colin, 68
Higgins, Doug, 45
Higgins, Joe, 125
Higgins, Michael, 115
High Noon, 158
High Rolling in a Hot Corvette, 211
High-Ballin', 134
Higino, Raimundo, 166
Hildoldt, Lise, 122
Hildyard, Jack, 199
Hilger, Karen, 18
Hill, Arthur, 221
Hill, Debra, 137
Hill, George Roy, 159
Hill, James, 208
Hill, Mariana, 126
Hill, Steven, 221
Hill, Terence, 221
Hill, Walter, 59
Hiller, Wendy, 159, 221
Hilliard, Harriet, 221
Hilling, John, 179
Hills Have Eyes, The, 208
Himes, Carol, 70
Himes, John, 128
Hinchman, Bert, 135
Hindle, Art, 120
Hindman, Earl, 111
Hines, Patrick, 111
Hiney, William M., 125, 137
Hingle, Pat, 221
Hinton, Darby, 129, 132
Hiott, Steve, 131
Hi-Riders, 132
Hirotsu, Mitsuo, 178
Hirsch, Judd, 115
Hirsch, Paul, 28, 115
Hirsch, Tina, 59
Hirschfeld, Gerald, 10
Hirt, Eleonore, 156
Hitchcock, Mike, 135
Hitchcock, Pat, 126
Hitchhike to Hell, 137
Hively, George, 102
Hively, Jack, 128
Hoban, Russell, 135
Hobbs, Ron, 150
Hobson, Al, 133
Hoddy, Steve, 127
Hodges, Clay, 102
Hodges, Michael, 54
Hoelscher, Heinz, 211
Hoenack, Jeremy, 136
Hoffer, William, 96
Hoffman, Basil, 90
Hoffman, Dustin, 23, 221
Hoffman, Guy, 194
Hoffman, Leslie, 35, 87
Hoffman, Mike, 14
Hoffman, Todd, 137
Hoffmeister, John, 42
Hogan, Susan, 130
Hokanson, Mary Alan, 82
Holbrook, Hal, 50, 51, 211, 221
Holchak, Victor, 125
Holcomb, Sarah, 66
Holden, Diana, 124
Holden, William, 54, 55, 159, 221
Holdridge, Lee, 32, 116, 118, 212
Holender, Adam, 131
Holland, Anthony, 20
Holland, Eric, 125
Hollander, Adam, 137
Holliday, Judy, 158
Holliday, Polly, 8
Holliday, Sasha, 37
Holliman, Earl, 221
Hollis, Glen, 136
Hollis, Jeff, 135
Hollis, John, 122
Hollman, Winnie, 78
Holloway, Jean, 136

Holloway, Stanley, 221
Hollywood Disco Dancers, 139
Hollywood, Peter, 138
Holm, Celeste, 125, 158, 221
Holmes, Christopher, 62
Holmes, Pam, 207
Holston, Rand, 33
Holt, Bob, 135
Holt, Denis, 175
Holzman, Allan, 173
Homeier, Skip, 128, 221
Homolka, Oscar, 235
Hong, James, 86
Hong Kong Strongman, 208
Honthaner, Ron, 76
Hood, Don, 37, 137
Hood, Randall, 212
Hooker, Bill, 66
Hooks, Robert, 221
Hooper, 72
Hooper, Peter, 128
Hoover, Mike, 139
Hoover, Phil, 127
Hope, Bob, 158, 159, 221
Hope, Harry, 129, 134
Hope, Ruth, 164
Hopkins, Alan, 92
Hopkins, Allan, 115
Hopkins, Anthony, 108, 109, 179
Hopkins, Bo, 96
Hopkins, J. Allan, 43
Hopkins, Shirley Knight, 208, 223
Hopper, Dennis, 221
Hora, John, 139
Hordern, Michael, 175, 190
Horino, Tad, 86
Horne, Lena, 92, 221
Horner, Chris, 102
Horner, Harry, 59, 118
Horner, Shelley, 132
Horon, Judy, 129
Horton, Louisa, 131
Horton, Robert, 221
Horton, Russell, 77
Horvath, Charles, 235
Hoskins, Troy, 135
Hot Lead and Cold Feet, 76
Hot Tomorrows, 129
Hotton, Donald, 80
Hou, Chow Hiap, 210
Houck, Joy Jr., 125
Hough, John, 22, 119
Hough, Stan, 125
Houghton, Don, 211
Houghton, James, 35
Houghton, Katharine, 221
House Calls, 20
House, Dana, 127, 132
Houseman, John, 56, 57, 159, 222
Houser, Jerry, 108, 222
Houston, Donald, 222
Houston, Robert, 208
Hoven, Louise, 130, 132
Hovey, Tim, 222
How Green Was My Valley, 158
Howard, Andrea, 130
Howard, Bob, 36
Howard, Clint, 133
Howard, Dennis, 86
Howard, Ken, 222
Howard, Mel, 78, 116
Howard, Peter, 42
Howard, Ron, 222
Howard, Ronald, 222
Howard, Trevor, 122, 189, 205, 222
Howden, Mike, 76
Howell, Chris, 128
Howells, Ursula, 222
Howerd, Frankie, 62, 63
Howes, Sally Ann, 222
Hoy, Maysie, 96
Hsi-ying, Wen, 211
Hsu, Victor, 130
Hsueh, Nancy, 20
Hubbard, Janet, 125
Hubert, Axel, 97
Huckabee, Cooper, 68
Hud, 159
Huddleston, Bob, 137
Huddleston, David, 50
Hudkins, John, 102
Hudson Brothers, 133
Hudson, Garth, 38
Hudson, Jarvais, 118
Hudson, Rock, 87, 222
Huet, Henri-Jacques, 194
Huff, Brent, 128
Huffman, David, 39, 124, 222
Hughes and Harlow: Angels in Hell, 125
Hughes, Barnard, 222
Hughes, Beulah, 42

Hughes, Charles, 139
Hughes, Harold, 97
Hughes, Kathleen, 222
Hughes, Wendy, 211
Hughes, Whitey, 133, 138
Hugo, Michel, 75
Hulbert, Jack, 235
Hulce, Thomas, 18, 19, 66
Hull, Josephine, 158
Hume, Alan, 173, 208
Hung, Hwa I., 211
Hung, Li, 204
Hunnicutt, Arthur, 222
Hunnicutt, Donnis, 137
Hunnicutt, Gayle, 105, 222
Hunt, Allan, 45
Hunt, Ed, 164
Hunt, Marsha, 222
Hunt, Peter H., 137
Hunter, John, 130
Hunter, Kim, 158, 222
Hunter, Tab, 222
Huppert, Isabelle, 194, 195
Hursey, Sherry, 137
Hurst, David, 192
Hurst, Rick, 52
Hurt, John, 96, 99, 190
Hurt, Marybeth, 64, 65, 141
Hurwit, Lawrence S., 133
Husky, Ferlin, 129
Hussey, Olivia, 84, 85
Hussey, Ruth, 222
Hustis, Pat, 100
Huston, Craig, 46
Huston, Jimmy, 125, 135
Huston, John, 158, 222
Huston, Walter, 158
Hutchinson, James Jr., 31
Hutton, Betty, 222
Hutton, Lauren, 95, 222
Hutton, Robert, 222
Hyams, Peter, 50
Hyde, David, 126
Hyde-White, Wilfrid, 222
Hyer, Martha, 222
Hyland, Mary, 70
Hylands, Scott, 18
Hyman, Dick, 137
Hyman, Ed, 31
Hyman, Richard, 125
I Wanna Hold Your Hand, 35
I Want to Live, 159
Iacangelo, Peter, 96
Ibbetson, Arthur, 26, 175, 209
Ice Castles, 124
Idziak, Slawomir, 207
If Ever I See You Again, 130, 131
Iglehart, James, 137
Igneri, Pasquale, 43
Igneri, Vincent, 43
Iizumi, Seikichi, 198
Illouz, Maurine, 176
Illumination, 212, 213
Imhoff, Gary, 135
Imi, Tony, 119, 179
In Old Chicago, 158
In the Heat of the Night, 159
Inch, Jim, 132
Incident at Muc Wa, 86
Indian Summer, 212
Informer, The, 158
Ingalls, Dee, 124
Ingalls, Joyce, 83
Ingels, Marty, 222
Ingham, Jill, 122
Ingham, Robert E., 54
Ingmarsdotter, Sylvia, 196
Ingram, Donna Patrice, 92
Inheritance, The, 210
Inn, The, 182
Innes, Michael, 17
Inness, Jean, 235
Insinnia, Albert, 53
Interiors, 64
International Velvet, 179
Invasion of the Body Snatchers, 120
Investigation of a Citizen above Suspicion, 159
Ioannou, John, 42
Ipale, Aharon, 137
Irby, Glen, 18
Ireland, John, 131, 222
Irizarry, Gloria, 116
Irricari, Gloria, 70
Irving, Amy, 28, 29
Irwin, Mark, 164
Isaac, Leon, 137
Isaksson, Ulla, 168
Ishihara, Hatsune, 134
Ishii, Turno, 211
Island of the Damned, The, 209
Isle, Evans, 128
Israel, Irving, 135

It Happened One Night, 158
It Lives Again, 130
It Shouldn't Happen to a Vet, 209
It's Alive, 130
It's Not the Size That Counts, 212
Ives, Burl, 159, 222
Iwashita, Kiyoshi, 198
Iwashita, Shima, 198
Jabara, Paul, 130
Jabbour, Gabriel, 148
Jack, Del, 139
Jackman, Tom, 52
Jackson, Anne, 222
Jackson, Clinton, 92
Jackson, Glenda, 20, 21, 159, 189, 222
Jackson, Gordon, 175
Jackson, Kathryn, 45
Jackson, Leonard, 115
Jackson, Michael, 92, 93
Jackson, Sherry, 135
Jacob Two-Two Meets the Hooded Fang, 139, 212
Jacobi, Derek, 175
Jacobi, Lou, 222
Jacobs, Allan A., 134
Jacobs, Jacqueline, 131
Jacobs, Jim, 48
Jacobs, Jon Ian, 80, 81
Jacobs, Lawrence-Hilton, 130
Jacobs, Newton P., 128, 131
Jacobsen, Henning, 129
Jacobson, Jill, 135
Jacobson, Steven, 137
Jacobson, Tom, 128
Jacoby, Joseph, 107
Jacoby, Scott, 131, 132, 222
Jacquet, Jeffrey, 22
Jaeckel, Richard, 129, 222
Jaeger, Claude, 191
Jaffe, Herb, 74
Jaffe, Sam, 222
Jaffrey, Saeed, 209
Jagger, Dean, 158, 222
Jake, 52
Jamerson, Thomas, 68
James, Allan, 122
James, Anthony, 22, 133
James, Brion, 53
James, Carol, 58
James, Clifton, 222
James, Dennis, 8
James, Jim, 211
James, Ken, 211
James, Kent, 58
James, Lisa, 45
James, Peter, 110
James, Rachel Nicholas, 213
Jamison, Peter, 35, 133
Jamison-Olsen, Mikki, 34
Janczar, Tadeusz, 163
Jandl, Ivan, 158
Janes, Loren, 94
Janis, Conrad, 70
Jankovic, Stole, 212
Jannings, Emil, 158
Jansen, Pierre, 194
Janss, Ed, 139
Janssen, David, 222
Jarman, Claude Jr., 158, 222
Jarre, Maurice, 30
Jarreau, Susan Player, 131
Jason, Peter, 59
Jason, Rick, 222
Jastrow, Terry, 33
Javet, Francoise, 176
Jaws 2, 44
Jay, Tony, 42
Jeakins, Dorothy, 16
Jean, Gloria, 222
Jeavons, Colin, 206
Jefferies, Philip M., 48, 54
Jeffers, Chris, 127
Jeffers, Michael, 83
Jeffrey, Cheryl, 80
Jeffrey, Peter, 96
Jeffreys, Anne, 222
Jeffries, Lionel, 222
Jemma, Ottavio, 213
Jendly, Roger, 210
Jenkins, George, 90
Jennifer, 130, 132
Jennings, Claudia, 128
Jennings, Will, 31
Jensen, Keith, 33
Jensen, Keith Lane, 87
Jenson, Linda, 137
Jephcott, Samuel C., 130
Jergens, Adele, 222
Jerome, Patti, 62
Jessel, George, 222

Jessie, DeWayne, 66, 125, 130
Jessop, Peter, 206
Jessup, Robert, 135
Jett, sue, 131
Jewison, Norman, 39
Jeyes, Jazzer, 199
Jezebel, 158
Ji, Chen Li, 210
Jinda, Siresh, 209
Job, Enrico, 160
Jobe, Bill, 44
Jobin, Peter, 130
Joe Panther, 138
Joelson, Jim, 125
Joffe, Charles H., 64
Johar, I. S., 84, 85
John, Gottfried, 211
Johnny Belinda, 158
Johnny Eager, 158
Johnny Rotten and the Sex Pistols, 209
Johnny Thunders & the Heartbreakers, 209
Johns, Anne, 137
Johns, Glynis, 222
Johns, Stan, 18
Johnson, Anthony, 70
Johnson, Arch, 70
Johnson, Ben, 135, 159
Johnson, Bernard, 125
Johnson, Beverley, 131
Johnson, Carlton, 92
Johnson, Celia, 222
Johnson, Craig, 92
Johnson, Dave, 82
Johnson, Donna R. W., 126
Johnson, Gene, 44
Johnson, George, 18
Johnson, Gray, 138
Johnson, Harold C., 95
Johnson, Karl, 80
Johnson, Kay Cousins, 132
Johnson, Lamont, 82
Johnson, Laurie, 208, 209
Johnson, Louis, 92
Johnson, Lynn-Holly, 124
Johnson, Mark, 102, 111
Johnson, Page, 222
Johnson, Rafer, 222
Johnson, Richard, 208, 213, 222
Johnson, Russell, 137
Johnson, Sandy, 137
Johnson, Sunny, 66, 137
Johnson, Van, 222
Johnson, Victoria, 164
Johnston, Amy, 70, 130, 132
Johnston, J. J., 132
Johnston, Jane A., 53
Johnstone, Anna Hill, 115
Joi, Marilyn, 135
Jolley, I. Stanford, 235
Jolley, Stan, 115
Jolliffe, Muriel, 88
Joly, Sylvie, 156
Jones, Al, 138
Jones, Alan, 60
Jones, Amy, 53
Jones, Anna, 210
Jones, Ben, 138
Jones, Bob, 189
Jones, Buster, 70
Jones, Carolyn, 222
Jones, Christopher, 222
Jones, Claude Earl, 35
Jones, Clifton, 190
Jones, Deacon, 46, 136
Jones, Dean, 97, 222
Jones, Don, 128
Jones, Eddie, 96
Jones, Freddie, 211
Jones, Grandpa, 129
Jones, Hank, 52
Jones, Jack, 222
Jones, James Earl, 222
Jones, Jay D., 95
Jones, Jeffrey, 95
Jones, Jennifer, 158, 222
Jones, John Randolph, 78
Jones, Lyall, 91
Jones, Parnelli, 127
Jones, Paula, 102
Jones, Robert C., 14, 46
Jones, Robert J. Jr., 54
Jones, Shirley, 159, 222
Jones, Terry, 205
Jones, Tiffany, 137
Jones, Tom, 222
Jones, Tommy Lee, 16, 78, 79, 222
Joplin, Scott, 125
Jordan, Bill, 70
Jordan, Curtis, 136
Jordan, Jo, 118
Jordan, Porter, 132
Jordan, Richard, 64, 65, 222
Jordan, Tom, 32

Jordan, Will, 35
Jordan, William, 127
Jorjani, Fereidun G., 136
Jory, Victor, 222
Joseph, Al, 78
Joseph, John, 139
Joseph, Paul A., 133
Josephson, Erland, 196
Josephson, Leo, 46
Jourdan, Louis, 36, 222
Jove, 130
Joya, Mario Garcia, 207
Jozefson, Jack, 70
Juban, Dennis, 18
Judgment at Nuremberg,
159
Juego, El, 209
Julia, 146, 159, 159
Julia, Raul, 78
Julian, Chuck, 122
Julien, Sandra, 204
Jump, Gordon, 20, 126
Junior, 65
Junkersdorf, Eberhard, 205
Jurado, Katy, 222
Jurasik, Peter, 97
Jurgensen, Randy, 111
Jurgensen, Albert, 210
Jurgenson, Aseneth, 66
Jurgenson, Randy, 122
Jury, Rick, 126
Just Crazy About Horses,
139
Justin, John, 170
Justis, Bill, 72
Justrich, Tracy, 62
Juttner, Christian, 22, 35
Juvet, Nathalie, 200
Jympson, John, 26
Kaclik, Nancy Coan, 94
Kagan, Jeremy Paul, 100,
125
Kahan, Stephen, 122
Kahane, B. B., 159
Kahler, Wolf, 192
Kahn, Madeline, 56, 57,
222
Kahn, Michael, 78, 124
Kahn, Sheldon, 106
Kahn, Shelly, 96
Kahnemoui, Mohammad,
110
Kaliban, Bob, 131
Kallimeyer, Liz, 82
Kalloaniotes, Helena, ¥25
Kalogeratos, Jerry, 137
Kalyagin, Alexander, 188
Kamel, Stanley, 53
Kaminsky, Mike, 136
Kampman, Steve, 130
Kane, Alice J., 24
Kane, Artie, 78
Kane, C. Vernon, 133
Kane, Carol, 222
Kane, Dennis, 137
Kane, Michael, 86
Kane, Thomas John, 82
Kane, Tom, 24
Kang, Kam, 208
Kani, John, 199
Kantor, Paul, 109
Kaplan, Jonathan, 222
Kaplan, Mady, 150
Kaplan, Nelly, 186
Kaprall, Bo, 33
Karalashville, M., 208
Karalexis, Serafim, 209
Karam, Elena, 39
Karen, Debbie, 211
Karen, James, 39
Karen, Michael, 211
Karin, Rita, 100
Karina, Anna, 180
Kark, Raymond, 126
Karlan, John, 136
Karlin, Fred, 127, 138
Karn, William, 31
Karnafel, Victoria, 150
Karp, Ivan, 24
Karras, Alex, 33, 139, 212
Karron, Richard, 8
Kasatsu, Clyde, 86
Kasem, Casey, 139
Kashfi, Rezi, 210
Kastner, Elliott, 26, 170
Kasznar, Kurt, 222
Katarina, Olivera, 212
Katon, Rosanne, 128
Katrakis, Manos, 184
Katt, William, 130, 222
Katz, Stephen, 132
Katzka, Gabriel, 74
Katzman, Alfred, 135
Kauer, Gene, 139
Kauffman, Judy, 135
Kaufman, Kurt, 80
Kaufman, Philip, 120
Kaufmann, Christine, 222
Kawaguchi, Matsutaro, 178
Kawazy, Seizaburo, 178

Kay, Sylvia, 91
Kaye, Danny, 159, 222
Kaye, John, 27
Kaye, Stubby, 222
Kazan, Elia, 158, 159
Keach, James, 33, 90
Keach, Stacy, 80, 127, 222
Keaton, Buster, 159
Keaton, Camille, 138
Keaton, Diane, 6, 64, 65,
144, 145, 159, 222
Keats, Steven, 222
Kedrakas, Nasis, 42
Kedrova, Lila, 159, 222
Keefer, Norman, 126
Keel, Howard, 222
Keeler, Ruby, 222
Kehoe, Pat, 59
Keillor, Warren, 164
Keitel, Harvey, 12, 126,
161
Keith, Brian, 72, 138, 222
Kellaway, Roger, 135
Keller, Jerry, 131
Keller, Marthe, 222
Keller, Paul D. III, 95
Keller, Sheldon, 102
Kellerman, Sally, 135, 222
Kelley, Thomas, 126
Kelley, Walter, 58
Kellin, Mike, 77, 96, 98
Kelly, Gene, 158, 222
Kelly, Grace, 159, 222
Kelly, J. B., 126
Kelly, Jack, 222
Kelly, Jim, 134
Kelly, Jimmy, 131
Kelly, John B., 130, 133,
137
Kelly, Louis H., 56
Kelly, M. G., 70
Kelly, Martine, 210
Kelly, Nancy, 222
Kelly, Patsy, 223
Kelly, Ron, 137
Kelsay, Ross, 126
Kemeny, John, 124
Kemp, Jeremy, 110, 208,
223
Kemper, Victor J., 8, 10,
78, 108
Kendall-John, Patricia, 42
Kenneally, Pam, 126
Kennedy, Arthur, 210, 212,
223
Kennedy, George, 84, 85,
119, 127, 159, 223
Kennedy, Jayne, 137
Kennedy, Patrick, 100, 125
Kennedy, Richard, 70
Kenney, Bill, 138
Kenney, Douglas, 66
Kenney, William J., 97
Kennis, Dan Q., 137
Kent, Cecil, 136
Kent, David, 136
Kentucky, 158
Kenzle, Ken, 125
Keramidas, Harry, 134
Kerby, Bill, 72
Kercheval, Ken, 39
Kern, Peter, 211
Kerns, Hubie, 126
Kerns, Sandra, 20
Kerr, Bill, 130
Kerr, Deborah, 223
Kerr, Elizabeth, 136
Kerr, John, 223
Kershaw, Clifford, 209
Kershaw, Doug, 88
Kershner, Irvin, 78
Kertesz, Akos, 201
Keshavarz, Mohammad Ali,
110
Kesner, Jillian, 133
Kessler, Zale, 56
Kester, Jim, 131
Ketchum, David, 125
Key, Alexander, 22
Key Largo, 158
Key, Ted, 52
Khambatta, Persis, 223
Khan, Amzad, 209
Kidd, Michael, 102
Kidder, Margot, 122, 123,
223
Kidnapped Co-Ed, 137
Kiebach, Jurgen, 205
Kieffer, Dorothy, 22
Kiel, Richard, 138, 202
Kier, Udo, 223
Kikumura, Akemi, 80
Kilar, Wojciech, 207
Kiley, Richard, 223
Kilian, Victor, 223
Killer's Delight, 136
Kilman, Peter, 71
Kilvert, Lilly, 77
Kim, Evan, 86
Kim, Young Eagle, 136

Kimball, Bruce, 131
Kincaid, Aron, 223
Kindberg, Ann, 128
Kindberg, Jack, 128
King, Alan, 223
King and I, The, 159
King, Arthur, 208
King, Damu, 137
King, Diana, 206
King, Donald, 92
King, Freeman, 70
King, Mabel, 92, 93, 125
King, Meegan, 128
King, Morgana, 43
King of the Gypsies, 115
King of the Hill, 127
King, Perry, 45
King, Tara, 59
King, Zalman, 130, 132
Kings, Tarka, 208
Kingsmen, The, 66
Kinnear, Roy, 190
Kinoshita, Robert, 13
Kinski, Klaus, 204
Kirby, Bruno, 137
Kirby, John, 137
Kirkland, Geoffrey, 96
Kirkwood, Gene, 90, 138
Kirschstein, Rudiger, 205
Kirshner, Jack, 133
Kit, Lee Man, 210
Kitt, Eartha, 223
Kitty Foyle, 158
Kivitt, Ted, 206
Klages, William M., 125
Klane, Robert, 130
Klausner, Lawrence, 107
Klavun, Walter, 111
Kleeman, Gunter, 138
Kleiman, Karen, 59
Kleimenhapen, Gay, 45
Klein, Allen, 42
Klein, I. W., 108
Klein, Robert, 72, 73
Kleiner, Burt, 139
Kleiser, Randal, 48
Klemperer, Werner, 223
Kline, Gerald, 78
Kline, James, 90
Kline, Richard H., 28, 74
Klingman, Lynzee, 137
Klotz, Florence, 26
Klotz, Georges, 184, 209
Klugman, Jack, 223
Klute, 159
Knatchbull, Norton, 84
Knight, Ashley, 208
Knight, Damien, 129
Knight, Eric, 212
Knight, Esmond, 223
Knight, Norma, 128
Knopf, Christopher, 125
Knotts, Don, 76
Knowland, Nic, 208
Knowles, Patric, 223
Knox, Alexander, 206, 223
Knox, Elyse, 223
Koch, Howard W. Jr., 46
Koenekamp, Fred J., 135
Kogure, Michiyo, 178
Kohner, Susan, 223
Kohut-Svelko, Jean-Pierre,
191
Koike, Kazumi, 178
Kolba, Vilmos, 30
Koller, Dagmar, 26
Kolsrud, Dan, 35, 106
Koltai, Lajos, 201
Komorowska, Maja, 207
Kongkham, Lynn, 150
Konieczny, Syzmunt, 163
Koock, Guich, 136
Koomen, Ann, 129
Koomen, Frank, 129
Kopestonsky, Father
Stephen, 150
Korman, Harvey, 223
Korty, John, 116
Korvin, Charles, 223
Koshiba, Mikio, 178
Kosleck, Martin, 223
Kotcheff, Ted, 91
Kotto, Yaphet, 12, 223
Kovacs, Laszlo, 38, 39, 83
Kovins, Ed, 131
Kozlowski, Diana, 126
Kraft, William, 87
Kramer, Bert, 118
Kramer, Frank, 206
Kramer, Jeffrey, 44
Kramer, Joel, 139
Kramer, Noel, 18
Kramreither, Anthony, 130
Krantz, Steve, 132
Krasny, Paul, 138
Kress, Harold F., 135
Kreuger, Kurt, 223
Krieger, Stu, 129
Krintzman, Robert D., 133

Kristofferson, Kris, 6, 58,
223
Kronsberg, Jeremy Joe, 114
Kruger, Hardy, 199, 223
Kuan-Chun, Hsi, 213
Kubis, Yvonne, 10
Kuby, Bernie, 20, 28, 106
Kuehl, H. August, 16
Kuehnert, Fred T., 70
Kukhlanidze, V., 208
Kulp, Nancy, 223
Kumagai, Denice, 86
Kumar, Sanjeev, 209
Kumushalleva, Savira, 213
Kuntzmann, Doris, 213
Kurant, Willy, 133
Kurtz, Swoosie, 116
Kurumada, Kim, 18
Kushida, Beverly, 75
Kuss, Richard, 150
Kutmanaliev, Orozbek, 213
Kuttabayev, Asankul, 213
Kux, William, 112, 128
Kwan, Nancy, 133, 211,
223
Kwan, Yi, 211
Kwouk, Burt, 60, 61
Kyle, David, 137
La Kome, Chris, 95
La Rochelle, Pierre Drieu,
210
La Strada, 159
Laborteaux, Matthew, 115
Labourier, Dominique, 205
Labyrinth-Burg, 130
Lachman, Edward Jr., 137
Lack, Steve, 207
Lackey, Douglas, 139
Lacy, Jerry, 223
Ladd, Cheryl, 223
Ladd, David, 199
Ladd, Diane, 223
Ladd, Margaret, 95
Lady Galadriel, 104
Lafleur, Jean, 208
Lafont, Bernadette, 194
Lagos, Poppy, 35
Lagrange, Valerie, 209
Lai, Francis, 116, 179, 209
Lai, Me Me, 206
Laing, John, 207
Laird, Joseph R., 129, 136
Lajarrige, Bernard, 194
Lalara, Cedric, 203
Lalara, Morris, 203
Lamarr, Hedy, 223
Lamas, Fernando, 56, 57,
223
Lamas, Lorenzo, 48, 223
Lamb, Gil, 223
Lamb, Larry, 122
Lambert, Jane, 28
Lambert, Robert K., 59,
111, 139
Lambeth, Larry, 137
Lambiotte, France, 210
Lambray, Maureen, 37
Lamm, Karen, 136, 137
Lamonea, Angelo, 59, 87
Lamont, Peter, 192
Lamour, Dorothy, 223
Lampkin, Ron, 125, 135
Lamy, Pierre, 211
Lancaster, Bill, 134
Lancaster, Burt, 86, 159,
223
Lanchester, Elsa, 223
Land, Geoffrey, 135
Land of No Return, 137
Landau, Ely, 42
Landau, Les, 42
Landau, Martin, 223
Landen, Dinsdale, 179
Lander, Toni, 206
Landgre, Inga, 168
Landis, John, 66
Landis, Rev. Bee, 32
Landon, Michael, 223
Landsburg, Valerie, 130
Landscape After Battle, 163
Lane, Abbe, 223
Lane, Charles, 102
Lane, David, 119
Lane, Rusdi, 56
Lang, Cindy, 56
Lang, Jennings, 20, 43
Lang, Robert, 18, 175
Langan, Glenn, 223
Lange, Hope, 223
Lange, Jessica, 223
Lang, Ted, 125
Langenskiold, Peder, 196
Langevin, Chris, 134
Langlois, Lisa, 194
Langlois, Yves, 194
Langrishe, Caroline, 91
Langton, Paul, 223
Lanier, Phillip, 125
Lanier, Susan, 208
Lankford, Kim, 131

Lannom, Les, 134, 135
Lanoux, Victor, 172, 209,
210
Lansbury, Angela, 84, 85,
223
Lansbury, Edgar, 132
Lansing, Michael, 102
Lansing, Robert, 127, 137,
223
LaPera, Sal, 43
LaPiere, Georganne, 132
LaPlatney, Martin, 127
Lapoten, Gary, 128
Laren, Michael, 75
Larner, Stevan, 70, 127,
137
Larsen, Ham, 139
Larsen, William, 46
Larson, Jay B., 129
Larson, John, 33
Larson, Nancy, 128
Larson, Robert, 33
Laserblast, 128
Laskaway, Harris, 115
Lasky, Byron, 211
Lassally, Walter, 107
Lassick, Sydney, 134
Lassie, 136
*Last Challenge of the
Dragon, The,* 210
Last Picture Show, The,
159
Last Supper, The, 207
Last Survivor, The, 206
"Last Time I Felt Like This,
The", 106
Last Waltz, The, 38
Last Wave, The, 203
Laszlo, Andrew, 82
Latallo, Stanislaw, 212
Lathrop, Philip, 45, 59, 118
Latka, George, 134
Laughlin, Teresa, 125
Laughlin, Tom, 125
Laughton, Charles, 158
Laure, Carol, 156, 157
Laurel, Stan, 129, 159
Laurie, Piper, 223
Lauris, George, 125, 127
Lauris, Priscilla, 66, 127
Lauter, Ed, 108, 109
Lautner, Georges, 204, 212
Lavallee, David, 127
Lavi, Arik, 204
Lavitan, Gladys, 137
Law, John Phillip, 223
Lawford, Peter, 223
Lawler, Bill, 136
Lawrence, Barbara, 223
Lawrence, Carol, 223
Lawrence, Dick, 23
Lawrence, Eddie, 223
Lawrence, Hap, 76
Lawrence, Jim, 207
Lawrence, Karen, 78
Lawrence, Marc, 68, 137
Lawrence of Arabia, 159
Lawrence, Paula, 78
Lawrence, Richard, 108
Lawrence, Robert, 126
Lawrence, Stephen, 131
Lawrence, Vicki, 223
Laws, Sam, 28
Lawson, Jennifer, 137
Lawson, Leigh, 212, 223
Lawson, Len, 127
Lawson, Nancy, 133
Lazarus, Frank, 122
Lazarus, Paul N. III, 50
Lazek, Heinz, 26
Lazenby, George, 134
le Carpentier, Jacques, 191
Le Forestier, Maxime, 209
Le Mesurier, John, 91
Leach, Britt, 94
Leachman, Cloris, 135,
159, 223
Lean, David, 159
Leavitt, Max, 83
LeBell, Gene, 35, 137
Lebenzon, Christopher, 125,
139
Lebeshev, Pavel, 188
LeBouvier, Jean, 8
Lecchi, Patricia, 36
Lecomte, Claude, 200
Lederer, Francis, 223
Ledin, Ulla, 168
Leduc, Richard, 210
Lee, Bernard, 212
Lee, Christopher, 22, 110,
164, 205, 211, 223
Lee, Gerald, 132
Lee, Howard, 125
Lee, Jennifer, 125
Lee, Michael David, 68
Lee, Michele, 223
Lee, Michelle, 223
Lee, Myron Bruce, 134
Lee, Penelope, 122

Lee, Stuart, 97
Leece, Mary Pat, 213
Leech, George, 199
Leek, Tiiu, 164
Lees, Gene, 135
Lefebvre, Jean, 204
Lefferts, George, 127
LeGault, Lance, 10, 137
Legend of Sea Wolf, The, 125
Legrange, Valerie, 209
Lehman, Robin, 139
Lehne, John, 27, 39
Leibman, Ron, 223
Leifert, Don, 131
Leigh, Janet, 223
Leigh, Mitch, 105
Leigh, Norman, 111
Leigh, Vivien, 158
Leikin, Molly-Ann, 32
Leiterman, Richard, 211
Lelouch, Claude, 209
Lembeck, Harvey, 223
Lembeck, Michael, 18
Lemmon, Jack, 128, 159, 223
Lemon, Max, 203
Lemond, Frenchie, 88
Lennon, James, 102
Lennon, John, 62, 134
Leno, Jay, 27, 36
Lenoir, Jack, 105
Lenz, Kay, 127
Lenz, Rick, 223
Lenzi, Bert, 210
Lenzi, Joseph Pepi, 54
Lenzi, Pepi, 58
Lenzi, Umberto, 206, 210, 212
Leon, Joe, 131
Leon, Valerie, 60, 61
Leonard, Michael, 134, 138
Leonard, Robert E., 46
Leonard, Sheldon, 111, 223
Leone, John, 132
Leone, Michael, 45, 86, 127, 132
Leotard, Philippe, 209
LePage, Brent, 137
Lepicier, Eugene, 194
Lerner, Ken, 129
LeRoy, Gloria, 96
Leroy, Philippe, 223
Leslie, Bethel, 223
Leslie, Joan, 223
Lesser, Len, 20
Lester, Mark, 30, 223
Let's Face It, C'est La Vie, 210
Letter to Three Wives, A, 158
Letts, Don, 209
Levee, Michael, 31, 101
Leven, Boris, 38
Levene, Sam, 223
Levene, Terry, 210
Leverington, Shelby, 129
Levien, Philip, 45
Levignac, Sylvain, 191
Levin, Boris, 134
Levin, Ira, 192
Levin, John, 134
Levin, Sidney, 56, 133
Levine, Floyd, 96
Levine, Harvey, 126
Levine, Joseph E., 108
Levine, Michael, 125
Levine, Mike, 139
Levine, Richard P., 108
Levinn, Sidney, 31
Levinthal, Malcolm, 133
Levitan, Charan, 126
Levitsky, Al, 134
Levy, Ariel, 42
Levy, Delphine, 174
Levy, Ori, 204
Lewis, Arthur, 119
Lewis, Bobby, 66
Lewis, Fiona, 28, 29, 137
Lewis, Geoffrey, 114
Lewis, Harvey, 137
Lewis, Jerry, 223
Lewis, Jerry Lee, 27
Lewis, Michael J., 175
Lewis, Monica, 43
Leyton, John, 206
Li, Bruce, 211, 212
Li, Chang, 210
Li, Chiang, 210
Liang, Bruce, 208
Liapis, Peter Paul, 133
Libertini, Richard, 88
Lichterman, Marvin, 131
Lieberman, Jeff, 132
Lieberman, Manny, 132
Lieh, Lo, 212
Lietot, Christine, 191
Life of Emile Zola, The, 158
Lifton, Bob, 131
Ligon, Tom, 223

Like a Queen, 182
Lilies of the Field, 159
Lilley, Merv, 203
Lillie, Beatrice, 223
Lillo, Marie, 126
Lilyholm, Leonard, 124
Lin Tse-Hsu: The Opium War, 211
Linblom, Gunnel, 168
Lincoln, Abbey, 223
Lincoln, Fred, 132
Lincoln, Henry, 138
Lincoln, Richard, 132
Lincoln, Steve, 136
Lind, Dagny, 168
Lindblom, Gunnel, 168
Linden, Carol, 133
Lindfors, Viveca, 77, 95, 223
Linero, Jeannie, 46
Ling, Hwa, 213
Ling, Shang Kuaw, 208
Link, James, 211
Linson, Art, 27
Lion in Winter, The, 159
Lipnick, Amanda Hope, 43
Lipson, Doreen, 164
Lipton, Robert, 206
Lisi, Virna, 223
Liss, Stephen, 128
Lisson, Mark, 71
Lithgow, John, 100
Little, Cleavon, 33, 223
Little, David, 115
Little Night Music, A, 26
Little Tramp, The, 128
Ljung, Oscar, 168
Llapur, Santiago, 207
Llaurado, Adolfo, 207
Llorens, Tony, 95
Lloyd, Charles, 137
Lloyd, Christopher, 94
Lloyd, Euan, 199
Lloyd, Frank, 158
Lloyd, Harold, 158
Lloyd, John J., 66
Lloyd, Kathleen, 126, 130
Lloyd, Norman, 33
Lloyd, Rosalind, 199
Lloyd, Sue, 60
Lloyd, Trevor, 199
Lo Bianco, Tony, 39, 96
Locke, Peter, 208
Locke, Sondra, 114, 125, 223
Lockhart, June, 223
Lockhart, Kathleen, 235
Lockhart, Warren, 135
Lockwood, Gary, 223
Lockwood, Margaret, 223
Loeb, Jerome, 174
Lofaro, Tommy, 212
Logan, Bruce, 134
Logan, Robert, 34, 139
Loggia, Robert, 60, 129
Lokkeberg, Georg, 196
Lollobrigida, Gina, 223
Lom, Herbert, 60, 61, 212, 213, 223
Lombardo, Francis, 58
Lombardo, Lou, 80
Lombardo, Tony, 95
Lomez, Celine, 211
London, Jack, 125
London, Julie, 223
Lonnberg, Anne, 210
Lonow, Mark, 130, 224
Lonzo, Michael, 212
Loomis, Nancy, 137
Looney, Peter, 116
Loop, Staci, 124
Loperena, Miguel, 116
Lopert, Tanya, 105
Lopez, Joe, 136
Lopez, Perry, 224
Lopez, Rigoberto, 207
Loquasto, Santo, 139
Lord, Jack, 224
Lord of the Rings, The, 104
Lord, Stephen, 126
Loredan, Mary Lou, 137
Loren, Sophia, 119, 159, 206, 224
Lorenz, Juliane, 211
Lost Weekend, The, 158
Louis, Grace, 206
Louise, Anna, 126
Louise, Tina, 127, 224
Love and the Midnight Auto Supply, 130, 131
Love at First Sight, 206
"Love Keeps Getting Stronger Every Day", 82
Love, Lucretia, 212
Lovejoy, Tim, 139
Lovelace, Linda, 224
Lovelett, Jim, 82
Lovelock, Ray, 211, 212
Lovett, Robert Q., 105

Lowe, Donna, 139
Lowell, Skip, 128
Lowell, Sondra, 129
Lowenadler, Holger, 168
Lowitsch, Klaus, 211, 224
Lowry, Jane, 131
Lowry, Joe, 108
Loy, Mino, 125
Loy, Myrna, 40, 224
Lozic, Zorica, 174
Lubicki, Claude, 174
Lubitsch, Ernst, 158
Lubtchansky, Nicole, 205
Lucari, Gianna Hecht, 204
Lucari, Gianni Hecht, 210
Lucas, Lisa, 24, 25, 224
Lucchesi, Vincent, 12
Luchini, Fabrice, 191, 194
Lucifer's Women, 127
Luedke, Cindy, 87
Lugagne, Francoise, 200
Luisi, James, 118, 136
Lukas, Paul, 158
Lukather, Paul, 76
Luke, Keye, 173
Lulu, 224
Lumet, Sidney, 92
Lumley, Joanna, 211
Lun, Kuan, 211
Lund, John, 224
Lund, Martin, 127
Lundren, Siv, 168
Lupino, Ida, 224
LuPone, Patti, 115
Lusby, Kool, 129
Lusk, Skip, 128
Lust for Life, 159
Lutenbacher, Don K., 37
Luthardt, Robert, 18, 31, 56
Luther, 205
Luther, Michael, 131
Lydon, James, 224
Lygizos, Danos, 42
Lynch, Richard, 128
Lynde, Paul, 13, 224
Lynley, Carol, 224
Lynn, Jeffrey, 224
Lynn, Joe, 92
Lynn, Sherry, 35
Lyon, Earle, 126
Lyon, Steve, 125
Lyon, Sue, 126, 130, 224
Lyons, Ivan, 91
Lyons, Nan, 91
Lyons, Robert F., 224
Lytle, Bill, 70
Lytle, Steve, 212
Lytton, Debbie, 76
Maas, Peter, 115
Maazel, Lincoln, 134
Mabry, Moss, 31
MacArthur, Courtney, 95
MacArthur, James, 224
MacAvoy, Gene, 125
Maccari, Ruggero, 182
Maccione, Aldo, 206
MacCorkindale, Simon, 84, 85
MacDonald, Doug, 129
MacDonald, Edith Blossom, 235
MacDonald, Richard, 39
MacDonald, Robert, 46
MacDonald, Russ, 136
MacDonald, Wallace, 235
Mace, Paul, 83
MacFarland, Mike, 129, 132
MacGinnis, Niall, 224
MacGraw, Ali, 58, 224
Machlis, Neil A., 48
MacInnes, Angus, 202
MacIntosh, Jay W., 62
Mack, Brice, 132
Mackenzie, Patch, 20
Macko, Denny, 59
MacLaine, Shirley, 224
MacLean, Alistair, 202
MacLeod, Murray, 100
MacLeod, Robert, 122
MacMahon, Aline, 224
MacMurray, Fred, 135, 224
Macnee, Patrick, 224
MacRae, Gordon, 224
MacRae, Michael, 10
Macri, Robert, 126
Madalone, Dennis, 87
Madame Rosa, 148, 159
Madden, Dennis, 129
Madden, Lee, 133
Maddox, Mary, 190
Madison, Guy, 129, 224
Mado, 162
Madsen, Harry, 92
Mag Wheels, 132
Magaro, Polli, 83
Maggiore, Charles, 42
Magic, 108
Magic of Lassie, The, 136
Magnani, Anna, 159

Magnin, Cyril, 68
Magnotti, Alexis, 138
Magnus, Harry, 199
Magnusson, Tony, 168
Magrini, Gitt, 213
Maguire, Charles H., 46
Mahar, Dan, 45
Maharis, George, 224
Maher, Joseph, 46
Mahieux, Alix, 209
Mahoney, Jock, 40, 127, 224
Mahoney, Tom, 128, 131
Maimone, Joseph Jr., 78
Maintenant, Cash, 129
Mairesse, Valerie, 210
Maistre, Francois, 194
Maitland, Scott, 44
Majors, Lee, 136, 224
Makel, Joseph F., 46
Malanowicz, Zygmunt, 163
Malanowski, Anthony, 131
Malcolm, Christopher, 202
Malden, Karl, 158, 224
Malet, Arthur, 46, 137
Malibu Beach, 131
Malick, Terrence, 88
Malikyan, Kevork, 96
Malkin, Barry, 82
Malle, Louis, 37
Mallett, Bob, 18
Mallett, Jane, 206
Malloy, John, 35
Malone, Dorothy, 159, 224
Mambetova, Nazira, 213
Man and a Woman, A, 159
Man for All Seasons, A, 159
Manasse, George, 101, 132
Manchester, Melissa, 124
Mancini, Henry, 20, 60, 91
Mandel, Alan, 20, 94
Mandel, Mel, 127
Mandelberg, Arthur, 125
Maneri, Sal, 43
Manes, Fritz, 114
Manfredi, Nino, 180, 181
Manfredini, Harry, 132
Manheim, Kate, 115
Manilow, Barry, 68
Maniolas, Jim, 131
Manitou, The, 75
Mankiewicz, Joseph L., 158
Mann, Daniel, 134
Mann, Delbert, 159
Mann, Kurt, 224
Mann, Michael, 20
Mann, Stanley, 54
Manners, Scott, 62
Mannino, Anthony, 126, 133
Mannino, Vincenzo, 212
Mannix, Bobbie, 138
Manns, Patricio, 204
Manoff, Dinah, 48
Manor, Chris, 115
Manos, George J., 46
Mansbridge, John B., 22, 52, 76
Manskey, Susan, 37
Mantee, Ann, 75
Mantee, Paul, 75
Mantegna, Joe, 130
Manuel, Richard, 38
Manz, Linda, 88, 89, 115, 224
Manza, Ralph, 8, 52
Maracek, Heimz, 26
Marachuk, Steve, 78
Marais, Jean, 224
Marcault, Claude, 200
Marcel, Terry, 60
March, Fredric, 158
March on Paris 1914, The, 129
March, Philippe, 105, 210
Marchand, Guy, 176
Marcus, DeVara, 133
Marcus, Paula, 48
Marden, Adrienne, 235
Marden, Richard, 110
Margo, 224
Margolin, Edward H., 127
Margolin, Janet, 224
Margolin, Stuart, 88
Margolis, Zora, 112
Marielle, Jean-Pierre, 212
Marin, Cheech, 80, 81
Marin, Jacques, 91, 224
Marinaro, Ed, 126
Marino, Ben, 80
Marinoff, Brenda, 208
Marischka, Georg, 192
Marisol, 207
Markell, Jean, 126
Markley, Ed, 132
Markopoulos, Iannis, 184, 208
Markowitz, Cheryl, 37
Marks, Beau, 44
Marks, Bruce, 206

Marks, Eddie, 10
Marks, Maurice, 20, 56
Marks, Sherry Lee, 131
Markus, Connie, 137
Markus, Sahbra, 88
Marley, Ben, 44
Marley, John, 72, 125, 130
Marlowe, Hugh, 224
Marlowe, Patricia, 33
Marly, Florence, 235
Marmande-Cerf, Michele, 211
Marmorstein, Malcolm, 22
Marner, Richard, 192
Maroff, Bob, 35
Marquez, Juan, 207
Marr, Sally K., 20
Marrhews, Richard, 211
Mars, Kenneth, 137
Marsani, Claudia, 213
Marsh, Terence, 108
Marsh, Tiger Joe, 52
Marshall, Alan, 96
Marshall, Anne T., 94
Marshall, Brenda, 224
Marshall, E. G., 64, 125, 224
Marshall, Edward, 36
Marshall, Frank, 59
Marshall, George, 12
Marshall, Mel, 125
Marshall, Penny, 224
Marshall, Rose, 129
Marshall, William, 224
Marston, Joel, 46
Marthouret, Francois, 200
Martin, 134
Martin, Armand, 138
Martin, Barney, 102
Martin, Charles, 136
Martin, Dean, 224
Martin, Dean Paul, 224
Martin, Dick, 130, 133
Martin, D'Urville, 207
Martin, Earl, 212
Martin, Eugene, 207
Martin, George, 62
Martin, Mary, 224
Martin, Nan, 32
Martin, Rosemary, 209
Martin, Sandy, 137
Martin, Stephen, 208
Martin, Steve, 62, 63
Martin, Strother, 40, 41, 80, 224
Martin, Tony, 224
Martinez, A., 128, 138
Martinez, Chico, 24
Martinez, Jimmy, 12
Martinez, Leo, 134
Martinez, Pablo, 208
Martino, Luciano, 212
Martucci, Ray, 100
Marty, 159
Martynow, Kurt, 26
Maruzzo, Joe, 115
Marvin, Lee, 158, 159, 224
Marx, Bill, 126
Marx, Brett, 134
Mary, Miz, 37
Mary Poppins, 159
Marzello, Vincent, 122
Masak, Ron, 128, 133
Mascellino, Philip, 36
Mascia, Tony, 36
Mascolo, Joseph, 44
Maslow, Walter, 131
Mason, James, 46, 192, 224
Mason, Marsha, 56, 57, 224
Mason, Pam, 130
Mason, Pamela, 224
Mason, Tom, 115
Massa, Bernie, 46
Massaccesi, Aristide, 212
Massard, Yves, 105
Massari, Lea, 210
Massen, Osa, 224
Massey, Daniel, 208, 224
Massey, Raymond, 224
Massip, Jose, 207
Masterman, David, 42
Masters, Ian, 139
Masters, Tammy, 33
Masterson, Graham, 75
Masterson, Peter, 224
Mastorakis, Nico, 42
Mastroianni, Marcello, 206, 224
Masur, Richard, 74
Matalon, Eddy, 211
Matheson, Margaret, 209
Matheson, Murray, 13
Matheson, Tim, 66, 67, 136, 137
Mathews, Kerwin, 135
Mathieu, Ginette, 205
Mathis, Johnny, 106
Matilda, 134

Matray, Ernst, 235
Matsuo, Toshi, 78
Mattey, Robert A., 44
Matthau, Charlie, 20, 21
Matthau, David, 33, 56, 100, 112
Matthau, Walter, 6, 20, 21, 31, 112, 113, 128, 159, 224
Matthews, Frederick, 18
Mattson, Denver R., 102
Mature, Victor, 224
Maturo, Sam, 137
Matusda, Hiroo, 211
Mauer, Howard, 208
Mauro, Albert M., 66
Maxsted, Jack, 208
Maxt, David, 122
Maxwell, Don, 138
May, Angela, 137
May, Bert, 112
May, Elaine, 46, 112, 113, 224
Mayehoff, Eddie, 224
Mayer, Louis B., 158
Mayes, Wendell, 86
Maynard, Bill, 209
Mayo, Bob, 62
Mayo, John, 100
Mayo, Virginia, 137
Mayron, Melanie, 77, 132
Mazars, Denis, 209
Mazen, Goen, 127
Mazurki, Mike, 136
Mazursky, Paul, 24
McBride, Harlee, 20
McCalister, George, 131
McCall, C. W., 58
McCall, June, 102
McCallon, Lynn, 45
McCallum, David, 224
McCalman, Macon, 90
McCambridge, Mercedes, 158, 224
McCann, Chuck, 68, 138
McCann, Sean, 211
McCarey, Crystal, 12
McCarey, Leo, 158
McCarthy, Kevin, 120, 136, 224
McCartin, Sean, 66
McCartney, Paul, 62
McCarty, Mary, 82
McCauley, Dan, 126
McClellan, Max, 132
McClory, Sean, 224
McClure, Doug, 208, 224
McClure, Marc, 35, 122
McConnell, Bill, 59
McCormick, Kevin, 118
McCormick, Pat, 95
McCourt, Malachy, 111
McCowen, Alec, 189, 224
McCoy, Arch, 132
McCoy, Colonel Tim, 236
McCoy, Tim, 236
McCracken, Jeff, 136
McCrary, Charles, 18
McCrea, Joel, 224
McCrory, Tom, 133
McCuller, Arnold, 27
McCullough, Patrick, 108
McDaniel, Hattie, 158
McDermott, Hugh, 224
McDonald, Lee, 12
McDonald, Mary Ann, 206
McDonough, Britt, 131
McDowall, Roddy, 13, 52, 128, 224
McDowell, Malcolm, 224
McElroy, Hal, 203
McElroy, James, 203
McEnery, John, 161, 206
McEnery, Peter, 224
McEveety, Joe, 76
McFarland, Spanky, 224
McFarland, Victoria, 12
McGara, Marven, 208
McGarry, William, 10
McGavin, Darren, 76, 130, 133, 224
McGill, Bruce, 66, 67
McGill, Myron, 128
McGillivray, David, 206
McGinnis, Carol, 126
McGoohan, Patrick, 119
McGovern, Don, 94
McGowan, Dorrell, 134
McGowan, Stuart E., 134, 138
McGrath, Paul, 235, 236
McGregor, Sandy, 211
McGrew, Skeets, 127
McGuinn, Roger, 125
McGuire, Betty, 10, 80
McGuire, Biff, 224
McGuire, Dorothy, 224
McGuire, Kathryn, 236
McHattie, Stephen, 127
McHugh, Thomas, 34

McInerney, Bernie, 115
McIntire, Tim, 27
McIntyre, Tom, 135
McKay, Gardner, 224
McKee, John R., 102
McKee, Lonette, 224
McKee, Richard, 68
McKenna, Virginia, 206, 224
McKennon, Dallas, 52, 76
McKenzie, Kevin, 71
McKenzie, Patch, 125, 134
McKenzie, Richard, 53
McKeon, Doug, 138
McKern, Leo, 17
McKuen, Rod, 224
McLaglen, Andrew V., 199
McLaglen, Victor, 158
McLarty, Gary, 66
McLaughlin, John, 132
McLaughlin, Lee, 56
McLean, Bill, 128
McLean, Coll Red, 44
McLean, David, 125, 128
McLean, Michelle, 124
McLerie, Allyn Ann, 224
McMahon, Thomas A., 110
McMaster, Niles, 130, 131
McMillan, Ken, 77
McMillan, Kenneth, 96, 116
McMillan, Susan O., 44
McMullen, Craig T., 124
McNair, Barbara, 224
McNally, Stephen, 132, 224
McNamara, J. Patrick, 28
McNamara, Maggie, 236
McNeely, Helen, 18
McNeil, Robert A., 204, 209
McNichol, Kristy, 40, 224
McPhee, John, 31
McPherson, Cynthia, 116
McPherson, Graham, 122
McQueen, Butterfly, 224
McQueen, Steve, 224
McRae, Frank, 83
McSwain, Faith, 128
McWilliams, Daphne, 92
Meadows, Audrey, 224
Meadows, Jayne, 224
Meagher, John, 203
Mean Dog Blues, 127
Meara, Anne, 192, 193
Medalis, Joe, 52
Medeiros, Anisio, 166
Medford, Kay, 225
Media Counterpoint, 137
Medina, Ofelia, 100
Medioli, Enrico, 212
Medoff, Mark, 132
Medusa Touch, The, 175
Medwin, Michael, 225
Meek, G. C. Rusty, 12
Meeker, Colleen, 132
Meeker, Ralph, 132, 225
Meeks, Jack, 43
Meffre, Armand, 205
Megna, John, 86
Mei, Po Fu, 212
Meisner, Gunter, 192
Mekka, Eddie, 225
Meland, Dean, 127
Melato, Mariangela, 204, 225
Melford, Jill, 42
Melgar, Gilbert, 70
Melhem, Alfred, 138
Mell, Marisa, 225
Melle, Gil, 158
Mellin, Bill, 136
Mellin, Kerry, 136
Melody in Gray, 198
Melton, Tim, 35
Melville, Sam, 130
Melvin, Murray, 30
Memmoli, George, 12, 129
Menard, Tina, 112
Menczer, Enrico, 206
Mendillo, Stephen, 115
Mendleson, Anthony, 192
Mendonca, Mauro, 166, 167
Mendoza-Nava, Jaime, 18, 125, 134, 136, 137
Menez, Bernard, 204
Menker, Robin, 130
Menning, Lee, 56
Menzel, Paul, 33
Menzies, Heather, 136
Mercadier, Marthe, 105
Mercado, Hector Jaime, 101
Mercer, Mae, 37
Mercer, Marian, 139
Mercier, Duane, 18
Mercouri, Melina, 184, 185, 225
Mercurio, Gus, 211
Meredith, Burgess, 68, 75, 107, 108, 225
Meredith, Lee, 225
Merholz, B. J., 94

Merino, Rick, 136
Merkel, Una, 225
Merli, Mike, 210
Merlin, Claudine, 156
Merlo, Ismael, 206
Merman, Ethel, 225
Merrick, Robert, 213
Merrill, Dina, 95, 225
Merrill, Gary, 225
Merritt, Theresa, 92
Merry, 104
Mersky, Kres, 137
Merta, Jack, 125
Mertens, Mary, 131
Mesguich, Daniel, 200
Message from Space, 211
Messina, Louis, 33
Metamorphoses, 131
Metcalf, Mark, 66
Metcalfe, Ken, 18
Metrano, Art, 134
Metz, Rexford, 114
Metzler, Fred L., 159
Meunier, Pamela, 24
Meury, Anne-Laure, 191
Meyers, Marilyn, 78
Meynier, Pascal, 209
Michaelford, James, 76
Michaels, Drew, 18
Michelangeli, Marcella, 204
Michell, Keith, 225
Michelle, Ann, 137, 210
Michelle, Vicki, 42, 210
Michener, James, 110
Michlin, Barry, 56
Middleton, Fran, 134
Midnight Cowboy, 159
Midnight Express, 96
Mifune, Toshiro, 225
Migicovsky, Allan, 130
Mignini, Caroline, 131
Mike Curb Congregation, The, 136
Mikhalkov, Nikita, 188
Mikhalkov-Konchalovsky, Andrei, 188
Mikolajska, Halina, 207
Milchan, Arnon, 175
Mildred Pierce, 158
Miles, Sarah, 170, 171, 225
Miles, Sherry, 212
Miles, Sylvia, 133, 225
Miles, Vera, 225
Milestone, Lewis, 158
Milford, Kim, 53, 96, 128
Milford, Penelope, 14, 15
Milian, Tomas, 210, 212, 213
Milius, John, 130
Milkis, Edward K., 68
Milkovich, Ed, 66, 97
Mill, Robert, 206
Milland, Ray, 116, 117, 158, 211, 225
Millar, Bill, 131
Miller, Ann, 225
Miller, Burton, 20
Miller, Chris, 66
Miller, Christian, 66
Miller, Claude, 204
Miller, David, 137
Miller, Denny, 136
Miller, Dick, 35, 136
Miller, Jason, 225
Miller, Jonathan, 205
Miller, Linda, 24, 130, 131
Miller, Martha, 207
Miller, Marvin, 225
Miller, Pamela, 83
Miller, Ron, 17, 22, 52, 76
Miller, Thomas L., 68
Mills, Hayley, 159, 225
Mills, Joey R., 78
Mills, John, 159, 170, 225
Milner, Martin, 225
Milo, Jana, 52
Mimieux, Yvette, 225
Min and Bill, 158
Minakami, Tsutomu, 198
Minazzoli, Daniele, 174
Miner, Stephen, 132
Ming, Kung, 210
Minnelli, Liza, 159, 225
Minnelli, Vincente, 159
Minor, Bob, 59, 134
Mintz, Fred, 129
Miou-Miou, 204, 212
Miracle, Irene, 96, 99
Miracle On 34th Street, 158
Miracle Worker, The, 159
Miranda, Isa, 225
Miravalles, Reynaldo, 207
Mirisch, Walter,, 106, 127
Mirojnick, Ellen, 137
Mirrors, 126
Mister Roberts, 159
Mitchell, Billy J., 122

Mitchell, Cameron, 128, 133, 225
Mitchell, George Alfred, 158
Mitchell, James, 50, 225
Mitchell, Joni, 38
Mitchell, Thomas, 158
Mitchum, Chris, 134
Mitchum, Christopher, 135, 136
Mitchum, James, 225
Mitchum, Jim, 211
Mitchum, Robert, 134, 170, 171, 173, 225
Mittelman, Mina, 37
Mitton, Tara, 101
Mitzner, Dean, 130
Mixaleas, Anthony, 42
Miyagawa, Kazuo, 178, 198
Miyata, Mitsuzo, 178
Mizoguchi, Kenji, 178
Mizrahi, Moshe, 148
Mnouchkine, Alexandre, 176
Mobley, Freeman, 18
Mockus, Tony, 39
Moder, Jane, 80
Moder, Mike, 80
Moe, Marilyn, 35
Mohner, Carl, 210
Mohrbach, F. Jo, 68
Moler, Ron, 129
Molin, Bud, 8
Molteni, Sonia, 213
Moment By Moment, 118
Monahan, Steve, 126
Monicelli, Mario, 182, 204
Monk, L. Jay, 138
Monks, John Jr., 83
Monks, Patrick J., 16
Monocheri, Bahram, 138
MonPere, Carol, 135
Monroe, Bill, 129
Monsieur Vincent, 158
Montagne, Edward, 138
Montague, Lee, 119
Montalban, Ricardo, 138, 225
Montana, Lenny, 126, 134, 138
Montanari, Sergio, 213
Montand, Yves, 225
Montanio, Rock, 129
Montenegro, Hugo, 137
Montez, Chris, 66
Montgomery, Belinda, 211, 225
Montgomery, Belinda J., 32
Montgomery, Earl, 46
Montgomery, Elizabeth, 225
Montgomery, George, 225
Montgomery, Goodee, 236
Montgomery, James, 126
Montgomery, Robert, 225
Montilor, Ovidi, 206
Monty, Jacques, 210
Monty Python Meets Beyond the Fringe, 205
Moody, Lynne, 133
Moon, Keith, 225
Mooney, Paul, 70
Moonjean, Hank, 40, 72
Moor, Bill, 225
Moorcroft, Judy, 30, 91
Moore, Constance, 225
Moore, Dick, 225
Moore, Dudley, 68, 69
Moore, Frank, 211
Moore, Jay, 115
Moore, Kevin, 132
Moore, Kieron, 225
Moore, Mary Tyler, 225
Moore, Millie, 86, 164
Moore, Neal, 18
Moore, Pamela, 204
Moore, Robert, 56
Moore, Roger, 199, 225
Moore, Terry, 134, 225
Moore, Tom, 125, 136
Morales, Santos, 18
Moran, Kelly, 125
Moran, Liza, 131
Moran, Tony, 137
More the Merrier, The, 158
Moreau, Jeanne, 225
Morell, Andre, 236
Morello, Joe, 125
Morena, Joseph, 112
Moreno, Belita, 95
Moreno, Rita, 159, 225
Moreton, Kevin, 209
Morga, Thomas, 102
Morgan, Andre, 173
Morgan, Andrew, 18
Morgan, Corney, 54
Morgan, Dennis, 225
Morgan, Donald M., 35
Morgan, Edwin T., 131
Morgan, Harry, 52
Morgan, Harry (Henry), 225

Morgan, Lynn, 48
Morgan, Maitzi, 135
Morgan, Michele, 209, 225
Morgan, Read, 16, 35
Moriarty, Evelyn, 102
Moriarty, Michael, 74, 225
Morick, David, 20
Morin, Michel, 208
Morioka, Ken-Ichiro, 211
Morison, Patricia, 225
Moritz, Louisa, 80
Moriyama, Rollin, 66
Morley, Angela, 190
Morley, Robert, 91, 225
Morley, Ruth, 101, 111
Morning Glory, 158
Moroder, Giorgio, 96
Morphett, Tony, 203
Morra, Mario, 180, 212
Morricone, Ennio, 88, 206, 210, 212
Morris, Greg, 225
Morris, Howard, 137, 225
Morris, Jeff, 94
Morris, Oswald, 92
Morris, Van, 38
Morrison, Ann, 236
Morrison, Van, 38
Morriss, Frank, 35, 130
Morrow, Byron, 97
Morrow, Vic, 211, 225
Morse, Barry, 206
Morse, Donl, 12
Morse, Robert, 225
Morse, Susan, 70
Mortimer, Trisha, 206
Moschin, Gastone, 210
Moses, Harry, 32, 128
Moses, Rick, 87
Moskowitz, Joel, 174
Moss, Arnold, 225
Moss, Delbert, 128
Moss, Gerald, 210
Moss, Kathi, 115
Moss, Michael, 133
Mostel, Zero, 190
Mosten, Murray, 126
Motown-Casablanca, 130
Motulsky, Judy, 135
Moulard, Eric, 156
Moulden, Prentiss, 135
Moulinot, Jean-Paul, 162
Moullin, Francois X., 105
Mountain, Charles, 54
Mouse and His Child, The, 134, 135
Moustache, 36
Movie Movie, 102
Moyer, Tawny, 112
Moyle, Allan, 207
Mphahlele, Madala, 211
Mr. Deeds Goes to Town, 158
Mr. Smith Goes to Washington, 125
Mrozowska, Zofia, 207
Mrs. Miniver, 158
Muir, Georgette, 126
Mule Deer, Gary, 80
Mull, Martin, 33
Muller, Jorge, 204
Mulligan, Richard, 225
Mulligan, Robert, 96, 106
Mullins, Michael, 133
Mullins, Peter, 60, 175
Munday, Mary, 108
Mundy, Meg, 78, 116
Munger, Robert L., 97
Muni, Paul, 158
Munk, Jonathan, 145
Munne, Pep, 213
Murder on the Orient Express, 159
Murphy, Charles, 135
Murphy, Dennis, 137
Murphy, Fred, 77
Murphy, George, 158, 225
Murphy, Gerard, 111
Murphy, John, 134
Murphy, Maurice, 236
Murphy, Michael, 24, 107, 225
Murphy, Mike, 128
Murray, Charlie, 102
Murray, Don, 225
Murray, George, 206
Murray, Ken, 225
Murray the K., 35
Murton, Peter, 84
Musante, Tony, 225
Musayev, Manasbek, 213
Mustang Ranch, 137
Mustang: The House that Joe Built, 137
Muti, Ornella, 183
Mutiny on the Bounty, 158
Mutrux, Floyd, 27
Mutrux, Gail, 23
My Fair Lady, 159
My Uncle, 159

Myers, Chuck, 14
Myers, David, 33, 38, 125, 139
Myers, Kevin, 136
Myers, Lawrence, 42
Myers, Pamela, 96
Myers, Ruth, 36, 108
Myers, Stanley, 42, 150, 205, 206
Myers, Susan, 31
Myers, Thomas, 59
Myggen, Bent, 72
Myhers, John, 134
Myrberg, Per, 168
Myrtil, Odette, 236
Nabokov, Vladimir, 211
Nachman, Andi, 80
Nadeau, Elyane, 134
Nader, George, 225
Nadoolman, Deborah, 66
Nagy, William J., 206
Nakajima, Toro, 211
Nakhapetov, Rodion, 188
Nalder, Reggie, 134
Nalpern, John, 131
Nan, Ten, 211
Nanas, Leo, 83
Naniwa, Chieko, 178
Napier, Alan, 225
Naraoka, Tomoko, 198
Narita, Hiro, 38
Narita, Mikio, 211
Narita, Richard, 56
Narke, Rob, 209
Nash, Alan, 126
Nat, Marie-Jose, 210
Nathanson, Bernard, 199
National Lampoon's Animal House, 66
National Velvet, 158, 179
Natkin, Rich, 18
Natkin, Rick, 18
Natwick, Mildred, 225
Naughton, James, 225
Nayfack, Joe, 125
Naylor, Cal, 204
Ndiaye, Tabara, 205
Nea: New Woman, A, 186
Neal, David, 122
Neal, Patricia, 159, 225
Near, Timothy, 130
Needham, Hal, 68, 72
Neely, Ted, 125
Neeman, Yitzhak, 204
Neenan, Audry, 130
Neff, Hildegarde, 225
Neil, Martin, 179
Nelson, Barry, 225
Nelson, Craig Richard, 95
Nelson, David, 80, 225
Nelson, Don, 76
Nelson, Ed, 127
Nelson, Frank, 135
Nelson, Gene, 225
Nelson, Gerri, 32
Nelson, Gwen, 209
Nelson, Harriet Hilliard, 225
Nelson, Lori, 225
Nelson, Mervyn, 192
Nelson, Novella, 24
Nelson, Rick, 225
Nelson, Ruth, 95
Nelson, Shawn, 136
Nero, Franco, 202, 213
Neron, Claude, 162
Nervig, Sandy, 138
Nesbitt, Cathleen, 225
Netter, Douglas, 199
Netter, Kate, 139
Network, 159
Neukum, John, 138
Neukum, John E., Jr., 136
Neuwirth, Bob, 125
Nevil, Steve, 128
Nevinson, Nigel, 36
New House on the Left, 158
Newcombe, John J., 54
Newhart, Bob, 225
Newley, Anthony, 139, 225
Newman, Barry, 225
Newman, David, 122
Newman, Eve, 32, 83
Newman, Laraine, 27
Newman, Leslie, 122
Newman, Nanette, 179
Newman, Paul, 6, 225
Newman, Susan Kendall, 35, 95
Newman, Walter, 96
Newmar, Julie, 225
Newport, Jim, 133
Newton-John, Olivia, 48, 49, 142, 226
Nicholas, Denise, 50
Nicholas, Paul, 62, 63, 226
Nicholls, Allan, 95
Nichols, Anthony, 138
Nichols, David, 12
Nichols, Mike, 159, 226
Nichols, Paul "Tiny", 76

Nichols, Stephen, 45
Nichols, Terry, 76
Nichols, Terry L., 102
Nichols, Tiny, 60
Nicholson, Al, 54
Nicholson, Jack, 7, 94, 159, 226
Niciphor, Nick, 132
Nickerson, Denise, 133, 226
Nickerson, James, 102
Nickerson, Jim, 35, 124
Nicksay, David, 8
Nicol, Alex, 226
Niebeling, Hugo, 206
Nielsen, Leslie, 173, 226
Nielsen, Peggy, 127
Nieto, Eduardo, 139
Night of the Askari, 205
Nighthawks, 213
Nightmare in Blood, 135
Nights of Cabiria, The, 159
Niki, Jeff, 78
Nikolaidis, Dimitri, 42
Niles, Chuck, 126
Nimoy, Leonard, 120, 121, 226
Nishida, Toshiyuki, 198
Nitzsche, Jack, 12
Niven, David, 17, 84, 159, 226
No Beast So Fierce, 23
No Problem!, 204
Noble, Thom, 209
Noguera, Luis R., 208
Noiret, Philippe, 91, 176, 177, 210
Nolan, Frederick, 119
Nolan, Jeanette, 75, 87
Nolan, Lloyd, 125, 226
Nolte, Nick, 74, 226
None but the Lonely Heart, 158
Norbert, Frederic, 191
Norman, Allen G., 137
Norman, Gene, 31
Norman, Jay, 115
Norman, Maidie, 102
Norman, Michel, 176, 204
Norman, Zack, 126
Norris, Christopher, 226
Norris, Chuck, 130, 132
Norris, George, 137
Norris, Patricia, 50, 88, 112
Norris, Patty, 102
Norseman, The, 136
North, Alex, 82
North, Heather, 226
North, Noelle, 128
North, Robert, 101
North, Sheree, 13, 226
Northcutt, David, 106
Northup, Harry, 12
Norton, B. W. L., 58
Norton, Cliff, 135
Norton, Ken, 226
Norton, Roseanna, 35
Norwood, Lance, 132
Nosseck, Noel, 130
Nourry, Pierre, 194
Novak, Debbie, 137
Novak, Kim, 226
Novak, Lenka, 128, 134
Novo, Richard, 80
Noyes, Jan, 126
Ntshona, Winston, 199
Nuckols, William, 129
Nugent, Elliott, 226
Nugent-Hart, Judith, 137
Nunn, Alice, 28
Nunn, Terri, 130
Nunzio, 43
Nureyev, Rudolf, 226
Nurse Sherri, 135
Nusbaum, Mike, 130
Nute, Don, 226
Nuyen, France, 226
Nye, Louis, 133
Nykvist, Sven, 115, 196
Nyman, Lena, 196, 197
Nytten, Bruno, 204
Oakes, Bill, 62
Oakes, Randi, 127
Oakie, Jack, 236
Oas-Heim, Gordon, 42
Oates, Warren, 111, 226
Oberley, Charlet, 43
Oberman, Milt, 128
Oberon, Merle, 226
Obie, 71
O'Blath, Carol, 130
O'Brian, Hugh, 226
O'Brian, Peter, 206
O'Brien, Bird, 93, 97
O'Brien, Clay, 226
O'Brien, Edmond, 159, 226
O'Brien, Margaret, 158, 226
O'Brien, Pat, 40, 125, 226

O'Brien, Richard, 46, 212
Obsessed One, The, 212
O'Callaghan, Richard, 190
O'Connell, Arthur, 226
O'Connell, Bob, 100
O'Connor, Carroll, 226
O'Connor, Donald, 226
O'Connor, Glynnis, 226
O'Connor, Kevin, 111
O'Dare, Kathy, 133
O'Dea, Denis, 236
O'dell, Bryan, 130
O'Donnell, Walter D., 20
O'Donovan, Edwin, 46
Ogier, Bulle, 205
Ogisu, Terry, 131
O'Halloran, Jack, 122
O'Hanlon, George, 226
O'Hanlon, George Jr., 133
O'Hara, Maureen, 226
O'Herlihy, Dan, 226
O'Herlihy, Gavan, 95
Oja, Patty, 78
O'Keefe, Michael, 127
Okon, Tom, 131
Okun, Charles, 150
Olbrychski, Daniel, 163
Old Arizona, 158
O'Leary, Jack, 128
O'Leary, John, 118
Olek, Henry, 45
Olenicoff, S. Rodger, 124
Olfson, Ken, 8, 20
Oliver!, 159
Oliver, Cisco, 18
Oliver, James, 131
Oliver, Kyle, 20
Oliver, Stephen, 131
Oliver's Story, 116
"Oliver's Theme", 116
Olivier, Claude, 176
Olivier, Laurence, 16, 128, 158, 159, 192, 193, 226
Olivor, Jane, 106
Olly Olly Oxen Free, 71
O'Loughlin, Gerald, 226
Olson, Gerald T., 131
Olson, Nancy, 226
Olson, Ronald B., 125
Omaggio, Rosemary, 210
O'Meara, Tim, 190
Omeirs, Patrick, 102
On the Waterfront, 159
Once in Paris, 105
One and Only, The, 8
One Flew over the Cuckoo's Nest, 159
One Man Jury, 136
One Way or Another, 207
Oneal, Ellen, 126
O'Neal, Patrick, 226
O'Neal, Peggy, 18
O'Neal, Ron, 226
O'Neal, Ryan, 59, 116, 117, 226
O'Neal, Tatum, 159, 179, 226
O'Neill, Dick, 70
O'Neill, Tricia, 226
O'Neill, Dick, 8, 20
O'Neill, Jennifer, 110, 226
O'Neill, Robert, 122
Ontiveros, Lupe, 100, 112
Opatoshu, David O., 74
Operation Thunderbolt, 204
Oppenheim, Jon, 115
Oppenheimer, Alan, 125
Orchard, Julian, 30
Orlandi, Felice, 59
Orme, Charles, 54
Ornitz, Arthur, 24, 116
Orsatti, Frank, 12
Orsini, Umberto, 210, 212
Ortega, Manuel, 138
Ortolani, Riz, 213
Orton, David, 202
Osawa, Tetsuzo, 211
Osborne, Nancy, 35
Oscarsson, Per, 208
O'Shea, Milo, 212
Osmond, Cliff, 133, 135, 138
Osmond, Donny, 133, 137
Osmond, Jimmy, 133
Osmond, Marie, 137
O'Steen, Sam, 23
Osterloh, Shelley, 126
Osterwald, Bibi, 132
O'Sullivan, Maureen, 226
Oswald, Jean Stringam, 126
Other Side of the Mountain Part 2, The, 32
O'Toole, Annette, 115
O'Toole, Peter, 226
O'Toole, Stanley, 192
Otterbein, Adam J., 138
Ottinger, Barbara, 131
Our Winning Season, 132

Out of the Darkness, 133
Outin, Nick, 46
Owen, Meg Wynn, 161
Owens, Laura Mish, 137
Owensby, E. E., 135
Owensby, Earl, 125, 135
Owsley, David, 44
Oyama, Ted, 132
Pace, Richard, 138
Pacino, Al, 226
Pack, The, 212
Padada, Tom, 126
Paddack, Allan L., 44
Page, Geraldine, 64, 226
Page, Kari, 78
Page, Ty, 137
Paget, Debra, 226
Pagett, Leslie, 112
Pagett, Nicola, 116, 117
Pagni, Eros, 182
Paige, Janis, 226
Pailus, Ken, 137
Paine, Cathey, 87
Pakravan, Shahnaz, 110
Pakula, Alan J., 90
Palance, Cody, 206
Palance, Jack, 136, 206, 226
Paley, Petronia, 137
Palin, Michael, 205
Palmer, Betsy, 226
Palmer, Donna, 78
Palmer, Gregg, 76, 226
Palmer, Lilli, 192, 226
Palmer, Maria, 226
Palmer, Norman, 16
Palmieri, Vice, 129
Palmisano, Conrad, 137
Palmisano, Nick, 136
Paluzzi, Luciana, 42
Pampanini, Silvana, 226
Pancake, Roger, 35, 52
Panday, Malc, 212
Panetta, Tony, 43
Panzer, William N., 137
Papa, Anny, 160
Papadouka, Olympia, 184
Papaioannou, Panos, 184
Papamichael, Dimitris, 184, 185
Papas, Irene, 226
Paper Chase, The, 159
Paper Moon, 159
Pappas, Lucia, 126
Pappe, Stuart H., 24, 116
Paradise Alley, 83
Paredes, Jean, 91
Parfrey, Woodrow, 135
Parke, Henry C., 129
Parker, Alan, 96
Parker, Ed, 135
Parker, Eleanor, 226
Parker, Fess, 226
Parker, Jack, 139
Parker, Jean, 226
Parker, John F., 122
Parker, John T., 126
Parker, Suzy, 226
Parker, Willard, 226
Parkins, Barbara, 226
Parks, Michael, 125, 130, 131
Parks, Van Dyke, 94
Parnell, Julian, 208
Parrish, Leslie, 126
Parrish, Tracy, 212
Parrondo, Gil, 192
Parry, Harvey G., 102
Parslow, Frederick, 203
Parson, Jennifer, 14
Parsons, Estelle, 159, 226
Parsons, Julie, 128
Paryla, Stefan, 26
Pascal, Christine, 204
Pascal, Olivia, 211
Pass, Mary Kay, 135
Passer, Ivan, 36
Pastore, Michael, 132
Pasztor, Erzsi, 201
Pataki, Michael, 134
Patch of Blue, A, 159
Paterson, Pat, 236
Patinkin, Mandy, 100
Patrick, Dennis, 226
Patrick, Nigel, 226
Patrucci, Daniel, 180
Patten, Robert, 33
Patterson, Cjon Damitri, 34
Patterson, Dick, 48
Patterson, Gyr, 129
Patterson, Lee, 226
Patterson, Neva, 70
Patterson, Pat, 236
Patterson, Richard, 128
Pattillo, Allan, 18
Patton, 159
Paul and Paula, 66
Pauleson, Jack, 136
Paull, Lawrence G., 12, 33
Paulsen, Pat, 133

Paulson, Dan, 90
Paval, Samy, 210
Pavan, Marisa, 226
Paxinou, Katina, 158
Payan, Manuel, 204
Paycheck, Johnny, 138
Payne, Roy, 206
Paynter, Robert, 170
Peace, Steve, 137
Peach, Mary, 226
Peake, Don, 208
Pearce, Damon, 92
Pearce, John, 18
Pearl, Barry, 48
Pearl, Daniel, 139
Pearl, Minnie, 129
Pearson, Beatrice, 226
Pearson, Jesse, 136
Pearson, Richard, 209
Peck, Ed V., 46
Peck, Gregory, 159, 192, 193, 226
Peck, Ron, 213
Peckinpah, Sam, 58
Pecsi, Ildiko, 201
Pedi, Tom, 52, 136
Peerce, Larry, 32
Peeters, Barbara, 133
Pehrsson, Inger, 196
Peiser, Hazel, 208
Pelegrin, Ines, 210
Pelikan, Lisa, 130, 132
Pelish, Thelma, 126
Pellegrin, Raymond, 213
Pellegrino, Nick, 35
Pellow, Clifford A., 90
Peluso, Claudia, 111
Penafiel, Luis, 209
Pendleton, Austin, 132
Pendleton, Dave, 130
Penfold, Mark, 36
Penghlis, Thaao, 101
Penland, Michael, 138
Pennell, Larry, 134
Pennock, Christopher, 112
Penny, Joe, 132
Penzer, Jean, 156
Peppard, George, 226
Perceval, 191
Perez, Laida, 18
Perez, Manuel, 207
Perez, Tomas Gonzalez, 207
Pergolesi, G. B., 160
Perich, Donna, 24
Perilli, Frank Ray, 128, 134, 137
Perkins, Anthony, 226
Perkins, Marion, 45
Perkins, Pat, 37
Perkins, Von Eric, 37
Perlmutter, David, 206
Perpiche, Cindy, 87
Perrault, Gilles, 200
Perreau, Gigi, 226
Perren, Freddie, 125
Perrine, Valerie, 122, 226
Perry, Dean, 56
Perry, Felton, 127
Perry, Jamie, 92
Perry, Jeffrey S., 95
Perry, Steve H., 31, 56
Persico, Benito, 160
Pert, William, 12
Perucci, Leonardo, 204
Pescarolo, Leonardo, 211
Pesce, Frank, 83, 126, 136
Pescow, Donna, 226
Pesci, Joseph, 137
Peters, Bernadette, 226
Peters, Brock, 226
Peters, Clive, 213
Peters, Jean, 226
Peters, Jon, 78
Peters, Michael, 125
Peterson, Alan, 70
Peterson, Diane, 132
Peterson, Henry, 136
Petley, Kate, 126
Petrie, Daniel, 16
Petrie, George, 32
Petrie, Mary, 16
Petrie, Susan, 130, 211
Petrou, David, 122
Petrova, Sonya, 212
Pettet, Joanna, 130, 133, 226
Petti, Robyn, 35
Pettit, Suzanna, 77
Petty, Tom, 33
Peverall, John, 150
Peyrinaud, Frank, 105
Peyrot, Yves, 210
Phalen, Robert, 16, 137
Phenix, Lucie Massie, 127
Philadelphia Story, The, 158
Phillips, Frank, 22, 76, 137
Phillips, MacKenzie, 226
Phillips, Michelle, 226
Phillips, Thalia, 39

Phipps, Sally, 236
Phipps-Wilson, V., 130
Piazzoli, Roberto, 213
Picard, Beriau, 138
Piccoli, Michel, 162
Piccolo, Ottavia, 162
Picerni, Paul, 226
Pickens, Slim, 125, 135, 138, 226
Picker, David V., 8, 116
Pickford, Mary, 158, 159, 226
Pickles, Vivian, 17
Pidgeon, Walter, 227
Pieplu, Claude, 204
Pierce, Arthur, 126
Pierce, Charles B., 136
Pierce, Roger Lawrence, 131
Pierson, Frank, 115
Pietropinto, Angela, 43
Piffath, Rod, 76
Pilon, Daniel, 164
Pine, Howard, 129
Pine, Howard B., 23
Pine, Larry, 35
Pine, Phillip, 227
Pinion, Efren C., 207
Pino, Jose, 204
Pinzon, Victor, 18
Pippin, 104
Piquer, Juan, 213
Piranha, 136
Pirosmani, 208
Pirro, Ugo, 210
Pischinger, Herta, 26
Pisier, Marie-France, 205, 38
Pistilli, Luigi, 212
Pitt, Arthur, 205
Pitt, William, 31
Piwowski, Marek, 207
Place in the Sun, A, 158
Place, Mary Kay, 227
Planchon, Roger, 200
Planet of the Apes, 159
Plans, J. J., 209
Plater, Alan, 209
Plato, Dana, 112
Platt, Howard T., 52
Platt, Polly, 37
Playten, Alice, 227
Pleasence, Donald, 62, 63, 133, 137, 227
Plemiannikov, Helene, 186
Pleshette, John, 20
Pleshette, Suzanne, 227
Plimpton, George, 125, 131
Plumb, Flora, 131
Plummer, Christopher, 179, 227
Plytas, Steve, 36
Podesta, Rossana, 227
Poer, John M., 37, 58
Pohle, Robyn, 128
Poinc, Eugene, 71
Poindexter, 22
Poire, Alain, 172
Poire, Jean-Marie, 204
Poitier, Sidney, 159, 227
Pola, Claude, 87
Polakof, James, 131
Poledouris, Basil, 130, 137
Polito, Gene, 80, 134
Polito, Lina, 227
Poll, Martin, 82
Pollard, Michael J., 227
Pollard, Samuel D., 139
Pollock, David, 134
Polon, Vicki, 77
Pomares, Raul, 207
Pomerantz, Jeff, 42
Ponti, Carlo, 206
Pontreomil, David, 209
Ponzini, Anthony, 127
Poole, Roy, 16
Poopsie, 206
Pope, Tom, 75
Popescu, Peter, 203
Poplin, J. S., 127
Popwell, Albert, 70
Pornodiva, 182
Porteous, Emma, 202
Porter, Eric, 208, 227
Porter, Russell, 16
Poseley, Jacquelyn, 137
Post, Mike, 13
Post, Ted, 86, 132
Posta, Adrienne, 212
Poston, Tom, 13
Potter, Martin, 170
Potter, Steve, 44
Pottle, Harry, 170
Potts, Annie, 53, 115
Poulton, Ray, 202
Pourriche, Armelle, 176
Poursattar, Mohammad, 110
Powell, Anthony, 84
Powell, Eleanor, 227

Powell, Jane, 227
Powell, Larry, 114
Powell, Robert, 208, 227
Powell, William, 227
Power, Derry, 208
Power, Richard, 205
Power, Taryn, 227
Powers, Mala, 227
Powers, Pamela, 161
Powers, Stefanie, 126
Prather, Joan, 13
Pratt, Charles A., 127
Pratt, Tony, 30
Preiss, Wolfgang, 192
Preissman, Ron, 28
Prentiss, Gregory, 100
Prentiss, Paula, 227
Presle, Micheline, 186, 187, 227
Presnell, Harve, 227
Pressman, Edward, 83
Preston, Billy, 62, 63
Preston, Robert, 227
Pretty Baby, 37
Prevost, Francoise, 209
Price, Peggy, 212
Price, Ray, 129
Price, Richard, 96
Price, Roger, 52
Price, Vincent, 212, 227
Price, Walt, 126
Prime of Miss Jean Brodie, The, 159
Primes, Robert, 139
Primus, Barry, 87, 211
Prince, Harold, 26
Prince, Michael, 42
Prince, Steven, 38
Prince, William, 52, 227
Principal, Victoria, 227
Prine, Andrew, 133
Pringle, Douglas, 211
"Prisoner", 78
Pritchard, Anne, 211
Pritchard, Sally, 127
Private Files of J. Edgar Hoover, The, 125
Private Life of Henry VIII, 158
Proietti, Luigi, 91, 95, 210
Protheroe, Brian, 122
Proudfoot, Patty, 80
Proulx, Monique, 125
Proval, David, 43, 227
Provine, Dorothy, 227
Provost, Martin, 186
Prowse, Juliet, 227
Prucnal, Anna, 200
Pruzelius, Gosta, 158
Pryor, Barbara, 125
Pryor, Nicholas, 54, 55
Pryor, Richard, 12, 92, 112, 113, 227
Puerto, Carlos, 213
Punk Rock Movie, The, 209
Purcell, Lee, 130, 136, 137, 227
Purcell, Noel, 227
Purdom, Edmund, 227
Putnam, David, 161
Puzo, Mario, 122
Pyke, Hy, 135
Pyle, Denver, 22, 227
Python, Shirley, 68
Quaid, Dennis, 18, 132, 135
Quaid, Randy, 96, 99
Quayle, Anthony, 206, 227
Queen-Mason, Edward, 211
Quick, Diana, 161, 170, 171
Quiet Man, The, 158
Quigley, Lee, 122
Quilligan, Veronica, 17
Quine, Richard, 227
Quinn, Almeria, 12
Quinn, Anthony, 42, 110, 158, 159, 210, 227
Quinn, Duncan, 110
Quinn, James, 38
Quinn, Pat, 24
Quinn, Tom, 43, 115
Raab, Gilles, 191
Rabbit Test, 13
Raben, Peer, 211
Rabier, Jean, 194
Racheva, Elena, 209
Rachmil, Michael, 50
Rader, Jack, 127
Radmall, Peter, 213
Rae, Charlotte, 13
Rae, Michael, 128
Raebeck, Wendy, 131
Rafelson, Roby Carr, 94
Raffaeli, Bruno, 209
Rafferty, Frances, 227
Raffill, Joseph C., 34
Raffill, Stewart, 34
Raffin, Deborah, 227
Rafia, Bozorgmehr, 110

Raft, George, 227
Ragland, Robert O., 129
Ragozzini, Ed, 125
Raho, Umberto, 180
Raimond, Lawrence, 131
Rain and Shine, 201
Rainer, Iris, 135
Rainer, Luise, 158
Raines, Cristina, 161
Raines, Ella, 227
Ralston, Jane, 129
Ralston, Teri, 16
Ramage, Jack, 101
Ramer, Henry, 164
Rametta, Guido, 203
Ramezani, Joe, 115
Ramirez, Luis Alberto, 208
Ramis, Harold, 66
Ramos, Rudy, 59
Rampling, Charlotte, 227
Ramrus, Al, 94
Ramsey, Anne, 94
Ramsey, Gordon, 131
Ramsey, Logan, 227
Rand, Corey, 23
Randall, Tony, 227
Randell, Ron, 227
Randles, Bob, 131
Randolph, John, 46
Randolph, Lillian, 108
Ranieri, Massimo, 206
Ransome, Prunella, 209
Rapaglia, Sal, 131
Rapp, Paul, 87
Rapper, Irving, 97
Rapson, Robert, 137
Rash, Steve, 70
Rashomon, 158
Rasmussen, Tom, 133
Rassimov, Ivan, 206, 212
Rastatter, Wendy, 132
Rasulala, Thalmus, 227
Ratliff, Jane, 137
Rattray, Eric, 42
Rattray, Heather, 34, 139
Ratzenberger, John, 122, 208
Ravel, Jean, 210
Rawlings, Terry, 190
Ray, Aldo, 134, 227
Ray, James, 23
Ray, Joseph, 43
Ray, Robyn, 136
Ray, Satyajit, 209
Ray, Tony, 24
Rayburn, Basil, 208
Raye, Martha, 227
Raymond, Gene, 227
Raymond, Maryse, 174
Razor's Edge, The, 158
Reagan, Ronald, 227
Reason, Rex, 227
Rebbot, Sady, 105
Rebecca, 158
Rebillon, Gisele, 209
Record City, 125
Redack, Jay, 13
Redd, Mary-Robin, 126
Reddy, Helen, 227
Redeemer, The, 129
Redeker, Quinn K., 150
Redford, H. E. D., 126
Redford, Robert, 6, 227
Redgrave, Corin, 227
Redgrave, Lynn, 227
Redgrave, Michael, 227
Redgrave, Vanessa, 147, 159, 227
Redlich, Forest, 211
Redman, Joyce, 227
Redondo, Emiliano, 213
Reed, Alan, 158
Reed, Carol, 159
Reed, Donna, 159, 227
Reed, Jerry, 134
Reed, Marshall, 125
Reed, Oliver, 30, 170, 171, 227
Reed, Rex, 122, 227
Reems, Harry, 227
Reeve, Christopher, 122, 123, 127, 141, 227
Reeves, Jim, 129
Reeves, Steve, 227
Reggiani, Serge, 209
Reid, Elliott, 227
Reilly, Diane, 124
Reineke, Gary, 211
Reiner, Carl, 8, 40, 41, 227
Reiner, Robert, 227
Reinke, Carla, 112
Reinking, Ann, 102
Reis, Beth, 137
Reisz, Karel, 74
Reith, Douglas, 179
Reitman, Ivan, 66, 211
Remick, Lee, 175, 227
Remsen, Bert, 95, 138
Renaday, Pete, 52

Renant, Simone, 176
Renard, Jacques, 205
Renoir, Jean, 159
Renucci-Wakhevitch, Jeanne, 206
Renzetti, Joe, 70
Replay, 210
Repo, 133
Reseher, Cayne, 71
Resenker, Bruno, 174
Resin, Dan, 131
Resnick, Patricia, 95
Resnick, Robert, 137
Restless, 208
Rettig, Tommy, 227
Return From Witch Mountain, 22
Return to Boggy Creek, 125
Revenge of the Pink Panther, 60
Revere, Anne, 158
Revill, Clive, 134, 227
Rey, Antonia, 115
Rey, Fernando, 227
Rey, Silvano, 207
Reyes, Stanley, 137
Reynolds, Burt, 6, 40, 41, 72, 73, 227
Reynolds, Clarke, 204
Reynolds, Debbie, 227
Reynolds, Gerald H., 94
Reynolds, Marjorie, 227
Rezende, Rui, 166
Rheaume, Dell, 120
Rhoades, Barbara, 227
Rhodes, Harry, 10
Rhodes, Jennifer, 133
Rhytis, Arthur, 82
Ricceri, Luciano, 182
Rice, Herbert, 130
Rich, Allan, 138
Rich, Irene, 227
Rich, Lee, 91
Richard, Jacques, 162
Richard, Pierre, 211, 212
Richards, Jeff, 227
Richards, Kim, 227
Richards, Kyle, 137
Richards, Lisa Blake, 46
Richards, Lou, 135
Richards, Martin, 192
Richards, Sal, 78
Richards, Ted III, 45
Richardson, John, 210
Richardson, Ralph, 190, 227
Richardson, Tony, 159
Richardson, W. Lyle, 133
Richardson, Warren, 31
Riche, Alan, 130
Richler, Mordecai, 212
Richman, Roger, 126, 136
Richmond, Anthony, 36, 42
Richrath, Gary, 33
Richt, Claus, 211
Richter, W. D., 120
Richwine, Maria, 70
Rickles, Don, 227
Rickman, Thomas, 72
Riddle, Nelson, 133
Riddle, Rock, 12
Ridgely, Bob, 135
Riedel, Georg, 168
Riegert, Peter, 66
Rielo, Luis, 208
Rifkin, Ron, 100
Rigaud, George, 210
Rigby, Terence, 190
Rigg, Diana, 26, 227
Riley, Jack, 137
Riley, Jeannie C., 133
Riley, Steve, 126
Rilla, Stefano, 206
Rimmer, Shane, 36, 208
Rinaldi, Peter M., 138
Rini, David, 112
Rique, Newton, 166
Riquier, Georges, 176
Risdon, Carlton, 94
Risi, Dino, 182
Risley, Ann, 116
Ritchie, Joe, 170
Ritchie, Michael, 134
Ritchie, Stan, 135
Riton, 156
Ritt, Martin, 31
Ritt, Tina, 33, 56
Ritter, John, 130, 227
Rituals, 211
Ritvo, Rosemary, 131
Rivera, Greg, 136
Rivera, Marika, 212
Rivera, Mike, 136
Rivers, Joan, 13
Rivers, Leslie Ann, 137
Rivette, Jacques, 205
Riviere, Carine, 174
Roach, John F., 83
Roarke, Adam, 125

Robards, Jason, 90, 146, 159, 227
Robbins, Gale, 227
Robbins, Harold, 16
Robbins, Jerome, 159
Robbins, Marty, 129
Robbins, Matthew, 53
Roberson, James, 125
Robert, Guy, 191
Robert, Ives, 172
Robert, Jean-Denis, 162
Robert, Pierre, 207
Robert, Yves, 172
Roberts, Arthur, 80, 97, 133
Roberts, Donald, 106
Roberts, Doris, 13, 105
Roberts, Eric, 115, 142, 227
Roberts, Marilyn, 126
Roberts, Mariwin, 205
Roberts, Pernell, 136
Roberts, Rachel, 68, 69, 208, 227
Roberts, Ralph, 228
Roberts, Randy, 23
Roberts, Tanya, 126
Roberts, Tony, 144, 228
Robertson, Cliff, 159, 228
Robertson, Dale, 228
Robertson, Ken, 213
Robertson, Malcolm, 203
Robertson, Robbie, 38
Robertson, Sandy, 87
Robinson, Bruce, 126
Robinson, Charlie, 127
Robinson, Chris, 228
Robinson, Dick, 127
Robinson, Edward G., 159
Robinson, Jay, 97
Robinson, Joe, 126
Robinson, Mabel, 92
Robinson, Raymone, 66
Robinson, Richard, 136
Robinson, Robert, 36
Robinson, Roger, 228
Robinson, Stuart K., 83
Roblee, Jan, 38
Robles, Hernan, 18
Robson, Flora, 208, 228
Robson, Mark, 236
Robson, Michael, 206
Rocco, Alex, 13
Rocco, Antonino, 131
Rochaix, Francois, 210
Roche, Eugene, 53, 68
Rochefort, Jean, 91, 172
Rochester, 228
Rocky, 159
Roddro, Jose Lopez, 192
Rodger, Strewan, 91
Rodgers, Aggie Guerard, 53
Rodgers, Michael, 102
Rodrigo, Xavier, 132
Rodriguez, Charles, 92
Rodriguez, Jose Antonio, 207
Rodriguez, Nelson, 204, 207
Rodriguez, Paul, 207
Rodriguez, Percy, 126
Rodzianko, Anna, 62
Roe, Jack, 23, 112
Roehm, Edward, 137
Roerick, William, 16
Roessel, Howard, 96
Rogak, Gina, 77
Rogalny, Marty, 131
Rogers, Charles "Buddy", 228
Rogers, Ginger, 158, 228
Rogers, Lesley, 95
Rogers, Roy, 228
Rogers, Wayne, 105, 228
Rohmer, Eric, 191
Roizman, Owen, 23, 62
Rojas, Orlando, 204
Roland, Gilbert, 228
Roland, Rita, 16
Rolf, Tom, 12
Rolfe, David W., 138
Rollins, Oneida, 44
Roman Holiday, 159
Roman, Ric R., 135
Roman, Ruth, 228
Roman, Shenda, 204
Romano, Andy, 136
Romano, Renato, 208
Romano, Tony, 126
Romanos, The, 35
Romer, Ana, 206
Romero, Cesar, 228
Romero, George A., 134
Ronard, Jason, 53
Ronay, Laci von, 26
Rondell, R. A., 66
Rondell, Reid, 124
Rondi, Brunello, 205
Rondo, George, 56
Ronstadt, Linda, 33

Rook, David, 208
Room at the Top, 159
Rooney, Mickey, 136, 158, 228
Roosevelt, Theodore, 137
Rooyen, DeWet Van, 199
Roscoe, Judith, 74
Rose, Al, 37
Rose, Alex, 35, 130
Rose, Jack, 133
Rose, Reginald, 82, 199
Rose, Reva, 20
Rose, Stephen Bruce, 128
Rose, Steven, 132
Rose Tattoo, The, 159
Rose, Wally, 102
Rosemary's Baby, 159
Rosen, Charles, 120, 130
Rosen, Martin, 190
Rosenberg, Edgar, 13
Rosenberg, Frank P., 127
Rosenberg, Marion, 150
Rosenberg, Melissa, 13
Rosenberg, Philip, 92
Rosenberg, Richard K., 131
Rosenberg, Stephen, 212
Rosenblum, Irving, 131
Rosenblum, Ralph, 64, 107
Rosenman, Leonard, 18, 104
Rosenthal, Laurence, 74, 119
Rosenthal, Robert J., 131
Rosher, Charles, 95
Rosher, Charles Jr., 102
Rosly, Judy, 206
Ross, Artie, 128
Ross, Beverly, 95
Ross, Diana, 92, 93, 228
Ross, Herbert, 112
Ross, Joe, 56
Ross, Katharine, 16, 135, 228
Ross, Ted, 92, 93
Rosseau, Don-Jack, 137
Rossen, Carol, 28
Rossi, Giorgio Carlo, 206
Rossiter, Leonard, 228
Rota, Nino, 84, 204
Roth, Ann, 14, 43, 112
Roth, Joe, 132
Roth, Lillian, 131, 228
Roth, Nathan, 131
Rothman, Marion, 90
Rothman, Stephanie, 133
Rothschild, Richard Luke, 54
Rothwell, Robert, 76
Rotunno, Giuseppe, 160
Rougerie, Jean, 156, 209
Rouland, Jean-Paul, 176
Rouleau, Philippe, 200
Rounds, David, 115, 228
Roundtree, Richard, 228
Roupe, Larry, 228
Routh, May, 62
Rowe, George, 211
Rowe, Greg, 203
Rowland, Beverly, 126
Rowland, Oscar, 126
Rowlands, David, 100
Rowlands, Gena, 111, 228
Rowley, Chris, 211
Roy, Gary, 136
Roy, Soumendu, 209
Royle, Carol, 42
Royster, Vermetta, 12
Rozsa, Miklos, 125
Ruban, Al, 100
Rubber Gun, The, 207
Rubel, Marc Reid, 137
Ruben, Joseph, 132
Rubenstein, Susan, 131
Rubin, Andrew, 31, 228
Rubin, Frank, 128
Rubin, Glynn, 68
Rubinstein, Arthur B., 107
Rubinstein, Donald, 134
Rubinstein, John, 192
Rubinstein, Martin, 130
Rubinstein, Richard, 134
Rucker, Bo, 122
Rudd, Paul, 16
Ruddy, Albert S., 134
Rudnick, Charles, 135
Rudolf, Gene, 126
Ruhl, Warney H., 16
Ruidoso, 31
Ruiz, Isaac, 125
Ruiz, Isaac Jr., 53
Ruiz, Jose Carlos, 74
Rule, Janice, 228
Runacre, Jenny, 161
Rundell, Tommy, 36
Running Deer, 100
Rupert, Michael, 228
Rush, Alice, 12
Rush, Barbara, 228
Rush, Deborah, 116

Ruskin, Sheila, 91
Russell, Harold, 158
Russell, Jackie, 32
Russell, Jane, 228
Russell, John, 228
Russell, Kurt, 228
Russell, Nipsey, 92, 93
Russell, Tanya, 126
Russell, Theresa, 23
Russell, William, 122
Russianoff, Penelope, 24
Russo, Daniel, 162
Russo, Gianni, 128
Russo, Matt, 122
Russo, N. W., 212
Russo, Neno, 68
Russo, Vincent, 43
Russon, Stanley, 126
Rutherford, Ann, 228
Rutherford, Margaret, 159
Ruud, Michael, 126
Ruud, Sif, 168
Ruymen, Ayn, 228
Ryan, Fran, 23, 133
Ryan, John P., 130
Ryan, Madge, 91
Ryan, Paul, 133
Ryan's Daughter, 159
Ryerson, Ann, 95
Sabiston, Peter, 125
Sacci, Chuck, 130
Sacharnoski, Rod, 135
Sachs, Norman, 127
Sackler, Howard, 44, 127
Sacks, Ezra, 33
Sacks, Michael, 125
Sadrinen, Eric, 208
Safan, Craig, 53, 132
Sager, Carole Bayer, 124
Sager, George, 127
Sahag, John, 78
Saint, Eva Marie, 159, 228
Saint-Clair, Barrie, 205
Saint-Cyr, Renee, 204, 212
Saito, Ichiro, 178
Sakata, Harold, 125, 134, 137
Saks, Gene, 8
Salamunovich, Mike, 135
Saldana, Theresa, 35, 43
Saldanha, Raul Faustino, 192
Salier, Edward, 131
Salisbury, Frances, 92
Salkind, Alexander, 122
Salkind, Ilya, 30, 122
Salles, Maurilio, 166
Salling, Norman, 40
Sallis, Peter, 91
Salmi, Albert, 228
Salt, Jennifer, 228
Salt, Waldo, 14
Salvador, Manuel, 209
Sam, 104
Same Time, Next Year, 106
Sammeth, Barbara, 68
Samosiuk, Zygmunt, 163
Samperi, Salvatore, 213
Samuels, David, 17
Samulekin, Alexander, 188
Samurai, 159
San Juan, Olga, 228
Sanchez, Alicia, 206
Sanchez, Leon, 138
Sand, Paul, 107
Sanda, Dominique, 210
Sanders, Beverly, 108
Sanders, Cornelia, 54
Sanders, George, 158
Sanders, Harlan, 127
Sanders, Jack, 16, 50
Sanders, June, 100
Sanders, Sandy, 136
Sandin, Will, 137
Sandor, Kuli, 204
Sands, Tommy, 228
Sandy, Gary, 132
Sanford, Paula, 18
Sanger, Jonathan, 102
Santa Lucia, Vincent Robert, 82
Santercole, Gino, 212
Santi, Jacques, 162
Santiago, Cirio H., 134, 137
Santoni, Reni, 133
Santos, Burt, 212
Santos, Cecile, 115
Sapounakis, Paul, 134
Sarandon, Chris, 228
Sarandon, Susan, 37, 115, 127, 132, 228
Sarchet, Kate, 128
Sarde, Philippe, 162
Sardo, Cosmo, 106
Sargent, Alvin, 23
Sargent, Bobby, 136
Sargent, Richard, 228
Sarlai, Imre, 201
Sarli, Maurice, 210
Sarony, Leslie, 209

Saroyan, Lucy, 12
Sarrazin, Michael, 110, 228
Sarstedt, Richard, 126
Sartain, Gailaird, 70, 138
Sasaki, George, 20
Sasquatch, the Legend of Bigfoot, 125
Sato, David, 112
Satterfield, Bush, 18
Satterfield, Katherine, 18
Saunders, Jan, 77
Saunier, Claude, 105
Saussure, Marie-Therese, 205
Sautet, Claude, 162
Sauvegrain, Didier, 200
Savadove, Larry, 205
Savage, Brad, 22
Savage, John, 149, 150, 151
Savalas, Sally, 212
Savalas, Telly, 50, 51, 228
Savani, Tom, 134
Save the Tiger, 159
Savile, David, 170
Saville, Philip, 208
Savini, Tom, 134
Savoy, Teresa Ann, 228
Sawade, Ron, 129
Sawaya, George, 35
Sawaya, Rick, 35
Sawyer, Connie, 68
Sawyer, David, 137
Sawyer, Tony, 212
Saxon, John, 138, 228
Saxton, John C., 211
Sayles, John, 136
Saylor, Shannon, 34
Sayonara, 159
Sbragia, Giancarlo, 206
Scaccia, Mario, 212
Scaccianoce, Luigi, 210
Scales, Prunella, 192
Scales, T. Carlyle, 107
Scalici, Jack, 8
Scalpel, 137
Scanlan, Jack, 112
Scanlan, Jerry, 46
Scarano, Silvio, 14
Scarano, Tony, 39
Scarantino, Bob, 43
Scardamaglia, Elio, 212
Scardino, Jack, 150
Scarpelle, 182
Scarpelli, Glenn, 43
Scarpita, Guy, 135
Scarroll, David, 137
Scarwid, Diana, 37
Schacht, Franne, 128
Schachter, Simone, 131
Schaefer, Hal, 173
Schaeffer, Irwin, 132, 139
Schafer, Kent, 126
Schaffner, Franklin J., 159, 192
Schain, Don, 137
Schall, Wendy, 125
Schamus, Ray, 134
Schechtman, Jeff, 136
Scheeland, Rich, 127
Scheider, Roy, 44, 228
Scheiderman, Herb, 137
Scheiwiller, Fred, 102
Schell, Maria, 122, 228
Schell, Maximilian, 159, 228
Schell, Ronnie, 52
Schellerup, Henning, 126
Schenck, Joseph M., 158
Schiavelli, Vincent, 24
Schifrin, Lalo, 22, 43, 52, 75
Schildkraut, Joseph, 158
Schiller, Joel, 70, 124
Schilz, Mark R., 83
Schizo, 206
Schlesinger, John, 159
Schlondorff, Volker, 205
Schmalholz, David, 132
Schmidt, Arne, 108
Schmidt, Arthur, 44
Schmidt, Burr, 129
Schmidt, Georgia, 94
Schmidt, Jacques, 191
Schmidt, Marlene, 133
Schmidt, Phoebe, 132
Schneider, Barry, 133
Schneider, Bert, 88, 128
Schneider, Daniele, 174
Schneider, Franz, 209
Schneider, Harold, 88, 94
Schneider, Maria, 228
Schneider, Romy, 162, 210, 228
Schockey, Raymond, 70
Schofield, Katharine, 42
Schoolnik, Stuart, 87
Schoppe, James, 59
Schrader, Leonard, 12
Schrader, Paul, 12

Schroeder, Barbet, 191, 205
Schrympf, Rudolf, 26
Schubert, Franz, 200
Schubert, Heidi, 129
Schubert, Patrice, 129
Schullman, Hal, 130
Schultz, Michael, 62
Schumacher, Joel, 64, 92
Schumacher, Paul, 129
Schumann, Eric, 205
Schussler, Franz, 26
Schussler, Johanna, 26
Schuster, Mary, 124
Schwab, Joseph, 118
Schwade, Sol, 116
Schwartz, Hal, 34
Schwartz, Jean-Paul, 176
Schwartz, Teri, 138
Schwartzberg, Louis, 139
Schwary, Ronald L., 31, 56, 112
Schwarzenegger, Arnold, 228
Scofield, Paul, 159, 228
Scola, Ettore, 182
Scooler, Zvee, 115
Scorsese, Martin, 38
Scott, Antony, 122
Scott, Bill, 72, 130
Scott, Bryan, 18, 19
Scott, Carl, 211, 212
Scott, Cedric, 95
Scott, Elliot, 208
Scott, Franklyn, 115
Scott, George C., 30, 102, 103, 159, 228
Scott, Gordon, 228
Scott, Jan, 40
Scott Joplin, 125
Scott, Kathryn Leigh, 42
Scott, Kirk, 136
Scott, Martha, 228
Scott, Randolph, 228
Scott, Ridley, 161
Scott, Secret, 37
Scott, Susan, 205
Scott, Tim, 88
Scott, Tom, 137
Scott, W. Patrick, 31
Scott, William P., 31
Scott-Taylor, Jonathan, 54, 228
Scrobogna, Federico, 180
Scuderi, Philip, 132
Sea Gypsies, The, 34
Sea Wolf, 125
Seabo, 135
Seagull, Barbara Hershey, 228
Sears, Heather, 228
Seberg, Jean, 228
Sechan, Edmond, 205
Secombe, Harry, 228
Secret Life of Plants, The, 139
Secrets, 228
Sedaka, Neil, 82
Sedgwick, Katrina, 203
Seelers, Arlene, 20
Seff, Richard, 45
Seffinger, Carol, 128
Segal, Erich, 116
Segal, George, 91, 228
Segal, Michael, 17
Segal, Stuart A., 129
Segall, Harry, 46
Segall, Stuart, 137
Segui, Pierre, 150
Seibel, Mary, 95
Seldes, Marian, 126
Selleck, Tom, 10
Sellers, Arlene, 36
Sellers, Elizabeth, 228
Sellers, Peter, 6, 60, 61, 228
Sellier, Charles E. Jr., 126
Selman, Linda, 101
Seltzer, Daniel, 24
Seltzer, David, 54
Seltzer, Dov, 204
Seltzer, Jack, 8
Selver, Veronica, 127
Selwart, Tonio, 228
Selzer, Milton, 12, 130, 133
Sembene, Ousmane, 205
Semprun, Jorge, 210
Sene, Nar Modou, 205
Senia, Jean-Marie, 205
Seniors, The, 135
Senna, Lorraine, 102
Sennett, Mack, 158
Senter, Jack, 22, 86
Sentis, Ivonne, 213
Separate Tables, 159
Seppe, Christopher, 137
September 30, 1955, 18
Sergeant Pepper's Lonely Hearts Club Band, 62

Sergeant York, 158
Sernas, Jacques, 228
Serpe, Ralph, 111
Serrador, Cia, 166
Serrador, Narciso Ibanez, 209
Serreaul, Michel, 156
Serres, Jacques, 205
Servant and Mistress, 209
Serve, Alain, 191
Server, Eric, 76
Settle, Phil, 126
Seventh Heaven, 158
Seyler, Athene, 228
Seymour, Anne, 228
Seymour, Jane, 228
Seyrig, Delphine, 204, 210
Shackleton, Allan, 204
Shaffer, Anthony, 84
Shaine, Rich, 131
Shames, Lisa, 37
Shampoo, 159
Shamshiev, Bolotbek, 213
Shan, Kuan, 210
Shan, Lian, 211
Sha-Na-Na, 48
Shane, 209
Shaner, John Herman, 94
Shannon, James, 115
Shapiro, Larry, 127
Shapiro, Mel, 139
Shapiro, Melvin, 27, 124
Shapiro, Stanley, 135
Sharif, Omar, 228
Sharkey, Ray, 74, 83, 129
Sharpe, Robert, 133
Sharrett, Michael, 76, 136
Sharrock, Ian, 17
Shatner, William, 137, 228
Shaulis, Jane, 68
Shaver, Helen, 134, 164
Shaw, George Newman, 137
Shaw, James, 92
Shaw, Philip, 179
Shaw, Robert, 202, 237
Shaw, Sebastian, 228
Shaw, Stan, 18, 228
Shaw, Susan, 237
Shaw, Susan Damante, 139
Shaw, Tom, 58
Shawlee, Joan, 228
Shawn, Dick, 228
Shawn, Jenny, 43
Shay, Mildred, 17
Shaye, Lin, 94
Shear, Wendy, 114
Sheard, Michael, 202
Shearer, Moira, 228
Shearer, Norma, 158, 228
Sheehan, David, 112
Sheen, Martin, 228
Sheffield, John, 228
Shektin, Louis, 173
Shelach, Riki, 204
Sheldon, Ernie, 134
Sheldon, Stanley, 2
Shelley, Paul, 209
Shelly, Bruce, 125
Shelton, Sloan, 92
Shen, chang Chien, 204
Shenanigans, 107
Shengelaya, Georgi, 208
Shepard, Sam, 88, 89, 125, 142
Shepherd, Cybill, 36, 228
Shepherd, Elizabeth, 54, 55
Sheppard, Paula, 131
Sherbet, 211
Sherman, Don, 138
Sherman, J. Michael, 137
Sherman, Richard M., 136
Sherman, Robert B., 136
Sherman, Robert M., 58
Sherman, Samuel M., 137
Shernen, Gayna, 80
Sherrill, Diane, 148
Sherrin, Ned, 207
Sherry, Diane, 122
Sherwood, Mark, 135
Shields, Brooke, 37, 115, 131, 142, 228
Shifrin, Su, 122
Shimono, Sab, 13
Shindo, Eitaro, 178
Shinoda, Masahiro, 198
Shiomi, Sue, 211
Shipler, Craig, 126
Shire, David, 23
Shire, Talia, 228
Shirley, Peg, 133
Shiva, Gil, 160
Shker, Sheik Renal, 206
Shoe Shine, 158
Shoemaker, Ann, 237
Shoemaker, Donald S., 204
Shoop, Pamela, 136
Shop on Main Street, The, 159
Shore, Dinah, 228
Showalter, Max, 62, 229

Shrady, Henry, 101
Shroud of Turin, 138
Shubert, Lynn, 125
Shull, Richard B., 212
Shulman, Max, 20
Shultis, Jackie, 88
Shuman, Felix, 54
Shuster, Joe, 122
Shutan, Jan, 134
Shuter, Sally, 208
Shyer, Charles, 20, 94
Sibert, Roderick Spencer, 92
Siddall, John, 60
Siddon, J. David, 127
Sidney, Sylvia, 54, 229
Siebert, Charles, 10, 132
Siegal, Robin, 131
Siegel, Jerry, 122
Siegel, Richard, 126
Sierra, Gregory, 127
Signorelli, Tom, 131
Signoret, Simone, 148, 149, 159, 229
Silayan, Vic, 137
Silberkleit, William B., 125
Silent Witness, The, 138
Silliphant, Stirling, 135
Silva, Henry, 212
Silvan, David, 138
Silvani, Al, 114
Silver, Alain J., 75, 114
Silver Bears, 36
Silver, Borah, 12
Silverkleit, David, 138
Silvers, Phil, 56, 229
Silvestri, Larry, 43
Simmons, George F., 56
Simmons, Jean, 229
Simmons, Matty, 66
Simms, William, 137
Simon, Lauren, 56
Simon, Neil, 56, 112
Simon, Raphael, 100
Simon, Roger L., 100
Simon, Simone, 229
Simonelli, George, 70
Simpson, O. J., 50, 51, 229
Simpson, Peter R., 34
Sin of Madelon Claudet, The, 158
Sinatra, Frank, 159, 229
Sincere, Jean, 26
Sinclair, Ivy, 137
Sinclair, Madge, 58, 138
Sinclaire, Chrystin, 137
Sinden, Donald, 229
Sing, Chan, 173
Sing, Chen, 211
Singer, Marc, 86
Singer, Raymond, 96
Singleton, Eddie, 12
Singleton, Rya, 12
Siouxsie & the Banshees,, 209
Siporin, Steve, 133
Sirianni, Joree, 56
Sirico, Anthony, 136
Siroco, Anthony, 126
Sisco, Sheila, 56
Sisson, Rosemary Anne, 17
Sivero, Frank, 134
Sizeler, Philip H., 37
Skaff, George, 45
Skala, Lilia, 229
Skateboard, 126
Skeaping, Colin, 122
Skeggs, Roy, 211
Skelton, Red, 229
Skerritt, Tom, 80, 124, 229
Skinner, Anita, 77
Skinner, T. B., 92
Skippy, 158
Slade, Bernard, 106
Slade, Mark, 126
Slan, John, 134
Slark, Fred, 18
Slate, Henry, 52
Slate, Jack, 102
Slaughter and the Dogs, 209
Slave of Love, A, 188
Slezak, Walter, 229
Slithis, 135
Slits, The, 209
Sloan, John R., 202
Slocombe, Douglas, 110
Slocum, Tom, 118
Slow Dancing in the Big City, 101
Small, Marya, 130, 132
Small, Michael, 59, 77, 90
Smalls, Charlie, 92
Smally, Bob, 70
Smiles of a Summer Night, 26
Smillie, Bill, 136
Smith, Alexis, 31, 229
Smith, Arthur, 124
Smith, Bill, 137

Smith, Billy Ray, 13
Smith, Bud, 111
Smith, C. A. R., 115
Smith, Carl, 129
Smith, Catherine Lee, 137
Smith, Charles Martin, 70, 125
Smith, Cheryl, 128
Smith, Chief Tug, 122
Smith, Clay, 125
Smith, Delos V., 62
Smith, Delos V. Jr., 212
Smith, Derek, 91
Smith, Earl E., 125
Smith, Emily, 127
Smith, Frank T., 76
Smith, Frederick A., 130
Smith, George W., 94
Smith, Geraldine, 136
Smith, Hubert, 133
Smith, Irby, 50
Smith, Joe, 33
Smith, John, 229
Smith, Kate, 229
Smith, Kent, 212, 229
Smith, Lane, 12
Smith, Lionel, 130
Smith, Liz, 209
Smith, Lois, 229
Smith, Maggie, 84, 85, 112, 113, 155, 159, 229
Smith, Marjorie, 91
Smith, Martha, 66, 67
Smith, Maura, 130
Smith, Maurice, 206
Smith, Oliver, 206
Smith, Paul, 96
Smith, Pete, 159
Smith, Queenie, 68, 237
Smith, Rainbeaux, 80
Smith, Roger, 229
Smith, Stevie, 189
Smith, Stirling, 126
Smith, Susanne, 126
Smith-Caffey, Maria, 43
Smithers, Jan, 132
Smithers, William, 128
Smithson, Fred, 18
Smokey and the Goodtime Outlaws, 138
Smolinski, Aaron, 122
Smolker, Peter, 139
Smooth Velvet, Raw Silk, 205
Smothers, Tom, 36
Snapshot, 130
Sneed, Maurice, 130
Snider, Jerry, 12
Snodgrass, Carrie, 28, 229
Snow, Jack T., 46
Snow, Mark, 126
Snowden, Leigh, 229
Snyder, Arlen Dean, 137
Sobieski, Carol, 31
Soboloff, Arnold, 52
Sobul, Jerald, 108
Sokol, Marilyn, 68, 69
Solano, Felipe, 206
Solar, Silvia, 210
Solas, Humberto, 204
Soldo, Chris, 62
Sole, Alfred, 131
Soles, P. J., 132, 137
Solo, Robert H., 120
Solomon, Bruce, 68, 229
Solomons, Ralph, 210
Solomos, Alexis, 184
Solovei, Elena, 188
Somebody Killed Her Husband, 82
Someone Is Killing the Great Chefs of Europe, 91
Somers, Suzanne, 229
Sommer, Elke, 126, 212, 229
Sommer, Josef, 116
Sommerfield, Diane, 137
Sommers, April, 134
Sommers, Jason, 127
Sondergaard, Gale, 158
Sondheim, Stephen, 26
Song of Bernadette, The, 158
Sonny, 229
Soo, Jack, 22
Sopenar, Alexander, 95
Sordi, Alberto, 182, 229
Sorensen, Rick, 52
Soriano, Maruja, 213
Sorkin, Lou, 127
Sorrells, Bill, 46
Sorvino, Paul, 96, 101, 111, 229
Sothern, Ann, 75, 229
Sotolongo, Jorge, 207
Soul Brothers of Kung Fu, 211, 212
Sound of Music, The, 159
Soutter, Michel, 210
Souza, Emory, 133

Spacek, Sissy, 229
Spagnuolo, Filomena, 43
Spann, Patricia, 83
Spanyik, Eva, 201
Sparer, Paul, 115
Sparks, Frank, 44
Sparks, Scott, 137
Sparrowhawk, Len, 199
Spartacus, 159
Sparv, Camilla, 42
Spawn of the Slithis, 135
Spear of the Nation, 207
Spear, Walter M., 129
Speedtrap, 129
Speedwagon, Reo, 33
Speer, Martin, 136, 208
Spenato, Guy, 43
Spencer, Bob, 205
Spencer, Bud, 212
Spengel, Craig, 35
Spengel, Kimberly, 35
Spengler, Pierre, 30, 122
Spengler, Volker, 211
Spenser, Jeremy, 229
Sperber, Wendie Jo, 35
Spielberg, Steven, 35
Spikings, Barry, 58, 150
Spillman, Harry, 97
Spinell, Joe, 43, 83, 136
Spinks, James, 54
Spira, Daniel, 115
Spivey, Sedena, 131
Spo-De-Odee, 125
Springer, Gary, 44, 229
Spurrier, Paul, 199
Squire, Janie, 136
St. Alban, Dominique, 210
St. George, Clement, 125
St. Jacques, Raymond, 97, 125, 228
St. Jacques, Sterling, 78
St. James, Malinda, 126
St. James, Susan, 228
St. John, Betta, 228
St. John, Jill, 228
St. Johns, Richard R., 134
Stack, Robert, 229
Stader, Peter T., 102
Stadlen, Lewis J., 229
Stafford, Art, 34
Stagecoach, 158
Stagg, Bima, 211
Staheli, Julie, 135
Stalag 17, 159
Stallone, Frank Jr., 83
Stallone, Sylvester, 6, 39, 83, 229
Stambaugh, David, 134
Stamp, Terence, 122, 229
Stander, Lionel, 134, 229
Stang, Arnold, 229
Stangertz, Goran, 168
Stanislavsky, Michael, 127
Stanley, Erika, 135
Stanley, Frank, 53, 100
Stanley, John, 135
Stanley, Kim, 229
Stanton, Harry Dean, 23, 125
Stanwyck, Barbara, 229
Staple Singers, The, 38
Stapleton, Jean, 229
Stapleton, Maureen, 64, 229
Starbird, 128
Starenios, Dimos, 42, 96
Stargard, 62
Starger, Martin, 102
Starhops, 133
Stark, Graham, 30, 60
Stark, Ray, 31, 56, 112
Starky, Max, 36
Starr, Jeffrey Louis, 134
Starr, Ringo, 38
Starship Invasions, 164
Steadman, John, 76, 208
Stearns, Michael, 137
Stebel, Sidney L., 126
Steed, Judy, 211
Steel, Anthony, 229
Steel, Gordon, 199
Steele, Barbara, 37, 136
Steele, Tommy, 229
Steelsmith, Mary, 13
Steely Dan, 33
Steenburgen, Mary, 94
Steere, Anthony, 16
Steiger, Rod, 39, 159, 229
Stein, Andrew, 128
Stein, Lee, 130
Stein, Peter, 139
Steinberg, David, 40, 41
Steinberg, Dianne, 62, 63
Steinbrocker, Dan, 133
Steindler, Maureen, 95
Steiner, Fred, 34
Steinmetz, Bill, 112
Steinmetz, Dennis, 125
Stell, Frank, 126
Stelling, William, 42

Stephens, Nancy, 137
Stephens, Robert, 161
Stephens, Vicki, 112
Stephenson, Craig, 126
Sterling, Jan, 229
Sterling, Robert, 229
Stevens, Andrew, 18, 28, 29, 229
Stevens, Connie, 229
Stevens, George, 158, 159
Stevens, Kaye, 229
Stevens, Mark, 229
Stevens, Morton, 136
Stevens, Robert C., 46
Stevens, Ronald Smokey, 92
Stevens, Rory, 131
Stevens, Roy, 122, 229
Stevens, Stella, 75, 229
Stevenson, Houseley, 127
Stevenson, McLean, 52
Stevenson, Michael, 42
Stevenson, Michael A., 56, 112
Stevenson, Parker, 229
Stevie, 189
Stewart, Alexandra, 229
Stewart, Bruce, 129
Stewart, Byron, 137
Stewart, Dennis C., 48
Stewart, Donald, 128
Stewart, Douglas, 120
Stewart, Douglas Day, 32
Stewart, Elaine, 229
Stewart, James, 136, 158, 170, 171, 229
Stewart, Jean-Pierre, 82
Stewart, Martha, 229
Stewart, Paul, 60
Stiers, David Ogden, 56, 108
Stiglitz, Hugo, 137
Stigwood, Robert, 48, 62, 118
Sting, The, 159
Stingray, 134, 135
Stocker, Walter, 125
Stocking, Roy, 80
Stockton, Kevin, 92
Stockwell, Dean, 229
Stockwell, Jake, 130
Stokes, Gary, 102
Stokowski, Leopold, 158
Stoler, Shirley, 150
Stone, L. Andrew, 39, 62
Stone, Oliver, 96
Stone, Peter, 36, 91
Stone, Philip, 209
Stone, Robert, 74
Stoor, Mieczyslaw, 163
Stop the World—I Want to Get Off, 139
Stoppard, Tom, 211
Storaro, Vittorio, 213
Storch, Larry, 125
Storm, Gale, 229
Story, George Gage, 126
Story of Louis Pasteur, The, 158
Storyville, 37
Stover, George, 130, 131
Strachan, Alan, 42
Stradling, Harry Jr., 58, 86, 97
Straight, Beatrice, 159, 229
Straight Time, 23
Strand, Joe, 150
Strange Things Happen at Night, 204
Strange-Mason, Aralee, 107
Strasberg, Susan, 75, 229
Stratton, Gil, 52
Strauss, Peter, 229
Stravinsky, John, 24
Streep, Meryl, 149, 150, 151, 229
Street, Elliott, 125
Streetcar Named Desire, A, 158
Streisand, Barbra, 6, 78, 159, 229
Streit, David, 77
Stricker, 208
Strickland, Amzie, 8, 133
Strickland, Gail, 74
Stride, Karen, 134
Strindberg, Anita, 212
Stringer, Michael, 42
Stritch, Elaine, 229
Strode, Woody, 229
Strohmeier, Tara, 131
Stroller, Louis A., 78
Strong, Jim, 126
Strongshield, Cyrus, 136
Stroud, Don, 70, 229
Strudwick, Shepperd, 229
Struthers, Sally, 229
Struycken, Carel, 62
Stryker, Amy, 95
Stuart, Arlene, 133
Stuart, John, 122

Stuart, Mel, 127
Stuyck, Pieter, 122
Suarez, Ramon, 209
Subject Was Roses, The, 159
Submission, 213
Subway Sect, 209
Sudygaliev, Nurgazi, 213
Suerstedt, Candace C., 33, 116
Sugai, Ichiro, 178
Sullivan, Barry, 110, 229
Sullivan, Jenny, 130
Sullivan, Jeremiah, 82
Sullivan, Joseph, 43
Sullivan, Mike, 136
Sullivan, Owen, 54
Sullivan, Susan, 136
Sully, Frank, 229
Sultan, Gene, 52
Summer, Donna, 130
Summer Paradise, 168
Summers, Bob, 126
Summers, Hope, 68, 138
Summers, Jerry, 87
Sun, Irene Yah Ling, 133
Sundays and Cybele, 159
Sundfur, Paul, 137
Sunset Cove, 129
Sunshine Boys, The, 159
Superman, 122
Suppa, Ronald A., 83
Surguine, Skip, 135
Surtees, Bruce, 102, 130
Surtees, Robert, 96, 106
Suso, Henry, 128
Suspicion, 158
Sussfeld, Jean, 162
Susskind, David, 229
Sutherland, Donald, 66, 120, 121, 229
Sutherland, Ian, 211
Sutton, Dudley, 170
Sutton, Henry, 56
Svenson, Bo, 229
Swados, Kim, 126
Swaim, Caskey, 100
Swanson, Gloria, 229
Sward, Ann, 133
Swarm, The, 134, 135
Swartz, Jerram, 62, 76
Swatek, Martha, 44
Sweater Girls, 128
Sweeney, Alfred, 68
Sweet Bird of Youth, 159
Sweet, Blanche, 229
Sweet, Dolph, 46, 86
Swenson, Chuck, 135
Swenson, Inga, 16
Swenson, Karl, 237
Swenson, Marcy, 135
Swetland, William, 126
Swift, David,, 17
Swift, Susan, 133
Swinburne, Nora, 229
Swink, Robert E., 127, 192
Swit, Loretta, 229
Swor, Kenneth, 127
Syberberg, Hans-Jurgen, 206
Sylbert, Anthea, 39
Sylbert, Paul, 46
Sylvander, Yvette, 137
Sylvander, Yvonne, 137
Sylvester, William, 46, 229
Sylvia, Gaby, 172
Symonds, Robert, 127
Syms, Sylvia, 229
Syslo, Tony, 129
Szabo, Etienne, 209, 210
Szabo, Lajos, 201
Szakacs, Zsuzsa, 201
Szemes, Zsuzsanna, 30
Szeski, Jerzy, 163
Szwarc, Jeannot, 44
Tabatabai, Khosrow, 110
Tabor, Eron, 138
Tabori, Kristoffer, 77, 229
Tacchella, Jean-Charles, 205
Tackett, Bill, 31
Tacorda, Sampa, 136
Taeger, Uta, 200
Taggart, Rita, 23
Tagoe, Eddie, 91
Taj Mahal, 125
Taka, Miiko, 100
Takaiwa, Tan, 211
Takanaski, Nabaru, 211
Takashi, 131
Take All of Me, 213
Takemitsu, Toru, 198
Talbot, Lyle, 229
Talbot, Nita, 229
Talsky, Ron, 76
Tamakuni, Sarah, 17
Tamba, Tetsuro, 211
Tambasco, Jerry, 43
Tamblyn, Russ, 229
Tamburro, Chuck, 87
Tammes, Fred, 211

Tan, Chao, 211
Tanaka, Haruo, 178
Tandy, Gareth, 122
Tandy, Jessica, 229
Tannenbaum, Gerald, 211
Tanner, Peter, 189, 208
Tantum Ergo, 182
Taplin, Jonathan, 38
Tarbes, J. J., 211
Tarpey, Tom, 33
Tarrare, Daniel, 191
Tasgal, Bill, 138
Taurog, Norman, 158
Tavoularis, Dean, 111
Tayback, Vic, 56, 57
Taylor, Chip, 207
Taylor, Delores, 125
Taylor, Don, 54, 229
Taylor, Dr. Leroy C., 138
Taylor, Dub, 138
Taylor, Elizabeth, 26, 159, 229
Taylor, Grigor, 211
Taylor, Jack, 213
Taylor, Kent, 230
Taylor, Les, 129
Taylor, Lisa, 78
Taylor, Meshach, 54
Taylor, Richard, 135, 213
Taylor, Rod, 212, 230
Taylor, Sharon, 137
Taylor-Young, Leigh, 230
Teacher, The, 208
Teague, Anthony Skooter, 230
Team-Mates, 137
Teboul, Philippe, 174
Tedrow, Irene, 68
Teifer, Gregory, 173
Teige, Jan, 133
Teige, Laura, 133
Teigh, Lila, 96
Tellone, Rita, 78
Temple, Paul, 97
Temple, Shirley, 158, 230
Tempter, The, 212
Tenaya, 75
Tenser, Marilyn J., 131
Tenser, Mark, 128
Teodorescu, Ion, 68
Ternstrom, Solveig, 168
Terrian, Anita, 94
Terry-Thomas, 230
Terzieff, Laurent, 230
Tessler, Sheela, 134
Tester, Ted, 110
Testi, Fabio, 210
Texas Detour, 130, 133
Thacker, Russ, 230
Thank God It's Friday, 130
Thatcher, Torin, 230
That's Country, 129
Thaxter, Phyllis, 122, 230
the Bee Gees, 63
Their Only Chance, 127
Theiss, William Ware, 94
Theodore, Sondra, 126, 134, 135
Theodorakis, Mikis, 212
They Shoot Horses, Don't They?, 159
They Went That-A-Way and That-A-Way, 138
Thiedot, Jacqueline, 162
Think Dirty, 207
Thoma, Maralyn, 136
Thomaidou, Anna, 184
Thomas, Danny, 230
Thomas, Hilary, 28
Thomas, Mark, 18
Thomas, Marlo, 230
Thomas, Melody, 28, 136
Thomas, Philip, 230
Thomas, Phillip, 87
Thomas, Ralph, 212
Thomas, Richard, 18, 19, 230
Thomas, Victor, 212
Thomas, William, 31
Thomas, William Jr., 115
Thomerson, Timothy, 95, 125
Thompson, Donald G., 133
Thompson, Galen, 133
Thompson, Garth, 102
Thompson, J. Lee, 42
Thompson, Jack, 230
Thompson, Marshall, 230
Thompson, Raymond, 122
Thompson, Rex, 230
Thompson, Richard, 31
Thompson, Sada, 230
Thompson, Tommy, 95
Thordsen, Kelly, 237
Thorne, Dyanne, 208
Thornton, Scoody, 134
Thorson, Linda, 42
Thost, Bruno, 205
Thousand Clowns, A, 159

Three Faces of Eve, The, 159
Through a Glass Darkly, 159
Thulin, Ingrid, 230
Thurley, Martin C., 208
Ti, Pei, 211
Tidy, Frank, 161
Tien, Haiao, 211
Tierney, Gene, 230
Tierney, Lawrence, 230
Tiffin, Pamela, 230
Tiger From Hong Kong, 204
Tigress, The, 208
Till Death, 125
Till, Eric, 209
Tilley, Kate, 133
Tilvern, Alan, 122
Tinti, Gabriele, 205, 212
Tintle, David, 44
Tintorera, 137
Tisch, Steve, 137
Tittinger, Gregg, 135
To Each His Own, 158
To Kill a Mockingbird, 159
Toback, James, 126
Tobias, Charles, 204
Todd, Richard, 170, 230
Tognazzi, ugo, 182
Tokar, Norman, 17, 52
Told, John, 139
Tolkien, J. R. R., 104
Toll, Pamela, 20
Tolo, Marilu, 42, 230
Tolsky, Susan, 125
Tom Jones, 159
Tomalin, O'Brian, 127
Tomarken, Peter, 46
Tomassi, Vincenzo, 206, 212
Tomko, Henen, 150
Tomlin, Lily, 118, 230
Tompkins, Angel, 136, 138
Tompkins, Peter, 139
Tonelli, David, 162
Toni, Aldo, 210
Tonoyama, Shoji, 198
"Too Close to Paradise", 83
Too Hot to Handle, 137
Toolbox Murders, The, 128
Topkapi, 159
Topol, 230
Torme, Mel, 137
Tormented, The, 212
Torn, Rip, 10, 11, 125, 230
Tornquist, Alfredo, 204
Torres, Daniel Diaz, 207
Torres, Jose L., 116
Torres, Liz, 230
Torrey, Mary, 33
Tosi, Mario, 16
Toste, Father Frank, 116
Totter, Audrey, 230
Tottman, Jayne, 122
Touch of Class, A, 159
Tovali, Luciano, 180
Towing, 130
Townsend, Bud, 128
Townsend, Primi, 206
Toy, The, 211
Tozzi, Fausto, 237
Tracey, Ray, 138
Tracy, Spencer, 158
Trauner, Alexander, 174
Travalena, Fred, 70
Travers, Bill, 208, 230
Travis, Mark, 139
Travis, Neil, 44
Travis, Richard, 230
Travolta, Ellen, 48
Travolta, John, 6, 48, 49, 118, 230
Traxler, Stephen, 135
Treasure of the Sierra Madre, The, 158
Tree Grows in Brooklyn, A, 158
Treggonino, Joe, 36
Tremayne, Les, 230
Trent, John, 206
Trent, Sylvia, 207
Treu, Wolfgang, 206
Trevor, Austin, 237
Trevor, Claire, 158
Trice, Ron, 130
Trikonis, Gus, 133
Trimble, Lawrence, 122
Trintignant, Jean-Louis, 210, 230
Tripi, Joseph, 43
Tromberg, Sheldon, 129
Trovajoli, Armando, 182
Trowe, Jose Chavez, 138
Troy, Hector, 78
Troyes, Chretien de, 191
True Grit, 159
Trujillo, Roberto, 20
Tryon, Tom, 230
Tscheppe, Hubert, 26

Tso-Nan, Lee, 213
Tsopei, Corinna, 230
Tsugawa, Hiro, 131
Tsuji, Shintaro, 131, 135
Tubb, Ernest, 129
Tubor, Mort, 138
Tucci, Michael, 48
Tucker, Burnell, 122
Tucker, Forrest, 230
Tucker, Michael, 24, 78
Tucker, Michel, 160
Tuerpe, Paul, 122
Tunick, Jonathan, 26
Tuntke, William, 127
Turco, Paolo, 180
Turenne, Louis, 116
Turner, Jesse, 138
Turner, Lana, 230
Turner, Simon, 170
Turpitt, Dean, 31
Turton, Stuart Craig, 213
Tushingham, Rita, 230
Tutin, Dorothy, 230
Tuttle, Lurene, 75, 230
Tuttle, William, 159
Twain, Mark, 30
Twelve O'Clock High, 158
Twiggy, 230
Two Women, 159
Twofeathers, Bill, 136
Tyler, Beverly, 230
Tyrrell, Susan, 18, 230
Tyson, Cicely, 230
Uccello, Paul, 31
Uda, Hatsuo, 45
Uemura, Banjiro, 211
Ufford, Kelsey, 124
Uggams, Leslie, 230
Ullmann, Linn, 196
Ullmann, Liv, 196, 197, 230
Ultra Violet, 24, 230
Umeki, Miyoshi, 159
Uncle Joe Shannon, 138
Unger, Anthony B., 202
Unger, Joe, 86
Unger, Oliver A., 202
Unmarried Woman, An, 24
Unsworth, Geoffrey, 122
Up in Smoke, 80
Upson, Denise, 137
Upton, Morgan, 135
Urioste, Frank J., 18
Urtreger, Rene, 174
Ustinov, Peter, 84, 85, 135, 159, 230
Violette, 194
Uytterhoven, Pierre, 210
Vaccaro, Brenda, 50, 230
Vacek, Jack, 129
Vacek, John Sr., 129
Vacey, Sandra, 125
Vahanian, Marc, 115
Vaidou, Litsa, 184
Valassi, Betty, 184, 185
Valberg, Birgitta, 168
Valdes, Omar, 207
*Valdesta*_, 137
Valentine, Karen, 76
Valera, Roberto, 207
Valladeres, Richard, 115
Vallee, Rudy, 230
Valli, Alida, 212, 230
Valli, Romolo, 206
Vallone, Raf, 42, 230
Vampire Hookers, 134
Van, Bobby, 230
Van Cleef, Lee, 206, 230
Van De Ven, Monique, 230
Van Der Wyk, Richard, 126
Van Devere, Trish, 102, 103, 230
Van Doren, Mamie, 230
Van Dreelan, John, 137
Van Dyke, Dick, 230
Van Fleet, Jo, 159, 230
Van Greenaway, Peter, 175
Van Leeuwen, Chako, 136
Van Lyck, Henry, 205
Van Ost, Valerie, 211
Van Pallandt, Nina, 95
Van Patten, Dick, 230
Van Patten, Jimmy, 76
Van Patten, Joyce, 230
Van Runkle, Theodora, 46
Van Scott, Glory, 92
Van Zandt, Billy, 44
Vanders, Warren, 76
Vandis, Titos, 16
Vane, Kenny, 27
Vans, Gene, 136
Varazi, Avtandil, 208
Vasile, Turi, 180
Vasseur, Didier, 211
Vaudaux, Maurice, 194
Vaughan-Hughes, Gerald, 161
Vaughn, Robert, 119, 164, 230
Vaughn, Skeeter, 128
Vaziri, Susan, 110
Veazey, Cindy, 132

Veber, Francis, 211, 212
Vega, Isela, 230
Vega, Marlina, 32
Veigl, Anna, 26
Vejar, Michael, 129
Venable, Sarah, 134
Venegas, William B., 124
Vennera, Chick, 130
Ventura, Jean-Claude, 176
Ventura, Lino, 175, 230
Venture, Richard, 16
Venus, Brenda, 33, 128
Venuta, Benay, 230
Vera-Ellen, 230
Verdon, Bliss, 115
Verdon, Gwen, 230
Vereen, Ben, 230
Verges, Betty, 211
Verne, Jules, 213
Vernick, William, 129
Vernon, John, 66, 67
Vernon, Richard, 211
Verona, Michael Ross, 35
Verroca, Frank, 35
Verzier, Rene, 134
Vestoff, Virginia, 95
Vicci, Laurent, 205
Vick, Helen, 66
Vickers, Mike, 208
Victor, Barry, 136
Victor, Charles, 9
Victor, Mark, 115
Vidette, John, 211
Vidor, King, 159
Vigoda, Abe, 56, 57
Viharo, Robert, 133
Vilers, Vania, 210
Villagra, Nelson, 204, 207
Villalonga, Marthe, 172
Villar, Robert, 35
Villaron, Dulce Maria, 207
Ville, Victoria, 105
Villechaize, Herve, 8, 9, 129, 230
Villery, Eddie, 112
Vincent, Chuck, 137
Vincent, Jan-Michael, 72, 73, 130, 230
Vincent, Mike, 136
Vincent, Pamela, 213
Vincent, Virginia, 208
Vinson, Robert, 136
Vint, Alan, 127
Vint, Jesse, 128
V.I.P.'s, The, 159
Virgin Spring, The, 159
Virgin Witch, The, 210
Vitale, Anthony, 136
Vitale, Frank, 207
Vitale, Milly, 230
Vitier, Sergio, 207, 208
Vitte, Ray, 130
Viva Italia!, 182
Viva Zapata, 158
Vivaldi, Antonio, 163
Vives, Camilo, 207
Vlachos, Stefanos, 184
Vogel, Jesse, 212
Vogel, Klaus, 210
Vogel, Mitch, 133
Vogel, Nicolas, 162
Voglis, James, 184
Vohs, Joan, 230
Voight, Jon, 4, 7, 14, 15, 153, 159, 230
Volonte, Gian Maria, 230
Volpe, Lenore, 43
von Brandenstein, Patrizia, 77
Von Hanno, Eva, 196
Von Hoeltke, Jerry, 102
von Sternberg, Nickolas Josef, 125
von Sydow, Max, 119, 230
von Trotta, Margarethe, 205
Vorgan, Gigi, 44
Vosoughi, Behrooz, 110
Voutsinas, Andreas, 184, 185
Voyagis, Yorgo, 182
Vreeland, Elizabeth, 139
Vreeland, Russell, 87
Vrocco, Peter, 8
Waddy, Gyle, 92
Wagner, Ed, 115
Wagner, Jane, 118
Wagner, Lindsay, 230
Wagner, Ray, 18
Wagner, Robert, 230
Wagner, Winifred, 230
Wahler, Bob, 45, 132
Wahrman, Charles, 203
Wain, Charles, 203
Wainwright, James, 125, 127
Waite, Genevieve, 230
Waite, Ric, 32
Waits, Tom, 83
Wajda, Andrzej, 163
Wakao, Ayako, 178

Wakayama, Tomisaburo, 134
Wakhevitch, Georges, 206
Wald, Jeff, 83
Walden, Robert, 50, 132
Waldman, Frank, 60
Waldron, John, 70
Walken, Christopher, 149, 150, 151, 154, 159, 230
Walker, Charles, 137
Walker, Clint, 230
Walker, Debra Fay, 12
Walker, Jack David, 128
Walker, Jimmie, 13
Walker, Johnny, 131
Walker, Kathryn, 77
Walker, Keith, 125
Walker, Kenneth, 131
Walker, Nancy, 230
Walker, Peter, 206
Walker, Rodney Lee, 12
Walker, Sandra, 68
Walker, Scott, 97
Walker, Will, 59, 128, 129
Walker, William, 137
Wallace, Bob, 130
Wallace, Dee, 208
Wallace, Elizabeth, 138
Wallace, Regina, 237
Wallace, Rick, 137
Wallach, Eli, 77, 102, 230
Wallach, Roberta, 33
Wallenstein, Joe, 27
Wallis, Shani, 230
Walls of Malapaga, The, 158
Walsch, Franz, 211
Walsh, Bob, 138
Walsh, Chuck, 68
Walsh, David M., 20, 68, 112, 125
Walsh, Joseph, 59
Walsh, M. Emmet, 23
Walsh, Sean Fallon, 12
Walston, Ray, 230
Walter, Ernest, 30
Walter, Jerry, 135
Walter, Jessica, 230
Walter, Mariane, 128
Walter, Tracey, 12, 94
Walters, Barbara Ann, 94
Walton, Tony, 92
Wanamaker, Sam, 84, 125, 230
Wang, Don, 213
Wang, Singloy, 211
Wanger, Walter, 158
Wanoskia, Galbert, 31
War, 130
War and Peace, 159
Warburton, Cotton, 52
Ward, Burt, 231
Ward, Kelly, 48
Ward, Lalla, 30
Ward, Roger, 211
Ward, Simon, 206, 231
Warden, Jack, 46, 84, 85, 231
Warden, May, 209
Warfield, Joe, 100
Warlock, Richard, 52
Warlords of Atlantis, 208
Warner, David, 36, 231
Warner, Harry M., 158
Warner, Jack, 237
Warner, Jack L., 237
Warner, Kent, 34
Warren, Jennifer, 124, 231
Warren, Lesley Ann, 231
Warren, Nancy, 56
Warren, Sammy, 12
Warren, W. S. Tiger, 126
Warrick, Ruth, 231
Warschilka, Edward, 20
Warwick, Dionne, 206
Warwick, Norman, 122
Warwick, Richard, 179
Washbourne, Mona, 189, 231
Washburn, Deric, 150
Washington, J. Dennis, 58
Wasson, Craig, 18, 86
Watanabe, Yoshinori, 211
Watch on the Rhine, 158
Waterman, Dennis, 208
Waters, Charles, 84
Waters, Chuck, 35
Waters, Muddy, 98
Waters, Robert E., 134, 137
Watership Down, 199
Waterston, Sam, 50, 51, 64, 65, 231
Watkins, Michale, 38
Watling, Jack, 231
Watlington, Dennis, 150
Watson, Douglass, 231
Watson, Jack, 199, 206
Watson, Mills, 80
Watson, Paula, 35

253

Watson, William, 135
Watt, Colter, 139
Watt, Mildred, 127
Watts, Queenie, 206
Way of All Flesh, The, 158
Way of the Wind, The, 204
Waye, Anthony, 110
Wayman, Sam, 139
Wayne County, 209
Wayne, David, 231
Wayne, John, 7, 159, 231
Wayne, Patrick, 130, 133, 231
We Will All Meet in Paradise, 172
Weathers, Carl, 202
Weaver, Carl Earl, 27
Weaver, Dennis, 231
Weaver, Fritz, 100
Weaver, Lee, 20, 46
Weaver, Marjorie, 231
Webb, Alan, 161, 231
Webb, Jack, 231
Webber, Merrily, 32
Webber, Robert, 31, 60, 231
Weber, Billy, 88
Weber, Sabina, 126
Weber, Sharon, 134
Webster, Ferris, 114
Wedding, A, 95
Wedgeworth, Ann, 231
Weeks, Andy, 132
Weeks, Todd, 132
Weill, Claudia, 77
Weingrow, Howard, 131
Weintraub, Fred, 127, 212
Weintraub, Jerry, 18
Weintraub, Joseph, 137
Weir, Ingrid, 203
Weir, Peter, 203
Weis, Don, 133
Weisberg, Eric, 131
Weisel, Lee, 211
Weisser, Norbert, 96, 99
Weissman, Bernie, 130
Weissmuller, Johnny, 231
Weist, Gary, 107
Welch, Raquel, 30, 208, 231
Weld, Tuesday, 74, 231
Weldon, Ann, 130
Weldon, Joan, 231
Weller, Mary Louise, 66, 67, 133
Welles, Gwen, 231
Welles, Orson, 129, 159, 231
Wellman, Cissy, 33
Wellman, William Jr., 130
Wells, Carole, 56
Wells, Danny, 137
Wells, Dawn, 125
Wells, Kitty, 129
Wells, Richard, 58
Wells, Win, 42
Welsh, John, 136
Wemple, Joe, 139
Werner, Karen, 66
Werner, Oskar, 231
Wertimer, Ned, 212
Wertmuller, Lina, 160
Wertmuller, Massimo, 160
West, Adam, 72, 212
West, Carinthia, 42
West, Mae, 231
West Side Story, 159
Westerner, The, 158
Weston, Brad, 76
Weston, Eric, 134, 139
Weston, Jack, 231
Weston, Robert R., 231
Westover, Winifred, 237
Westrope, Tony, 213
Wexler, Haskell, 14
Wexler, Jerry, 37
Whalen, Fred L., 52
Wharton, Anne, 80
Wheeler, Charles F., 52
Wheeler, Hugh, 26
Wheeler, John, 62
Whelan, Robert, 122
Whelehan, William J., 54
Where Time Began, 213
Where's Willie, 129
Whip Ship, The, 213
Whispering Death, 205
Whitaker, Barbara, 139
Whitaker, Johnny, 231
White, Carol, 231
White, Caryn, 211
White, Charles, 231
White, Craig, 70
White, Deborah, 125
White, Deloy, 138
White, Jason, 179
White, Jesse, 52, 231
White, Onna, 159
White, Ouida, 18
White, Robert, 137

White, Roberta, 133
White, William H., 129
Whitecloud, Jim, 76
Whitely, Jon, 159
Whitemore, Hugh, 189
Whitlock, Albert, 92
Whitman, Stuart, 231
Whitmore, James, 137, 231
Whitmore, James Jr., 18
Whittaker, James, 127
Whitten, Bill, 125
Whittington, Dick, 100
Whitworth, James, 208
Who Is Killing the Great Chefs of Europe?, 91
Who'll Stop the Rain?, 74
Who's Afraid of Virginia Woolf?, 159
Wicki, Bernhard, 211
Widdoes, James, 66
Widdoes, Kathleen, 231
Widmark, Richard, 10, 135, 231
Wieland, Joyce, 211
Wigert, Knut, 196
Wiggins, Chris, 134
Wilbur, George P., 102
Wilcox-Horne, Colin, 18, 19, 44, 231
Wilcoxon, Henry, 39, 231
Wild Geese, The, 199
Wilde, Cornel, 136, 231
Wilder, Billy, 158, 159
Wilder, Gene, 231
Wilder, Glenn, 12
Wilder, Yvonne, 231
Wilderness Family Part 2, 139
Wilding, Michael, 231
Wiles, Mark, 136
Wilke, Robert, 88
Wilker, Jose, 166, 167
Wilkerson, Ralph, 126
Wilkes, Donna, 44, 137
Wilkinson, John, 88
Wilkinson, M. Scott, 126
Willesee, Mike, 134
Wilhelm, John, 137
Williams, Alfred T., 136
Williams, Barry, 139
Williams, Billy Dee, 125, 231
Williams, Brook, 199
Williams, Cara, 136
Williams, Carol, 124
Williams, Cindy, 231
Williams, Dick, 231
Williams, Dwight, 101
Williams, Elmo, 110
Williams, Emlyn, 231
Williams, Esther, 231
Williams, Grant, 231
Williams, Jan, 52
Williams, John, 28, 44, 76, 122, 231
Williams, Lorraine, 110
Williams, Otto, 211
Williams, P. W., 43
Williams, Pat, 135
Williams, Patrick, 8, 31, 56
Williams, Paul, 40, 43, 56, 57
Williams, Peter, 110
Williams, Sam, 205
Williams, Sylvia "Kuumba", 137
Williams, Ted, 92
Williams, Trevor, 37
Williamson, Fred, 207, 231
Williamson, Malcolm, 190
Williamson, Nicol, 56, 57
Williard, Carol, 16
Willingham, Noble, 18
Willis, Gordon, 18, 64, 90
Willis, Nancy, 132
Willmus, Teresa, 124
Willoughby, Leueen, 122
Willrich, Rudolph, 131
Wills, Chill, 237
Wills, Sheila, 130
Willson, Paul, 212
Wilson, Billy, 139
Wilson, Bob, 88
Wilson, Brian, 137
Wilson, Bruce, 127
Wilson, Claude, 18
Wilson, David, 127, 137
Wilson, Demond, 231
Wilson, Flip, 231
Wilson, Freddie, 170
Wilson, George, 137
Wilson, Georges, 176
Wilson, Ian, 138
Wilson, Kathy, 44
Wilson, Keith, 179
Wilson, Mary Louise, 115
Wilson, Nancy, 231
Wilson, Ned, 97
Wilson, Rogert L., 94
Wilson, Scott, 231

Wilson, Trey, 134
Winburn, James, 102
Windburn, Jim, 137
Winde, Beatrice, 116, 231
Winding, Andreas, 186
Winding, Victor, 206
Windom, William, 127, 129, 231
Windsor, Frank, 91
Windsor, Marie, 231
Winetrobe, Maury, 124
Winfield, Paul, 231
Wing, Chen, 211
Winger, Debra, 130
Wings, 158
Winifred Wagner, 206
Winitsky, Alex, 20, 36
Winkler, Henry, 7, 8, 9, 231
Winkler, Irwin, 90, 138
Winn, Kitty, 231
Winner, Michael, 170
Winslow, Dick, 102
Winter, Catherine, 209
Winter, Lex, 134
Winter, Vincent, 122, 159
Winters, Deborah, 132
Winters, Jonathan, 231
Winters, Roland, 231
Winters, Shelley, 115, 159, 231
Wintersole, William, 10
Wintle, Julian, 208
Winwood, Estelle, 231
Wise, Alfie, 72
Wise, Robert, 159
Wiseman, Joseph, 16
Wishbone Cutter, 125
Witherick, Albert, 17
Withers, Googie, 231
Withers, Jane, 231
Without Words, 182
Wiz, The, 92
Wolf, Emanuel L., 16
Wolf, Frank, 208
Wolf, Fred, 135
Wolf, Ian, 135
Wolf, Marcia, 80
Wolf, Richard A., 126
Wolfe, Kedric, 20
Wolfe, Robert L., 130
Wollet, Michael, 150
Wolsky, Albert, 24, 48, 118, 126
Woman at Her Window, A, 210
Woman's Decision, A, 207
Women in Love, 159
Wonder, Stevie, 139
Wonderful Wizard of Oz, The, 92
Wong, C. H., 211
Wong, Harry D. K., 46
Woo, James Wing, 100
Wood, Janet, 68
Wood, John, 82
Wood, Lana, 129
Wood, Mario, 208
Wood, Natalie, 231
Wood, Patricio, 208
Wood, Peggy, 237
Wood, Ron, 38
Wood, Salvador, 207, 208
Wood, Teri Lynn, 62
Woodard, Bronte, 48
Woodlawn, Holly, 231
Woods, James, 231
Woods, Ren, 130
Woodville, Kate, 129
Woodward, Joanne, 40, 159, 231
Woodward, Morgan, 129
Woody, Dave, 125, 136
Wooland, Norman, 231
Wooley, Peter, 71
Woolf, Charles, 135
Woolf, Jack, 134
Woollard, Tony, 208
Woolner, Larry, 133
Woolsey, Ralph, 212
Word Is Out, 127
Worden, Hank, 62, 138
Words, Sylvester, 126
Worf, David, 131
Workman, Lindsay, 136
Woronov, Mary, 8, 231
Wragge, Martin, 211
Wrather, Bonita Granville, 136
Wray, Fay, 231
Wright, Amy, 77, 150
Wright, Bob, 42
Wright, Heather, 208
Wright, John, 58
Wright, Patrick, 136
Wright, Richard, 76
Wright, Ron, 128
Wright, Teresa, 158, 231
Written on the Wind, 159
Wrye, Donald, 124

Wrzeninska, Barbara, 207
Wyatt, Allen H., 87
Wyatt, Jane, 231
Wyatt, Walter, 66
Wybult, Tadeusz, 207
Wyeth, Sandy Brown, 59
Wylder, Nan, 112
Wyler, William, 158, 159
Wyman, Jane, 158, 231
Wymore, Patrice, 231
Wyner, George, 134
Wynn, Keenan, 128, 136, 231
Wynn, Kitty, 126
Wynn, Mary, 115
Wynn, May, 231
Wynter, Dana, 231
Wynter, Mark, 122
Xavier, Nelson, 166
Xing, Chen, 210
X-Ray Spec, 209
Yablans, Frank, 28
Yablans, Irwin, 137
Yablans, Mickey, 137
Yacov, Rony, 204
Yade, Moustapha, 205
Yahraus, William H., 139
Yallop, Julia, 138
Yanez, David, 32
Yang, Yueh, 204
Yankee Doodle Dandy, 158
Yannatos, Mihalis, 96
Yara, Sara Gomez, 207
Yarmy, Dick, 136
Yashima, Mitsu, 68
Yates, Cassie, 33, 39, 58, 133
Yates, Kenneth A., 128, 129
Yavneh, Cyrus I., 132
Yee, Yeu-Bun, 38
Yesterday, Today and Tomorrow, 159
Yin, Ching, 211
Yoda, Yoshikata, 178
York, Dick, 231
York, Marylou, 126
York, Michael, 231
York, Rebecca, 102
York, Susannah, 122, 231
Yorston, David, 122
You Can't Take It with You, 158
Youb, Samy Ben, 148, 149
Young, Alan, 52, 231
Young, Burt, 58, 138
Young, Clint, 112
Young, Faron, 129
Young, Freddie, 189
Young, Gig, 159, 237
Young, Loretta, 158, 231
Young, Neil, 38
Young, Ray, 132
Young, Robert, 231
Young, Yvonne, 135
Youngblood, 130
Youngfellow, Barrie, 135
Yourcenar, Marguerite, 205
Yu, Chang, 213
Yu, Kam Szu, 211
Yu Ling, Barbara, 211
Yuan, Chuan, 212
Yule, Ian, 199
Yung, Li, 211
Z, 159
Zabor, Jacques, 200
Zacharias, Alfredo, 138
Zacharias, Ann, 186, 187, 231
Zacharias, Michel, 138
Zaentz, Saul, 104
Zakkai, Jamil, 115
Zaloom, Joe, 115
Zaltzman, Rochelle, 204
Zanger, Zigi, 205
Zanninou, Zanninos, 96
Zanuck, Richard D., 44
Zanussi, Krzysztof, 207, 212
Zapponi, Bernardino, 182
Zarchi, Meir, 138
Zarchi, Tammy, 138
Zarchi, Terry, 138
Zardi, Dominique, 162, 194
Zaremba, Jerry, 70
Zastupnevich, Paul, 135
Zbeda, Joseph, 138
Zee, Eleanor, 62
Zehetbauer, Rolf, 119, 211
Zeitlin, Denny, 120
Zelnik, Jerzy, 163
Zemeckis, Robert, 35
Zens, Will, 128
Zepfel, Don, 18, 44
Zerbe, Anthony, 74
Zero to Sixty, 130, 133
Zetterling, Mai, 231
Zichy, Frederik, 205
Zide, Mickey, 205
Zieff, Howard, 20

Ziesmer, Jerry, 134
Ziman, Jerry, 56, 112
Zimbalist, Efrem Jr., 231
Zimbalist, Stephanie, 136
Zimmerman, Don, 14, 46, 138
Zimmerman, Jonathan, 124
Zimmerman, Laura, 37
Zineth, Mohammed, 148
Zinneman, Tim, 23
Zinnemann, Fred, 159
Zinner, Peter, 150
Ziskin, Laura, 78
Zivojinovic, Bata, 212
Zomina, Sonia, 43
Zorba the Greek, 159
Zsigmond, Vilmos, 38, 150
Zuckerman, Steve, 135
Zukert, William, 97
Zukor, Adolph, 158
Zuniga, Frank, 139
Zurlini, Valerio, 212
Zvanut, James, 132
Zwerling, Darrell, 48
Zze. Yang, 210